Named

Camilla Balshaw

Named

A Story of Names and Reclaiming Who We Are

Bedford Square Publishers

First published in the UK in 2025 by Bedford Square Publishers
London, UK

bedfordsquarepublishers.co.uk
@bedfordsq.publishers

A CIP catalogue record for this book is available from the British Library.

ISBN
978-1-83501-071-6 (Hardback)
978-1-83501-072-3 (eBook)

2 4 6 8 10 9 7 5 3 1

Typeset in Bembo Std by Palimpsest Book Production Ltd,
Falkirk, Stirlingshire
Printed in Great Britain by CPI Group (UK) Ltd, Croydon CR0 4YY

The manufacturer's authorised representative in the EU for product safety is Easy Access System Europe, Mustamäe tee 50, 10621 Tallinn, Estonia
gpsr.requests@easproject.com

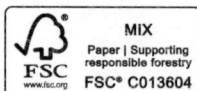

FSC
www.fsc.org
MIX
Paper | Supporting responsible forestry
FSC® C013604

For Mike

Still no one knows it just the same,
That Rumpelstiltskin is my name.

The Brothers Grimm

Families are like branches on a tree.
We grow in different directions,
yet our roots remain one.

Anonymous

CONTENTS

AUTHOR'S NOTE

Named is a voyage of names through the prism of my life. It is a story based on the memories of my experiences. The names and other identifying features of some people, places and events have been changed to ensure they are not identifiable.

INTRODUCTION

What are we without a name?

Our names are entwined with our identity. They are repeated in countless transactions, conversations and written correspondence. Our names are stamped on our passports, utility bills and employment IDs. They carry a lot of information. When we hear a name, we attach an age, gender, class, nationality or ethnic origin to the name's bearer, and, although we might not like to admit it, when we hear a name it influences our first impressions of someone. Yet most of us don't question our names. They are just there, aren't they? They are a necessary identifier to differentiate us as individuals. And, let's not beat about the bush; they are a legal requirement. Without them, how would we function as a society?

So allow me to introduce myself. My name is Camilla. Of course it is. It's the name written on the front cover of this book. But growing up, I was called an entirely different name. This was explored in an essay I wrote for the *Observer*, which, over time, grew into this book. As broadcast media has shown, more of us are questioning what makes us who we are and where we belong, so writing this story has felt increasingly relevant and timely. I knew I wanted to write a personal and factual exploration of the use of names through the lens of other people's experiences as well as my own. So it is a memoir of sorts. My story is the beating heart of this book. But it is so much more than that. By telling my story, I consider wider universal themes of how we fit into this world. The dynamics of identity, belonging and not belonging, families and the intricate relationships between mothers, fathers and daughters. My parents' shadows loom over the pages of this book. They are the key to unlocking the door to my name. Without them, this story can't be told.

This is by no means a complete account of all the naming practices worldwide. This book can't discuss everything, and I do not wish to overstep beyond my experiences and knowledge. I wrote this book to invite you, the reader, to consider your name. I hope it might spark conversations about what our names mean to us, because this seemingly simple part of our collective identities is anything but. There is a story behind every name; although this is my story, part of it may be your story, too.

And finally, remember, whatever the circumstances of your name, take comfort in it. This name you carry around with you is your trusted escort and friend. Cherish it, change it or reclaim it.

One

Mandy, Mandi, Mandeee

If I'm gonna tell a real story, I'm gonna start with my name.
—Kendrick Lamar

Norfolk, December 2014

I wake up with a jolt.

The downstairs phone is ringing. Who the hell is calling the landline on a Sunday morning? No one calls the landline any more except for crank callers, salespeople, and my mother before she discovered the joys of texting, emojis and WhatsApp.

'Shall I get it?' my husband, Mike, asks, yawning.

'I'll go,' I say.

I fling off the duvet, grab a jumper and run downstairs.

'Hello,' I say, picking up the receiver before it slides into a recorded message. 'Hello?'

'Camilla?' the person on the other end of the phone says, in an uncertain way, like he almost doesn't believe it. 'This is Teju,' he continues, but it's difficult to understand what he is saying over the clank-clank of crockery and the opening and shutting of cupboards in the background.

'I'm sorry. What was your name?' I ask, tasting last night's vegetable curry on my breath.

He laughs, apologises for the noise and says his wife can never make coffee quietly.

'I'm Teju. I'm your cousin, and we are *proper* cousins,' he chuckles. 'We are not first cousins removed or anything like that. My dad is your father's older brother.'

It's my turn to laugh. My family consists of my mother, brother, sister and me – that's it. There are no cousins.

'I'm calling on behalf of him,' he says.

'Who?'

'Your dad.'

The word 'dad' hangs in the air as though it's drying out in the breeze. What is a dad? How can he call someone I haven't seen or heard from in nearly four decades a dad?

'Are you still there?' he asks.

I don't reply. Instead, I focus on the beads of condensation trickling down the kitchen window, the perfect distraction from the shock and the wibbly-wobbly sensation in my legs.

'I said I'm calling on behalf of your dad. He—'

'Is this some kind of joke?'

'No,' he replies. 'Your dad asked me to find you. I realise it's a lot to take in after such a long time.'

I expel air through my nostrils. That's about all I can muster. I try to say something and my throat seizes up. I can't get my words out. I struggle to breathe, which is ridiculous – I teach yoga, for God's sake; I'm supposed to be good at this breathing lark.

I figure the best thing to do is let him talk. Then, glancing down, I notice in my haste to reach the phone I put my jumper on back to front. I'm barefoot. The kitchen floor is bloody freezing, and part of me wants to scream, 'I'm not interested,' or, more accurately, 'Leave me alone,' and slam down the phone.

But I don't hang up. I remain silent.

I listen to this man who claims to be my cousin witter on about my 'dad', and it takes every ounce of inner resolve not to mention some of my so-called 'dad's' nicknames. He is not *my dad*. He is *The Nigerian*. But how can I yell out 'The Nigerian?' This Teju person has a Nigerian accent, and I'm not a child. I am a grown woman in my 40s with a mortgage and responsibilities.

'I haven't called your brother yet. I thought I'd start with the youngest first,' he says good-naturedly. 'Then I'll contact your sister Adunni and your brother Abdul.'

'It's Dunni,' I say, correcting him. 'She prefers Dunni.'

'Ah – I see.'

'Why now?' I ask, leaning against the kitchen counter. 'Why did he ask you to find us now after all these years? Is he unwell or something?'

Teju says that other than a mild stroke a few years ago, he's in robust health.

'None of us is getting any younger.' He pauses. 'I think your dad wants to make up for lost time.'

'Is that so?' I reply sarcastically.

As a tactic to get rid of this stranger, I ask for his email and number. But he mishears. He says *my dad* would be pleased to know I'd agreed to call him.

'Oh – but your dad's hearing isn't great,' he says helpfully. 'You'll need to speak up—'

'No,' I say, raising my voice. 'I want *your* contact details, not his.'

I pick up yesterday's newspaper, scramble around the top drawer for a pen and scribble down the digits.

When I finish, there is a heavy silence.

'It's been good talking to you, Camilla,' he says. 'I hope we can speak again soon.'

Annoyingly, my overly polite gene raises its head. I mumble, 'Well, thanks for calling,' and I immediately regret it.

'Wait a minute. Can you clear something up? I'm a bit confused,' he says in an apologetic tone. 'Your dad called you—'

'Please stop calling him my dad!' I bark.

'Sorry,' he says. 'Uncle Rimi calls you Amanda, and when I last saw him he said you were known as Mandy, but he told me I should search for Camilla. Would you prefer I called you Amanda? I called you Camilla just now, didn't I, or do you like Mandy?'

'Yes – no,' I stutter.

'So when will you call back?' he asks.

I cradle the receiver against my ear and don't reply.

'When do you think you'll call back?' he asks again.

'Soon,' I lie, and I hang up.

*

What would you say if I asked you to guess the first recorded written name in history? Perhaps you'd reel off a series of names from the past – names like Thor, Eve or Andromeda – all perfectly acceptable guesses.

But to answer this question, let me take you back to the summer of 2020. It was a grim time. Lockdowns in the UK were just a few months old as the world dealt with the collective horrors of Covid. But in July, in the midst of the prevailing horrors, a large and remarkably fine pictorial clay tablet was sold at an auction in London. Known as the Kushim clay tablet, it was one of 77 pictographic tablets found in what is now southern Iraq. The tablet, etched with dots, brackets and drawings, appeared to depict business deals for multiple shipments of barley.

It read:

29,086 measures barley 37 months Kushim.

In his book *Sapiens: A Brief History of Humankind*, the cultural writer and historian Yuval Noah Harari refers to this clay tablet.

He believes the most probable reading of this sentence should be: 'A total of 29,086 measures of barley were received over the course of 37 months. Signed, Kushim.' This means that the tablet sold at auction in Iraq was one of the earliest references to naming, so, if Kushim was indeed a person, he may be the first individual in history whose name is known to us.

And, five millennia later, just like Kushim, I too was named.

My name was Mandy.

Here I am, aged ten, on a Sunday afternoon in 1980, sitting cross-legged on the carpeted floor in the back room of our terraced house in Luton, a multicultural town some 30 miles northwest of London.

In those days, life on a Sunday revolved around preparing for school on Monday. There were baths. After bathing, the 'kink' in my hair was pressed with a hot comb until it was as straight as a ruler. But not yet. It was a few minutes after two, and so far I'd spent the afternoon watching an MGM musical, and boy, did it brighten life up. Sundays back then were *the* day of closure. And that's no exaggeration. It felt like nowhere was open.

My brother, Abdul, five years older than me, was out, and Dunni, my sister, four years older, was upstairs 'doing her homework'. Except, in reality, she wasn't doing her homework. We shared a bedroom and, when I left her, she was lying on her bed, her hands behind her head, staring at the poster of Mel Gibson on her side of the bedroom wall.

Carmen, my mother, sat behind me, and I knew by the acrid smell wafting from the sofa that she was painting her nails. Remember that name – Carmen. It's important to this story.

By then, we no longer lived among the tight-knit community of the Marsh Farm council estate, built in the 1960s as part of the town's post-war expansion. Our new home was on Bradley Road, which meant if I wanted to see my best friend Jess it was a 15-minute cycle ride away. Still, we had moved up in the world. Our new bay-windowed terrace house had a galley kitchen, a too-hot-in-summer, too-cold-in-winter conservatory, a 'posh' front room reserved for guests and a back room/dining room for eating and watching television. Television was limited to three channels and was a massive part of family life, and the back room, like the rest of the house, was immaculate. Today, we'd call Carmen an early 80s devotee of the yet-to-be-born Marie Kondo approach to cleaning and clutter control. But money was tight. My mother worked hard to furnish our home in a cost-effective style, and she favoured an interior design aesthetic of pastels and scatter cushions. Ours wasn't a typical West Indian home. When I went to my Jamaican friends' houses, there were were trinkets on the tables, plastic-covered sofas, Jamaican flags pinned on a wall, and mantelpieces groaning with photographs of family members from 'back home', AKA Jamaica. In the summer holidays, my friends who could afford the airfare travelled with their parents to visit the island. On their return, they swaggered down the corridor, reeking of the Caribbean and greeting one another in a brand-new way. Instead of, 'How are you?' they said, 'Wah gwan.' I envied their holidays with their Jamaican families and their use of Jamaican patois. We had no family in Jamaica, and even if we *did* have family in Jamaica – how could we afford to go to the Caribbean? Our summer holidays were spent roaming the back garden of Bradley Road or, if my mother could afford it, in the seaside towns of Margate and Clacton. And believe me, there was no 'wah gwan' in Essex or Kent. Plus, my mother wasn't a fan of Jamaican patois, and we kids weren't encouraged to speak it. So, perhaps because of this, we were labelled by some West Indian families as a little bit 'other' and a little bit 'hoity-toity', which we were most certainly not.

'Poor Judy,' my mother said as the credits for *Meet Me in*

St Louis rolled. 'The Hollywood system worked that unfortunate woman to the bone.'

Intrigued, I asked her what she meant, but she didn't explain. Looking back, I suppose Judy Garland's ongoing battle with prescription drugs, alcohol and failed marriages wasn't the most appropriate conversation to have with a ten-year-old.

Instead, she shared a titbit.

'Her real name was Frances,' she said, applying the final application of cherry nail varnish to her nails. 'She changed it to Judy. I read all about it in the *Woman's Weekly*.'

Of course, changing your name in Hollywood was as common as weeds in a garden. But back then, I was unaware this was even possible. I knew you could change your mind about which television programme you wanted to watch, books you wanted to read or socks you wanted to wear – but changing your name? Wow! My ten-year-old head thought, if Judy could change her name, why can't I? Why do I have to be Mandy?

You see, until a few weeks ago, Mandy had been a perfectly acceptable name. Sometimes I even experimented with its spelling. Out went boring Mandy, in came Mandi, and one morning, sifting through Abdul's vinyl collection, I came across an album by the pop group Imagination. The lead singer was called Leee. So, for a few days, I became Mandeee.

But now I saw myself and my name differently. And this nugget about Judy changing her name blew my mind. It was like being locked in a sweet shop, watching Gene Kelly films, or, better still, locked in the mobile library parked near the Co-op.

Turning to my mother, I said in an eager tone that, like Judy, I wanted to change my name, but my mother seemed preoccupied. She raised a hand to her face, puckered her lips and blew air onto her freshly painted nails.

I tried again.

'I don't think I want to be called Mandy any more,' I said, hurrying to get the sentence out before I lost my nerve.

'Everyone knows you as Mandy,' she replied, frowning and blowing on her fingernails. 'Mandy's your special Jamaican name.'

'But we live in Luton, not Jamaica,' I shot back.

My mother told me not to be feisty and made that sound with her lips and teeth, a warning sign not to proceed further, but I ignored this.

In a faltering voice, I explained I wanted to be like Judy, without disclosing the reason why. How could I say that wasn't the name I had pulled from the bottom drawer in my mother's bedroom a few weeks ago?

I'd told no one about it. It was my secret. There was no way I could tell Abdul or Dunni. They'd want to know why I was rifling through our mother's underwear drawers, even though my mid-morning rumble was completely innocent. I was looking for a book. My best friend, Jess, who, like me, was a little bit show-off and shy, told me she'd found a copy of a book with a rude word on the front in her mother's drawers. She said the book was by someone called Jackie Collins. My mother was a reader, and I knew she read Jackie Collins, so one Saturday morning I opened her chest of drawers, hoping to find a copy of *The Bitch*. Instead, I found a birth certificate.

'I don't think I want to be called Mandy any more,' I said again to my mother. 'I want to change it.'

'Everyone knows you as Mandy. You can't change it. That's your name,' she replied with the faintest flash of irritation.

No, it's not, I wanted to say. That wasn't the name I pulled from your underwear drawer. The name on my birth certificate didn't say Mandy. It said Camilla.

But I didn't. I kept my mouth firmly shut.

Camilla was my secret, and, whisper it: I *loved* the name Camilla. The moment I saw that name on my birth certificate, something shifted and squatted inside me.

I scribbled *Camilla* in lower case and upper case using

freshly sharpened pencils and coloured pens down a whole page in my notebook, like one of the naughty kids in my primary school who were always being punished by the teachers. Except this wasn't a punishment. This was pure pleasure. When I was alone, I stood in front of my bedroom mirror and, in a grown-up voice, I said, 'I am Camilla,' and then in a louder voice, 'My name is Camilla,' dragging out the three syllables of my newly discovered name as though I were chewing on a toffee. But I wasn't Camilla. Who was she? I was Mandy. Friends and teachers at my primary school called me Mandy. If I visited the doctor or the dentist, I was Mandy. Camilla was a name in a drawer.

I tried another approach.

'Why are Dunni's and Abdul's names so different to mine, Mum?'

Silence.

'I think I'd like to change it,' I said, choosing my words carefully. 'Can I?'

At this point, my mother's glare became more of a frown, but it didn't alter her features. Of average height and slight build, she was knockout beautiful (you could cut your fingers on her cheekbones) and extremely well put together. If a fashion stylist peeked into her wardrobe, they would swoon and ask if they could borrow one of her outfits.

Without answering my question, she took one of her infamous tangents.

'I brought you three kids up without any help from *him*,' she said, spitting out the pronoun of the man I hadn't seen or heard from in over three years.

'Yes, Mum.'

'That man,' she said. 'I can't call him your father because he didn't act like a father. He called himself a playboy.'

'What's a playboy?'

'He was a good-for-nothing,' she continued. 'I didn't leave

Jamaica to train as a nurse and get lumped with him and all the other Nigerians.'

'No, Mum.'

'Nurse, did you come on a banana boat from Africa?' she said, affecting the voice of one of her White-British patients. 'Have you been on an aeroplane? Can you swim? Do you use a knife and fork in Africa? My name is S-A-R-A-H. Can you say it? S-A-R-A-H. Are people called Sarah in Africa?'

She shook her head at the murk of that particular memory.

'I explained to the patient that I was a Jamaican, thank you very much. But none of the patients on my ward had heard of Jamaica,' she said, making that sound again with her lips and teeth. 'But they knew all about Africa. They knew all about Tarzan and Jane and lions and tigers and naked men and women running around a mud hut clutching spears with a bone poking through their nostrils. Don't you ever marry a Nigerian, Mandy!'

'I want to change my name,' I said. 'I don't like it.'

'Babies can't name themselves, you know,' she said. 'You have a name. It is Mandy. You'll learn to like it. You haven't eaten your sandwich,' she said, pointing to the plate of floppy white bread layered with thick butter and strawberry jam on the floor beside me.

I took a bite but I was confused. I couldn't understand why I was called Mandy, not Camilla. Or what this had to do with him. Why did she mention *him*? And why didn't my mother just say, 'Of course, love, if you don't want to be called Mandy, then so be it. Change it.'

'Did The Nigerian?' I asked, whispering his nickname as though he were in the next room, not thousands of miles away in Nigeria. 'Did Sanni like the name Mandy?'

By the early 1980s, Sanni's names were interchangeable. He was never 'Dad'. He could be a pronoun one minute, a nick-name the next or we called him 'Sanni' – the surname me, my mother and my siblings shared with him. When they divorced my mother didn't revert to Francis, her surname before marriage, and, because she referred to him by our surname, we children copied the new moniker.

She pursed her lips and said Sanni was a good-for-nothing who didn't pay maintenance money for us kids and, with any luck, was as bald as a coot, begging on the streets of Lagos.

'Why don't you finish your jam sandwich or do one of your impressions, Mandy? Go on, love,' my mother asked, changing the subject again.

Now, of course, I realise this was her attempt to placate me and place a full stop on the subject of names and the thick forest of my parents' divorce – and her strategy worked.

In those days, I was known in our household for two things. I was a voracious reader. My childhood was full of books. I read by any means necessary – torch, street light from outside my bedroom or candle. I was also an enthusiastic mimic. Looking back, I realise part of my talent for mimicry and impersonations came from a desire to perform and make my mother laugh. Little wonder I enjoyed belting out Shirley Bassey's 'Goldfinger' or impersonating the botanist and television presenter David Bellamy at my mother's request.

I got up and impersonated Frank Spencer, the curious and rather odd character from the television series *Some Mothers Do 'Ave 'Em,* which, if you come across it now on one of those classic television channels, like most sitcoms from the 80s, hasn't aged well. Still, my rudimentary imitation of 'Ooh Betty, the cat's done a whoopsie on the carpet' made her chuckle, and seeing my mother chuckle was like a cloudy day, and then boom, the sun came out. I was lost in her joy, but the disquiet I felt about my name lingered.

Two

All Change, Please

A person's name is to him or her the sweetest and most important sound in any language.

—Dale Carnegie

The dictionary defines the word 'name' as a word or set of words that a person, thing or place is known, addressed as or referred by. This sounds relatively simple, doesn't it? We have a name to identify us. Names are one of the first things we learn about people, and they play a significant role in our initial impressions of someone. They are part of who we are. It is human nature to give something a name, and we humans just *love* naming things. Ask around; you'll be surprised at the random things people choose to name.

The average person in the US and the UK has two given names (a first name and a middle name), followed by a surname (last name or family name). However, not all countries follow the three-name configuration. It varies around the world. In Jamaica, double middle names are common, while in other nations, such as Italy, China and many East Asian countries, middle names are relatively uncommon. Still, regardless of our cultural backgrounds, our given name individualises us. It unlocks the door to our identity.

For Jeremy Schultz, a UK-based psychotherapist, names are central to his work. He says, 'I often ask my clients about their names, how they were chosen, and by whom, as this reveals important information about their family of origin, such as who they "belong" to or who holds the power.' Schultz goes on, 'I am curious about how my client has responded, consciously or unconsciously, to these pressures and how family narratives may have influenced their identity, relationships or sense of themselves in the world.' And Schultz should know. Like me, he chose to reclaim his name, which, in his case, was a Jewish surname, Anglicised from Schultz to Shaw to sound less Jewish.

But for now, I want to stick with the concept of an unforced name change. You change your name because you want to, and that's what I wanted to do as a ten-year-old.

In the UK, when you reach the age of 16, you have the right to change your name unless it is for fraudulent or deceptive purposes. But there is a cost. You will need to pay £30 for a deed poll document, as well as additional administration charges.

So, what compels someone to voluntarily change their name?

Some people change their names in response to their feelings. Perhaps they've outgrown a babyish nickname that doesn't represent who they are.

For others, changing a name marks a new chapter in their lives, and it can be a substantial or subtle change to distance themselves from a difficult family or upbringing.

In the 2023 film *Past Lives*, the central character, Na Young, emigrates to Canada from Korea and changes her name to Nora Moon to assimilate and make it sound less foreign there. The late sumo wrestler Akebono, who was born in Hawaii and became the first non-Japanese sumo grand champion, changed his name from Chadwick Haheo Rowan to Akebono Tarō after becoming a Japanese citizen.

At the turn of the twentieth century, in the US, many Italian, Slavic and Jewish immigrants changed their names in their desire to mix within the dominant American society. Italian immigrants translated their names into English, dropped the final vowel to make them sound less Italian, clipped or shortened their given names or altered the spelling. Sigismund Schlomo Freud dropped the Schlomo and replaced Sigismund with Sigmund to avoid anti-semitic discrimination. While another psychoanalyst, and friend of Freud, Otto Rosenfeld, changed his name to Otto Rank.

After emancipation from slavery in the 1860s, many former enslaved people adopted new names and surnames to represent a newfound identity and self-narrative. Some replaced a name or surname given to them by their former slave owners, like the African-American anti-slavery and women's rights activist Isabella Baumfree, who changed her name to Sojourner Truth.

In some Chinese-speaking communities across East Asia and South Korea, people change their names because they believe it ushers in good fortune or luck.

In India, names can signify social and caste status, and Dalits are at the bottom of this rigid caste system. So, to combat this, some Dalits escape the discrimination associated with their name by converting to Christianity and choosing an Anglicised name.

Some people change their name to show allegiance to a Confirmation name in Catholicism or as part of a new religious or spiritual calling. Changing a name marks a shift in their lives and their dedication to this new path.

In marriage, people change their names to show commitment to a new partner, and in divorce they change their names to outwardly disconnect from their partner and their past.

And, of course, there are those who change a name simply for the fun of it.

Why else would someone change their name from Craig Moore to Bowser I-Just-Wanna-Drift Moore? Or, how about the person in Texas who changed his first name to reflect his political apathy at the Trump and Biden presidential candidacy? In 2024 Dustin Ebey became Literally Anybody Else.

However, regardless of the 'fun element', according to Deed Poll UK most people change their names because they feel their name at birth doesn't fit who they are. But what does that mean?

Part of our need to understand ourselves is developed when we look back through the lens of our formative childhood experiences. When I ask my mother now about the afternoon we watched Judy Garland, and I announced I wanted to change my name, she says, 'All that name talk, love. You were always off in your own little world.' And I suppose I was. But this feeling of wanting to change a name can be experienced at any age.

The former Chancellor of the Exchequer, George Osborne, was 13 when he announced he no longer wanted to be known by his first name, Gideon. In an interview, Osborne explained the reason for the name change. He said, 'I never liked the name, and I couldn't think of anyone I liked or who was successful who was called Gideon.' The writer Zadie Smith, like Osborne, was in her early teens when she changed her name from Sadie to Zadie. Dana Elaine Owens, better known as the rapper, singer and actor Queen Latifah, came across the name Latifah in a book about Arabic names when she was eight years old. Before she became widely known as Chimamanda Ngozi Adichie, the celebrated Nigerian author revealed in a recent interview that she was not born Chimamanda. Her birth name was Ngozi Grace. As a Catholic, she chose Amanda as her confirmation name (even though it wasn't a saint's name). She was inspired by this name after reading about a character called Amanda in a novel. However, at university in the US, her class was full of Amandas. It was a popular name, so she created the Igbo name Chimamanda by adding 'Chim' to 'Amanda' and the rest is history. A literary superstar was born.

When I discovered the origins of Chimamanda's name, it was interesting to realise we shared a commonality in our given names. Mandy is the diminutive of Amanda, and, growing up on Bradley Road, Mandy and Amanda were used interchangeably depending on the family member. Dunni called me Amanda. Abdul preferred Mandy, as did my mother, although, on occasion, if I did something wrong, I was Amanda. Sanni called me Amanda, and when he called me by this name it had a peculiar intonation and rhythm. He emphasised the first letter. I was 'Ah-manda' and, growing up, I remember thinking - why does my name sound so strange on his lips?

If we think about someone changing a name, it is often about those legally changing their surname after marriage and divorce. When I spoke to Mary, a retired teacher from the UK, she explained how she had changed not only her surname but her given name too. 'I left the UK with an overnight bag and never returned,' she explained. 'I knew that my ex-husband would try any means, legitimate or otherwise, to find me, so I changed my name. It had to be untraceable, so I changed my first name, Eileen, to my second name, Mary, and dropped the letter "s" from my surname. Woods became Wood, and after a lot of form filling, the transition from "Eileen Woods" to "Mary Wood" was complete.'

For those going through the adoption process, once a child is adopted, changing their name is not encouraged unless there are safeguarding issues. For Tracy, an adoptive mum of two children, changing her children's names was never an option. 'My husband and I felt strongly about this,' she said. 'Considering all their losses before coming to us, their name is the only lasting gift given to them by their family. Their names are theirs to keep and not for us to take.'

Full disclosure: I am not what you'd call a religious person but, for purposes of research, I found myself flicking through the pages of the Bible. And I made a startling discovery. Names were frequently changed, which is an incredible fact, given that parts of the Bible are believed to have been written over 1000 years ago. It blows my mind to think we human beings have been changing our names for at least 3,000 years.

According to the Reverend Alice Goodman, who lives in the UK, changing names marked a sense of transformation or a turning point. 'But there are many, many more changes of male names than of women in the Scriptures,' she explains. 'Besides Sarai, whose name is changed to Sarah, the other female name change is Naomi, who says, "No longer call me 'Naomi', but call me 'Mara'."' However, Goodman says, 'Nobody followed her instruction. She remained Naomi throughout the book.' Despite the gender imbalance, what I learned about the many name changes in the Old and New Testaments was how symbolic they were. Changing a name was an act of transformation in acknowledging the person you've become, just like it is today.

The scientific study of the origin, history and use of proper names is known as onomastics. A few years ago, I attended a symposium with a group of onomasticians from Europe, North America and Africa.

In one of the seminars, Dr Julia Sinclair-Palm, an associate professor at the University of Calgary, discussed naming and changing names in the trans community. 'Choosing a name is often one of the first ways trans people begin to assume a different gender from the one they were assigned at birth,' she explained. 'It is one of the most powerful steps in acknowledging the person you've become, as this change reflects the process of identity formation. It is a joyful process.'

This mirrors how Jai, a 22-year-old student living in the UK, described his naming story. 'My name is just a few letters different from my birth name,' he said. 'It is a small change, but it's positive. It's my name. It reflects who I am and now, finally, I feel like I am wholly me.'

For Sophie, a nurse in the US, changing her name was a badge of pride. 'When you are trans, you can write your own story and the names you choose are your Declaration of Independence from everything you have ever known.'

When you tell people you are writing a memoir that examines our names and identities, they are intrigued. I've discovered it is the *number one* social gathering icebreaker. Try it. Ask around. You'll be surprised how inquiring about someone's name opens a floodgate of name stories. At a recent gathering, one person told me her name was changed by her mother. She said her mother changed it when she found out her husband (later ex-husband) named their daughter after his ex-girlfriend. Another explained how she almost changed her name in her teens due partly to her fractious relationship with her parents. Someone else explained how his name – he was called Barry – was one of the growing number of extinct 'untrendy' male names. 'Like Gary, Nigel and Craig,' he said. 'Now everyone is called Axel or Finn or Will. Barry just isn't cool.' And a few years ago, at a party in London, a well-dressed woman in her late 40s or early 50s sloped towards me, glass in one hand, vape in the other, and asked if I was the person writing the 'name book'.

'Guilty as charged,' I replied.

Without pausing for breath, she launched into her name story.

She said she used to be called Lesley, after an old raggedy doll that belonged to her older sister. Her mother wanted to throw the doll away because it was threadbare, had only one eye and was losing its stuffing, but her sister insisted their mother could only throw the doll away if she called her new baby sister Lesley.

'But Lesley is super dull. The name didn't feel right to me. And then I thought, why should I have a name that I don't really want? So when I was a teenager, I changed it,' she said, blowing sweet-smelling smoke into my face. 'I changed it to Emma. Emma's a straightforward name, isn't it?'

I didn't answer because what exactly is a straightforward name? If pressed, I'd say Lesley was a pretty straightforward name. Growing up in the 80s and 90s, everyone's mother was named Lesley, or else Mary, Julie, Carol or Karen. Karens were everywhere. And in those days, the name wasn't slang for a particular type of person who called the police on Black people. What was wrong with Lesley? And how could I tell this dinner-party stranger, Emma, that much as I liked the name Emma I was drowning in Emmas?

Once, out of curiosity, I scrolled through the contacts on my phone and made a startling discovery. I knew a lot of Emmas. I mean a lot. I've taught yoga to a lot of Emmas. I've hung out with a lot of Emmas. It is a popular name. In a recent study, Emma was perceived as a warm and competent name and, in 2016, when the dating app Tinder released its list of the most popular swipe-right names, top of the list in the US was Hannah and second was, you guessed it, Emma. No wonder, at this dinner party, Emma *loved* talking about changing her name and becoming an Emma.

But if you don't change your name, what are the consequences? Does an inner conflict continue to churn away inside?

Acting on the desire to change your name isn't easy. It is a big step – a giant leap. You will worry you'll offend the people who named you and about how others will react. When I spoke to Queenie-May, 26, from the UK, she explained how growing up, her name was considered 'different'. 'The kids at school used to bully and tease me about my name,' she said. 'I thought it was an odd name too, so from around the age of 11, or thereabouts, I really started to dislike my name,' she explained. 'I wanted to change it to something more gender-neutral. I liked the name Alex, but my mother was totally against the idea. She saw changing my name as a rejection of her.'

For some, like Kebbah, a musician based in London, who changed his name from Kevin to Kebbah to reflect his African ancestry, changing his name resulted in a long estrangement from his father. When we discussed this, Kebbah said, 'In my father's paradigm, changing my name was against everything he stood for. He said it was similar to losing a son. Thankfully, over the years, we've found common ground. He calls me Kevin' I wouldn't say I like it, but I've accepted if I want a relationship with my father, I must become this other person momentarily.'

Can I make it clear that there is nothing wrong with the name Mandy? It is a fine name. It has five letters, two syllables, and a certain creative pedigree.

As a child, I read about the adventures and exploits of Milly-Molly-Mandy. In 1919, Irving Berlin wrote the song 'Mandy'. The actor Nicolas Cage starred in a movie called, you guessed it, *Mandy.* In the 70s, the singer Barry Manilow crooned about Mandy as did the pop group Westlife, the French pianist Richard Clayderman and, slight curveball, a group called Mandy & Randy, who released a techno-inspired track called 'Mandy' in 2002. And a few years ago, I tuned in to a comedy on the television about a hapless heroine called Mandy Carter, AKA *Mandy*. So I'll say it again: It is a fine name. Who wouldn't want to be named Mandy?

Well – me.

But perhaps you are thinking – Why the fuss? What's the big deal? Shouldn't I get over myself? Move on. Sure, discovering another name on your birth certificate as a ten-year-old was discombobulating, but it's no big deal. It's only a name, right? Well, yes, it is only a name, but recent studies on naming suggest the impact our names have on our sense of identity. In his paper *Names, Identity and Self*, the US psychologist Kenneth L Dion refers to studies carried out in the US about the link between our names and how we see ourselves. The findings uncovered a definite correlation between names and one's sense of self. Dion discovered people who liked their first names also liked themselves more generally. In one study, American college students were asked to answer three questions. The first of these was who are you? – and the reference to one's name was the most frequent response. Sixty-three per cent of the respondents explicitly referenced their names when indicating who they were. Names matter. They are our central identifier, and yet, from the moment I discovered that name on my birth certificate, if I were asked the question – who are you? – I would struggle to know how I should answer.

Norfolk, January 2015

It is a few minutes past eight, and I am meeting Jenny, one of my Norfolk forest walking buddies, for an early morning stroll.

Jenny lives between LA, London and Norfolk. She was married and divorced to the same rock star, not once but twice, and is in her 60s. I am 45 and, despite our 20-year age gap, we've bonded over our shared experience of growing up without a father and our love-hate relationship with Norfolk. Part of me loves Norfolk's man-made broads, ancient woodlands, big skies and beaches. But Swaffham, the market town I've called home for the last five years, is a sleepy place. Although, saying that, there was once a scandal. The town's local married MP, a certain Liz Truss, embarked on an affair with another married MP, and a political commentator described the ensuing fallout as 'the most momentous thing to have happened in Swaffham since a cardboard box blew down the high street'.

I steer my car into the only available parking space and wave at Jenny, standing next to her car in tight white jeans, a Puffa jacket and aviator shades.

It is a Thursday, and the car park has a distinct 'New Year's resolution' vibe. It is busy, and everyone is in a hurry except me. I don't want to rush this walk.

I get out of the car, give Jenny's dog, Bindi, a ruffle, and think about Mike and his never-ending requests that we 'should get a rescue dog'.

'Are you all right?' Jenny asks, a note of concern in her voice.

'I'm fine,' I reply. 'Why, do I not seem all right?'

She smiles, slips her arm in mine, and we set off along a muddy path, wet with footprints and with an overpowering stench of horse manure.

'Come on, the suspense is killing me,' she says. 'Did you contact him?'

'Who?'

'The Oxford guy,' she says. 'The cousin who called you who lives in Oxford. What was his name?'

'Teju,' I say, noticing how unfamiliar his name sounds on my lips.

It's been a month since my so-called cousin's telephone call, and Jenny is one of the few people I've told about him. And, thank goodness she's a little more measured than one friend.

This friend became over-excited at the idea that I had a long-lost cousin, which was, I think, due in part to watching too many episodes of *Long Lost Family*, the television show where estranged or family members who've lost contact for one reason or another reconnect. I tuned in once, and I am embarrassed to admit I was sucked into its emotional vortex. By the end of the programme, my tissue was sodden, and I was a blubbering wreck.

I tell Jenny I haven't called Teju back.

She pulls at Bindi's dog lead.

'So does that mean if you don't contact this Oxford cousin, you'll think about contacting your father?' she asks.

The wind picks up. I stuff my hands deep into my coat pockets and think about everyone who's asked the same question over the years. When people find out you've not seen or heard from a family member, they are compelled to ask, 'Will you ever contact or try to find them?' And I utter the same response I give to Jenny.

'No,' I reply finally, and we continue trudging along the muddy path in silence. And silence suits this walk. The walking here is beautiful, and as I walk, head down, biting my lip, I'd be lying if I said I've not thought about Sanni during our long estrangement, although it's difficult to conjure up an image of someone I last saw four decades ago. My memories of him are hazy. He was such an absent presence it's hard to imagine him as a complete person. He was like an extra in a movie with a walk-on part and a few lines, and I suppose over the years I blocked him from my subconscious. Sanni was like a big ball of dust, and he was better left under the carpet. He was an erratic presence in our lives, and, because of this, my siblings and I held our mother tightly, and she held us more tightly still.

But as I stroll forward, fragments of memories rise and bubble on the surface.

I remember he was tall, well over six foot, slim, elegant, and, to my young eyes, supremely confident in his own skin.

I remember he wore expensive cologne that smelt of spices.

I remember the rustle of paper as he read *The Times.*

I remember he didn't teach me how to ride a bike.

I remember he didn't read me bedtime stories.

I remember the scant occasions I saw him after my parents divorced. One morning he was supposed to be taking us children out for the day – at least, that was the plan. I stood at the window, waiting, watching, but he never turned up.

I remember my mother's tears when a neighbour called her at work and told her Sanni was at our house in Marsh Farm. He came with a van and a key and helped himself to most of our furniture. Later, when I asked my mother why, she said, 'That's the kind of man he is, Mandy.'

Jenny stops for Bindi to pee.

'I can't wait for spring,' she says, pulling at the collar of her jacket.

'Look,' I say, pointing at two doe-eyed muntjacs peering out in the distance from a cluster of silver birches. 'They say you're never more than six feet away from a rat in London. Well, in Norfolk, you're never more than six feet away from a muntjac.'

Jenny grins, and I smile, too, but I can't shake the memories of this man I last saw decades ago. He was younger then. He's in his 80s now. What does he look like as an older person? As an older person, he could pass me right here, right now, on this path, and I wouldn't know who he was. A few moments ago, when I parked my car in the car park, I could have parked right next to *his* car. For all I know, Sanni could be among the few Black people in Norfolk I've given the secret nod. I call it the 'secret nod' because it acknowledges any person of colour in predominantly White spaces, AKA Norfolk, which, according to the last census, was 96 per cent White-British.

And let's say I *did* contact him. What would I say? Hello, The Nigerian. Hello, Sanni. Hello Dad. Hello… hello, what?

Years ago, before I started writing this book, I was on a train, travelling from Norfolk to London. In those days, like today, I carried a notebook around with me, and as the train chugged along, speeding through the countryside, I jotted down the names of all the people, past and present, in my life. Friends. Ex-boyfriends. Teachers. Family. Neighbours. Acquaintances. I didn't know where all those names would take me, but there was something deeply comforting about writing their names on the paper. They were part of the story of my life. But there was one person missing from that list. Then, like now, I knew he didn't deserve to be named. I can't allow myself to call him by his name.

That's what I tell myself.

Three

Miss Abara

A name is more than just a combination of letters; it's a reflection of your identity and aspirations.

—*Unknown*

My parents split up when I was around six and, when they divorced, there was no sit-down-and-let-the-children-know-we-are-splitting-up moment. Life wasn't like that in the 1970s. But even so, before their divorce, I knew something was wrong – very wrong. Growing up, I sensed my mother and Sanni were like night and day. She preferred quiet nights at home. He liked parties, whisky, politics, late nights and good times. On the rare occasions he was in the house, there was no holding of hands or displays of affection between them. I don't remember ever seeing them kiss. His erratic presence was marked by the clues he left around the house. Glass ashtrays filled with cigarette butts – the lingering aroma of his aftershave in the living room. And then, like a puff of smoke, he was gone.

Of course, grudges and gripes are nothing new when people get divorced. But young as I was, after their divorce, I recognised there were two opposing teams. In the blue corner was Team Mum. In the red, Team Sanni. There was no lurking in the middle. Dunni was on Team Mum. Abdul was on Team Mum. I was on Team Mum. There was only Team Mum.

So how did my parents meet?

Well, I know they met in London some time in the early 1960s. My mother had arrived in the UK in the winter of 1959, which was some years after Sanni, according to her, and five years after rationing officially ended. She was 19 years old and harboured an ambition to be a nurse and, unlike most of her friends, she came to England by plane. My mother said she'd heard rumours about some of the young people who travelled to the UK by ship. 'It took 22 days to sail to England,' she once remarked. 'That's a long time. No wonder when some of those young Caribbean ladies docked, it wasn't only their passports they were carrying,' she added, shaking her head in disgust.

Besides telling me Sanni had been in the UK for some time before she arrived, my mother didn't tell me much. I've since learned that he came from a very wealthy and privileged background and that, like most Nigerians with financial clout, he had been packed off to study at university in London. After he finished his studies, he didn't go back to Nigeria because, according to my mother, by then he'd had his head turned by the bright lights of the metropolis. Shortly after that, he met my mother and, when they married in the 60s, a union between a Jamaican and a Nigerian was uncommon. Even now, if I explain my heritage to an elderly person from the Caribbean, they'll scrunch up their nose and say, 'Your mother is Jamaican, and your father is Nigerian. That's an interesting and unusual mix!'

One cloudless afternoon, a week or so after discovering my birth certificate, I helped my mother peg out the washing in the back garden at Bradley Road.

It was a hot day, and my mother was in a good mood, which, on reflection, is probably why I asked her about Sanni.

'Did you have a big wedding?' I asked, wondering if this question would elicit the usual response. Silence. But it didn't. She answered in short, staccato sentences.

'There was one guest at the wedding,' she said, clipping two pegs onto Abdul's T-shirt. 'Sanni's cousin. He was a diplomat. He lived in London.'

'What's a diplomat?' I asked, passing her two pegs from a bag.

'A fancy job,' she replied.

I thought about asking if there were any photographs of this fancy diplomat or photographs of the day, but I knew there were none. In his smash-and-grab furniture raid at our old council house in Marsh Farm, Sanni helped himself to all our belongings. But even before that, there were no photographs of their wedding day on the mantelpiece. There were no pictures of my mother's family in Jamaica or photos of Sanni's wider family in Nigeria.

'Pass me another peg, love?' she asked, swatting away a fat fly from her face. 'I don't know why I married Sanni. He was tall, I'll give him that, but he was no Sidney Poitier.'

'Who is Sidney Poitier?'

'An actor, a *very* handsome actor.'

'When you married Sanni, did you wish Grandma Panama had come to the wedding?' I asked.

'Someone else liked me, you know,' she said, ignoring the question. 'He was called George. He had blue eyes and buck teeth. We used to go on dates. He'd open the door for me and buy me flowers.'

'Did you want to marry George?'

'Stop asking so many questions, Mandy,' she said. 'Go and get some more pegs from the conservatory.'

I sloped off, wondering what happened to buck-toothed George and what Grandma Panama, this mythical figure I'd never met, thought about her daughter marrying Sanni.

I wondered about the circumstances of their first meeting and who made the first move. Did Sanni sidle up to my mother and ask, 'What's your name?' Or did she?

Asking someone their name is about as personal as you can get. It is how we initiate conversation and build connections. 'What's your name?' is a universal question in any language. Behavioural psychologists describe it as social transference, and we all do it. Whether you live in Peru or Ghana, asking someone for their name and telling someone your name in response marks an important shift in your relationship. You are no longer strangers to each other. Telling someone your name is your opportunity to identify yourself as you wish others to identify you. And we tend to introduce ourselves by our given name, depending on our situation or cultural background. Little wonder the late American psychologist Gordon Allport said, 'The most important anchorage to our self-identity throughout life remains our own name.' You won't get arrested or go to jail if you don't possess a name, but at the same time, you can't legally identify yourself without one. How many times a day do you write your name? How many times a day do you say your name? How many times does someone ask you your name? But despite the ubiquitous nature of the question, in some communities referring to someone by their first name is *too* casual. A little bit *too* familiar. In South Asian, Caribbean and African communities, etiquette dictates that a person of the younger generation must not address an older person by their first name. If you do, it is tantamount to a crime. Older women are called 'aunty' (even when unrelated), and this is followed by their given name. Years ago, deep into my 30s, outside C&A, in the iconic 70s-built Arndale Shopping

Centre in Luton (later rebranded as the Luton Point), I called one of my mother's close friends, not *Aunty Sonia*, but just Sonia. As soon as I uttered the faux pas, I wished I could take it back. But it was too late. Aunty Sonia waved her finger in my face and shouted, 'Who do you think you are, young lady? Why are you calling me by my name? Are you an adult now? Wait till I tell your mother.'

No wonder she was aggrieved; I had broken the code. We were not mates! Plus, Aunty Sonia was from the Windrush generation. Like my mother, she grew up in a rural parish in Jamaica in the 50s. Back then, addressing an older person with a title was considered essential. Older people were treated with reverence and respect. They were Miss, Mr, Sir, Aunty, Uncle – never a given name.

When we consider using a given name within a family structure, things become even more interesting. Studies show there is often a reluctance to use a person's given name within the family. In most cultures globally, the parent-child relationship typically means children use a generic term for their parents, usually Mum or Dad, while the parents use the children's given names, as do the children between each other. And yet, growing up, one of my friends' parents actively encouraged her not to refer to them as Mum or Dad. She called her parents Mark and Tricia and not Mum and Dad, because they were anti-authority types and encouraged her to refer to them as human beings, not just a mother and a father. At the time, I thought, wow, now that is radical. However, in a study carried out in the US, students were asked to address their parents in an unconventional (for them) manner. If they usually referred to their parent as 'Mum' or 'Dad', they were asked to refer to them by their given names instead. On their return to class, most of the students reported their parents were upset with this new way of referring to them. Some parents felt ill at ease with the unknown status position that the new name implied, while others forbade their kids from using their given names. One female student reported being slapped by her mother because she did not appreciate her daughter calling her father by his first name!

Many years ago, I worked with a woman called Rebecca, but everyone called her Becky or Becca. She was older than me, perhaps in her late 30s, and she was a full-time sales assistant. I was a Saturday girl. That's what they called us in those days. And I enjoyed my job. I worked in the coats department in Debenhams, in the Arndale Centre. Although the money wasn't great, it was my first 'proper job' while I studied for my A levels.

Becca, as I preferred to call her, sucked discreetly on a Polo mint while we busied ourselves organising ladies' camel coats into their proper sizing on the hanging rails.

'My grandmother was a wise old soul,' Becca said, offering me a mint from her pocket. 'When I was growing up, she gave me four pieces of crucial advice. And she said if I followed them, I'd get on in life.'

Intrigued, I asked what those pieces of advice were.

'She told me to ask plenty of questions and mirror other people's body language,' Becca replied.

'That's two. What was the third?'

'Well, this is kind of random, but my gran said you should liberally use the name of the person you are talking to,' she explained. 'She said people liked hearing their first names because it makes them feel special, so I always try to slip in someone's name when I talk to them. It works. Honestly. You should try it.'

I asked her what the fourth was, and she said, 'Speak your mind. Don't bite your tongue.'

I didn't give Becca's grandmother's advice about names much consideration at the time, but now, 35 years later, I think, clever grandmother, she's right; people *do* like hearing their first names. During the last general election, I watched a televised debate and was reminded of Becca and her grandmother. I was curious to find out how often a politician referred to an audience member by their given name. And I lost count. Every politician on the panel used the first-name trick my friend's grandmother advised.

'Well, *Paula*,' the politician replied, flashing an insincere smile at the person in the audience. 'That's a *fascinating* question. Thank you for raising such an important topic, *Paula*.'

At the time, I wondered what the effect of hearing her name had on Paula. Did it make her feel special? And did hearing her name make her warm to the politician who used it? Perhaps this explains why there's been an explosion of people in the public eye adopting this given-name strategy espoused by my work colleague's grandmother. Over the last few years, politicians in the UK have ditched the formal way of addressing each other and instead increasingly use given names. Certain sections of the media refer to the ex-prime minister, Boris Johnson, as 'Boris'. Their predisposition to call him by his first name gives the impression that 'Boris' is our special friend or a much-loved comedy character. Or is calling him 'Boris' somehow a strategic weapon? Do they assume by calling him this, he can sit alongside the Zendayas or the Britneys, where the more famous a person is, the less of their full name you need to identify? Or perhaps this over-zealous use of a given name harks back to the origins of naming. Most people had only one name in the earliest period we recorded names in Europe. But I don't play the game. I refuse to call any politician by their given name. The only politician I've referred to by their first name was as a politicised, fired-up teenager in the mid-80s. Back then, Margaret Thatcher was the prime minister, and I, along with hordes of others, waved a placard and shouted, 'Maggie. Maggie. Maggie. Out. Out. Out.'

History is complicated, and, if we consider the historical context of naming, things become further complicated. Historians and name scholars struggle to pinpoint or answer where first names come from. If we consider naming in English-speaking countries, given names in the UK were historically drawn from an established pool of names. Some names came from the Bible, others from Germanic and other Continental first names, surnames and place names, and others from classical literary sources.

As an eager-to-learn ten-year-old student at primary school with a burgeoning love of history, I remember being taught about the all-conquering Romans, and the Vikings with their influence on place names in the UK, by a witty and sharp, if not a little grumpy, teacher called Mr Barrowman, who, looking back, was probably something of a name-obsessive. In one lesson, he explained that the Romans were early adopters of the three-name structure. He said they used a first name, middle name and surname, and he picked up a stick of white chalk and, with a flourish, wrote the name Julius Caesar on the blackboard. However, according to Mr Barrowman, this was not the man's complete name. Pushing his spectacles up the bridge of his nose he asked us kids to guess the famous emperor's full name. The usual hands shot up, but none were correct. In an excited voice, Mr Barrowman explained that each Roman male child received a personal name known as the praenomen, a nomen, which was a clan or tribe name, and a cognomen, a family name.

'So,' he said, peering around the classroom. 'The praenomen of Julius Caesar was Gaius, which means, children, that his complete name was Gaius Julius Caesar', and he wrote the emperor's full name on the blackboard. The diligent kids copied it into their notebooks.

Although the Romans provided a template for the naming structure common today, most onomasticians agree that the

Norman Conquest (some nine and a half centuries after the fall of the Roman Empire) is a better place to start when considering the history of naming in the UK. The arrival of the Norman invaders in 1066 had a huge impact on personal naming. Before the Norman Conquest, 85 per cent of men's names were Old English, like Godwin and Alwin. But, 150 years later, only 5 per cent of names were Old English; by then, most names were from Normandy. Names like Hugh and Robert were common names for men, and, for women, Matilda and Rosamund. Although there is some debate among name scholars about the extent of the Normans' influence, there is universal acceptance that the Conquest certainly accelerated the use of surnames in the UK, and most agree that many of the given names introduced into England then remain in use today. The establishment of the Church of England in the 1530s, after Henry VIII broke away from the Roman Catholic Church, coincided with the publication in 1553 of the first modern English translation of both the Old Testament and the New Testament of the Bible. The English translation of the Bible meant more people could read it. The public was influenced by many of those biblical stories, so when it came to considering their own naming choices, many turned to those books for inspiration. Names have evolved with each passing decade. Newly created names emerge all the time, and popular culture has insidiously weaved itself into modern naming culture. The Bible might have been a source of naming influence in the 1500s, but now inspiration comes from social media or the latest must-watch television show.

Biblical names are tied to my childhood. I remember, at the end of the school year, biting my nails, waiting to be assigned a role in the school nativity play. Most years, despite my performing and mimicking abilities, I was unlucky. I would typically be assigned only non-speaking roles, like a cloud, which meant flicking my fingers to denote falling rain.

However, one year, I lucked out. My best friend Jess was given the role of bush number one, which, if my memory is correct, she played with great gusto and enthusiasm, and I was assigned the coveted role of Mary.

At that age, the name Mary didn't mean much; sure, she was the mother of Jesus and all that, but I was too busy basking in the glory of having an actual speaking role to take much notice of the significance of my character's name. Now, I realise those biblical names that surrounded me in my childhood, like Mary, Adam and Eve, were some of the most popular male and female names chosen throughout the centuries. Biblical names used as given names are stamped on our cultural psyche, as are names drawn from the Hebrew Scriptures like Sarah and Elijah. However, given the popularity of religious names, it's perhaps surprising that Jesus is an uncommon name in English-speaking countries, despite being relatively commonly used as both a given name or a surname in Spanish-speaking countries. In Islamic communities, Muhammed, or any of its spelling variations, is a popular boys' name for parents who wish to honour and respect the prophet of Islam. In 2014, Mohammed was the most common name for men in Norway's capital city, Oslo, and in the UK, from 2016 to 2021, Muhammad was the number one name for baby boys. Despite its popularity, Mohammad, like many other Muslim names or non-White-sounding names, can inspire shockingly racist and Islamophobic behaviour. On a recent overseas trip, the Labour MP, Mohammad Yasin, was stopped from boarding a flight to Canada. Other members of Mr Yasin's group did not have any issues, but the MP for Bedford was delayed and questioned for a considerable length of time. When the MP queried why, he was told it was because of his name.

★

On those endless, summer holidays in 1980 Abdul, Dunni and I roamed the long, narrow back garden of Bradley Road, shielding our eyes from the sun, trading insults. Dunni and I made fun of Abdul's height. In 1980, he was 15, sported a dome-shaped afro, and was already well over 6 feet. Abdul and I, and I am ashamed to admit this now, made fun of Dunni's darker complexion. Dunni and Abdul made fun of my nocturnal reading habits. They said if I continued reading with a torch under the bedsheets, I would go blind. And then we indulged in our favourite pastime: poking fun at each other's names.

You see, back then, having a colourful and loud African-sounding name marked you out as different, especially among the Black Caribbeans who made up the bulk of immigrant communities at that time. In those days, my White friends, Pakistani friends, Irish friends and pretty much everyone else wanted to be associated with the Caribbean, particularly Jamaica. In the 80s, this small island of waterfalls, lush palm-fringed beaches, reggae, cricket and ska was *the* epitome of cool. Jamaica fizzed with creativity and, although the racism my mother experienced was still prevalent, times were beginning to change, albeit slowly. By 1980, unlike my mother's patient in her hospital ward in the early 60s, most people could locate Jamaica on a map. In comparison, Africa was portrayed as a place where children were in perpetual peril. Growing up, it was presented poorly in Western media. The continent's rich diversity, traditions, history and culture was ignored. Instead it was depicted as a monolithic entity in constant need of salvation. Africa was a starved continent plagued by conflict, poverty and hunger. Their children had flies round their mouths and distended bellies. I did not wish to be associated with that. Or with its weird-sounding given names. Although, in fairness, Dunni and Abdul thought I'd got off lightly on the name front. They questioned, as I did, why they were named differently. Mandy wasn't foreign and weird-sounding, like their names. They didn't explicitly say it, but Mandy blended in with all the Pauls, Claires, Joannes and Jasons on Bradley Road. Their Nigerian names didn't.

At the end of the garden on Bradley Road, there was a railway line that carried cargo, not passengers. Over the clank of freight train wheels clattering over the tracks, my siblings and I lay on our backs on the grass. We basked in the warmth of the sun, and, as an enthusiastic mimic, I would perform a comically exaggerated impression of Sanni's Nigerian accent.

'Adunni,' I shouted at my sister, lowering my voice to mimic Sanni's deep intonation. 'Go to the shop and buy me some cigarettes, Adunni.'

'It's Dunni, not *A*dunni,' she said, shooing a wasp from her face.

'Babatunde,' I said, calling my brother by his middle name and maintaining the Nigerian inflection in my voice. 'Go and get my cigarettes.'

They both laughed.

Despite my poking fun at their names, my siblings found my impersonation of Sanni and his smoking habit amusing. Trudging to the shop to buy his cigarettes was one of the few memories I had of him. In those days unlike today, it was perfectly acceptable for a pimply-faced kid to stroll into the local shop and buy pack after pack of cigarettes.

As an act of retaliation, Dunni and Abdul invariably threw my middle name into the verbal battleground. They had nothing else at their disposal. Mandy wasn't a powerful enough weapon, but my middle name – 'foreign', 'weird' and Nigerian – was in the same ballpark as their names and so aligned the three of us on the playing field.

'Adebisi,' my sister said in a faux Nigerian accent. 'What kind of middle name is Adebisi?'

'Mandy Adebisi,' my brother said, attempting a Nigerian accent but failing miserably.

I got up, raised my arms over my head and attempted a

cartwheel, then a handstand, but in my enthusiasm I fell over, and landed on my backside.

Dunni giggled.

'Do you miss The Nigerian?' I asked my brother, tugging at the grass to hide my embarrassment at falling over, and my question about Sanni.

Abdul shrugged. 'No,' he replied.

I knew he wasn't being entirely truthful. I thought that, as the eldest child, Abdul was Sanni's favourite.

'Liar,' I said to my brother. 'You *do* miss him.'

'No, I don't,' he replied.

I waited for him to ask me the same question. He didn't. This wasn't unusual. We kids never talked about Sanni, and we never discussed how we felt about our parents' divorce, even though a big part of me wanted to talk about it. But I was the youngest. They were older, quiet and compliant, and indulging in Nigerian name-calling was safer than a meaningful conversation.

Later that day, as 4 o'clock approached, signalling our mother's return from her job working in a daycare centre, we called a truce on our name-calling and sloped back inside. Now, I shudder at the memory of those summer days spent poking fun at our Nigerian names and our cultural heritage. But back then, I knew no better. I didn't know in Nigerian culture your name was unique to you. I didn't know names were chosen to bolster a child. I didn't know there were three levels of naming, and each stage connected a child to its heritage, ancestry and culture. Abiso is a personal name, Amutorunwa is a name given around the circumstances of birth and Oriki is a praise name, which is often given to a child by the parents' grandparents. I didn't know that behind every name there was a story.

I learned this later.

*

In 1981, I was 11 years old, and things were changing rapidly in my life. I was tall and skinny and, due to my high level of myopia, I wore glasses. Thick-framed black National Health glasses are fashionable today but, believe me, they weren't then. And there was another change. Puberty was dragging me backwards through a mulberry bush. There was blood in my knickers. Although I wasn't dying. According to my friends at school, it was part of being a woman. But I felt different. Not just physically but mentally. Dunni and I shared a bedroom, and her side of the bedroom was similar to a monk's meditation space. Clean lines. No mess. No clutter. In comparison, my side of the bedroom was like the aftermath of a raucous party. Most mornings, my mother stood at our bedroom door, her arms folded in front of her chest, and said, 'Why are you incapable of closing a cupboard or a door, Mandy?'

And there was another change – a more significant change.

Team Mum had a new member. My mother's 'special friend', AKA boyfriend and soon-to-be-husband, John, swelled our team of four to five. Like my mother, John was born in a rural parish in Jamaica, but he was so light-skinned he could pass for White. The real humdinger, though, for us, was how we referred to him. Somehow, we got away with referring to him by his given name. He was never Dad or 'Uncle John'. From the get-go he told us that we children should call him John, and, surprisingly, my mother agreed, which, looking back, might have been due to the fact that he was divorced and had children of his own. He wasn't our dad, so calling him 'John' somehow reflected his new status. And John didn't seem to mind the casual and controversial moniker (at least among the Caribbean community) we kids used. And we took his given names to new heights. Like many Jamaicans of his generation, John had a double middle name, so for a few months, in the early days of their courtship, behind his back, I called him by his full name: John Walter Benjamin.

One rainy Friday evening in 1981, I was curled up in the corner of the sofa, waiting for the two paracetamols I'd taken earlier to block out the pain. My mother was ironing, and John sat on the armchair, his legs stretched out in front of him.

In his deep rumble of a voice, he said he was going to the conservatory.

Hearing this, my mother stopped ironing and glared at him. She knew this was code. John's penchant for the conservatory was because he would crack open a beer and tune in to his CB radio. CB radio, otherwise known as Citizens Band radio, was massive in the 70s and 80s due in part to the film *Smokey and the Bandit*. CB was a two-way form of radio communication that enabled its users to talk and exchange information. I suppose it was an early precursor to the smartphone and the internet. Users had a 'handle', similar to a 'user name', and, if my memory is correct, John's was Top Dog.

'Mi soon come,' he said, getting up.

John spoke differently from my mother. He had retained his Jamaican accent, while she spoke in a carefully enunciated tone. Her accent was a mild curry, while John's was a fierce and fiery Scotch bonnet pepper-laden stew.

'Why can't you speak properly, John?' she asked.

'I'm a Jamaican, Carmen,' he said, grinning. 'That is how we Jamaicans speak.'

My mother kissed her teeth. She wasn't a fan of Jamaican patois, but her kissing-teeth prowess was Olympic gold-medal-winning standard.

'Mi soon come,' John repeated, opening the back-room door and closing it behind him.

I pressed a hot-water bottle against my swollen abdomen,

trying to numb my period cramps, while my mother pulled out a creased white shirt from an Eiffel-Tower-high stack of unironed clothes. I don't know why the pile of clothes sticks in my mind. But it does, and the fact that ironing was my mother's number one Friday night pastime.

'What's a Yoruba?' I asked, taking care to pronounce the word correctly. 'We've got a new teacher.'

'Another one? What happened to the last one?'

'He left. Miss Abara is our new teacher until we get someone else,' I explained. 'Her husband is from Nigeria, and she said I was a Yoruba and that—' I winced at this new kind of pain that hit me, searing through my ribs, pelvis and groin. Attacking with impunity.

'You'll grow out of it soon, Mandy,' she replied, changing the subject. 'It will get better, love. It's just period pain,' and, with a triumphant smile, she bent down and placed a pair of knickers on the ironing board. Some mothers love to knit; others cook; some like bingo. My mother loved ironing underwear. She said we children might get run over, and there'd be nothing worse than lying in an ambulance in crinkled knickers or underpants.

'Miss Abara said Sanni was a Yoruba surname,' I explained, pressing the hot-water bottle against my stomach.

My mother's nostrils and mouth made an odd noise somewhere between a sigh and a snort.

'What's a Yoruba?' I asked again.

In response, she slammed the iron onto a magnolia bedsheet.

'Miss Abara asked if Sanni was a Muslim,' I continued. 'What's a Muslim? Is it bad?'

'You are a *Jamaican*, not a Yoruba or a Muslim,' she replied.

'But was Sanni a Yoruba?' I whined.

She nodded.

'And a Muslim?' I asked.

'Yes,' she said. 'But you're none of those things. You're a Jamaican.'

'Miss told us in Nigeria, there are lots of different groups of people,' I continued. 'She said there were,' I paused, taking care to pronounce the word properly, 'Igbo people, and another one, beginning with H.'

The iron clanked down with renewed force onto the magnolia bedsheet.

'Hausa,' I quipped. 'Miss said they were called Hausa.'

My mother sighed.

'Do you like the name Mandy, Mum?'

'Yes,' she said, frowning. 'It's a fun name, and it's got two syllables. I like names with two syllables.'

'So why didn't you call me Molly or Milly?' I asked. 'They've got two syllables.'

'Stop asking so many damn questions,' she said.

But I carried on regardless.

'Did Sanni like the name Mandy?' I asked, pressing the now-cold bottle against my stomach.

'He planned to kidnap you children, you know. It was all arranged. He planned to take you to Africa. It's true, love. You'd be speaking Nigerian if it wasn't for me.' She paused. 'Why don't you put the kettle on, Mandy?' she asked in a softer tone.

'But *why* Mandy?'

'When you say the name Mandy, it makes you smile.'

'No, it doesn't,' I replied, poker-faced.

'Sanni is a liar, love,' she said, placing the iron onto the iron rest. 'When your brother and sister were born, he didn't register their names correctly.'

'Is a register like the register we have at school?'

In a weary voice, she explained that a baby's name must be registered when it is born.

'But Sanni registered your brother and sister with the wrong names. I told him to register your brother as Tony and your sister as Sarah, but he didn't. He gave them mumbo-jumbo Nigerian names, and we don't have those kinds of mumbo-jumbo names in Jamaica. Thank you very much.'

'Oh,' I replied, picking at the fabric of my polo-neck.

'When you were born, I warned Sanni not to register you with a Nigerian name. I said I liked the name Mandy, and what did the brute do? He registered you as Camilla,' she said, spitting out the name I found on my birth certificate like she was spitting out a drawer full of knives. 'I was meek and mild about Dunni and Abdul's names, but there was no way he would get away with it again. What kind of name is Camilla? Camilla doesn't sound nice. Mandy sounds nice.'

Fast-forward a few decades, and maybe my mother was on to something.

In a 2022 YouGov poll, 30 per cent of American parents admitted they chose a given name for their children simply because they liked the sound of it.

'Camilla isn't a good name,' my mother continued, slamming the iron onto a helpless pair of John's Y-fronts.

'I like it,' I said, still processing the deluge of information she had shared and the fact that Camilla was no longer a secret. My name was out in the open.

'That man,' she said, wiping her eyes with the back of her hand. 'He didn't put food on the table or clothes on your backs. You kids are better off without him. You don't need a father. I never really knew my mother or father, and look at me. I'm all right.'

But that wasn't true. Sometimes, behind those complex brown eyes, she wasn't all right, especially when she told us about her upbringing in Jamaica. We kids knew a few scant facts. We knew our great-grandparents were called Imogen and Albert. We knew they left Jamaica some time in the 1900s to work on the Panama Canal, a sprawling artificial 82-km waterway built to reduce travelling time for ships between the Atlantic and Pacific oceans. My mother told us her grand-parents were lured by the prospect of better employment opportunities in Panama, so they settled there and had a baby girl, Evelyn. But after many years of living in Panama, my great-grandparents missed Jamaica, and the family came home. Life in Jamaica in the 1920s was tough. Imogen and Albert struggled to find work, and Evelyn had met a local Jamaican man called Leopold. She became pregnant, and my mother was born, but a decision was made: Imogen and Albert decided to go back to Panama, and they persuaded Evelyn to join them. But one member of the family didn't make the journey back to Panama. Evelyn dropped my mother off like a barrel of rum, leaving her with her best friend. This friend promised to look after my mother until Evelyn had made enough money in Panama to send for her child. Except Evelyn never did send for her daughter. Later that night, I lay in bed thinking about Evelyn. I wondered what it meant for my mother not to have *her* mother. If she cried, my mother had no one to soothe her. Who was there to hug her if she grazed her knee? If it was her birthday, who baked her a cake or sang her happy birthday to you? I thought about all these things and, when I did, I felt an overwhelming sense of sadness too.

'Sanni is a poor excuse for a father,' she said, a tear rolling down her cheek.

I told her not to cry, but it was my fault. What kind of daughter makes her mother cry?

Dunni flung open the back-room door, ready for the school disco, reeking of Shalimar perfume, dressed in a black T-shirt, white ra-ra skirt, and badly applied make-up.

She looked at me, then my mother, and asked what was wrong.

'Mum wanted to call you Sarah,' I said to my sister. 'When you were born, she wanted to call you Sarah and Abdul Tony, but Sanni wouldn't let her. Sanni called you Adunni, not Sarah, and my name is Camilla, not Mandy or Amanda, so I want you to call me Camilla from now on.'

'What are you talking about Amanda?' Dunni asked.

'I'm Camilla. I'm not Mandy or Amanda.'

'Don't call her Camilla,' my mother replied. 'And nothing's wrong, Dunni. Don't be late, love.'

My sister glared at me, and closed the door.

'Are you feeling better, Mandy?' my mother asked.

'No,' I replied, shaking my head.

'Why don't you put the kettle on?' she asked. 'A cup of something warm will help.'

Over the years, I have dug deep into this memory to determine whether it was one of those shifting moments when you consider who you are and where you belong. I didn't belong anywhere.

Norfolk, February 2015

A few weeks after my walk in the forest with Jenny, over the whirl of Mike's electric toothbrush, I stand at the bathroom door, phone in one hand, a slip of paper in the other.

'I'm thinking of contacting Teju, this cousin guy,' I say to Mike.

He spits white foam into the sink.

'What made you change your mind?' he says, wiping his mouth on a towel.

'I'm curious, I suppose,' I reply. 'It won't do any harm. I thought I'd send a quick "let's keep the lines of communication open" kind of message.'

'Good idea,' he says.

To be honest, I'd hoped for a different response. Because

I'm not 100 per cent certain I do want to contact Teju, and part of me hoped Mike would persuade me not to. I hoped he'd say it was a terrible idea. I hoped he'd say think about your poor mother. Why on earth are you dredging up her ex-husband's Nigerian family? I am on a rollercoaster. Round and round I go.

'I spoke to Dunni and Abdul last week,' I say, leaning against the door frame. 'Teju called Abdul. He didn't call Dunni. I suppose he didn't manage to track her down, but it doesn't matter. They don't want anything to do with him.'

'Why not?'

I shrug.

'They're just not interested,' I say. 'It's dredging up the past, and they don't want to do that, so we've agreed not to tell Mum about Teju or Sanni.'

In truth, Abdul was keen to tell her all about Teju and Sanni, but I persuaded him not to. We made a sibling pact. Do not tell our mother about our Nigerian cousin Teju calling on behalf of her wayward, good-for-nothing ex-husband.

Following Mike into the bedroom, I place my phone and the slip of paper with Teju's number on the bedside table.

'I'm not bothered about Sanni,' I say. 'I want nothing to do with him.'

'I think it's great you want to contact Teju,' he says, climbing in beside me. 'I've always been intrigued by your Nigerian heritage.'

'This isn't about Sanni,' I say again. 'I'm curious about the idea of having a cousin. You grew up with loads of cousins.'

'Yeah,' he replies, smiling. 'Too many.'

'Do you think it's too late for a text?'

He glances at the bedside clock.

'It's a bit late,' he says. 'But why not? I bet he's been waiting for you to contact him.'

So, that's what I do. I grab my phone and write,

Hello Teju,

But saying hello and greeting someone by their name is the easy part. The tricky part was figuring out what came next.

Four

Made in Luton

'I have no name. I am but two days old.' What shall I call thee?

—William Blake

'I'm going to have zillions and zillions of babies,' my best friend Jess said, placing the hairbrush she'd used as a makeshift microphone onto her floral bedspread.

It was a Saturday afternoon. I was around 11 years old and, like most Saturday afternoons, I'd hopped on my bike and cycled to Jess's house. She lived with her mum and three older brothers in a cul-de-sac near the Co-op. Jess never talked about her dad. I presumed he had died, because there was a faded photograph of a wispy-haired blond man on the side table next to Jess's bed.

'I'm going to call my first baby Agnetha,' Jess said in a matter-of-fact voice.

I didn't reply. I was too exhausted. Wrung out by Abba.

We'd spent the last hour or so singing a medley of Abba songs. We wore towels on our heads. Mine was red and lavender-smelling to denote Anni-Frid, AKA Frida's flame-coloured hair. Jess's blonde hair was styled in a bowl cut, and, to be honest, she didn't need a towel. Nevertheless, she wore a white towel on her head in homage to Agnetha's blonde locks.

I wasn't much of an Abba fan. I preferred warbling along to 'Rapper's Delight' by The Sugarhill Gang or 'Wordy Rappinghood' by Tom Tom Club, but I was at Jess's house, and she was an Abba fan, so I had no choice but to belt out 'Super Trouper', 'Waterloo' and 'Gimme! Gimme! Gimme!'

'I'm going to call *all* my babies after Abba,' she said.

'I'm going to call my baby Grace,' I replied.

'Who's Grace?' Jess asked.

'Grace Jones,' I said. 'She's a singer, and she's amazing.'

By the look on Jess's face, she wasn't convinced Grace Jones was amazing. But Grace was *my* baby name, at least; that's what I told Mike, my soon-to-be boyfriend and now husband, when I retold this story many years later.

Because of our work – I teach yoga as well as being a writer, and Mike is an acupuncturist – people who don't know us presume we met on a wellness retreat in Bali, when, in reality, we met as students on a sweaty dance floor on Whitworth Street in Manchester at the height of the early 90s club scene.

Mike was in his third year at Manchester University, studying politics and sociology. I was in my second, studying drama and history at another college up north. I had noticed him across the dance floor, but played it cool, until he edged towards me and, in his Lancashire accent, this guy with the hazel eyes asked *the* question; at least, I thought he asked the question. The bass in the club was so loud it moved your body back a couple of inches, so it was tricky to hear.

'What's your name?' he asked again.

I gulped my warm beer.

'My *real* name is Camilla, but everyone calls me Mandy,' I yelled back.

'Why?'

I shrugged.

'Well – Mandy is a lovely name, but Camilla's beautiful,' he said, smiling. 'Which name do you prefer?'

I told him I liked Camilla, but everyone knew me as Mandy.

'So I can't change it,' I said. 'And Camilla's . . .' I trailed off and started again. 'Camilla is . . .' I gave up and told him my mum liked the name Mandy.

He asked what my dad thought, and I told him not much because he wasn't around.

'He buggered off when I was a kid,' I said by way of an explanation.

'His loss,' he replied.

'So – what's your name?' I asked, trying to maintain an aloof tone.

'Mike,' he replied. 'And the reason I'm called Mike is because my older sister fancied a kid at her primary school, so she badgered my mum to call her new baby brother Michael.'

I played it cool. I lit a cigarette (the menthol kind). In those days, my first few months at university, I smoked. I stupidly thought, hey, these cigarettes taste of peppermint, so they must be good for you, right?

'So what do you prefer?' I asked him. 'Michael or Mike?'

'Both. I don't mind, but don't call me Mick,' he grinned. 'One of my tutors called me Mick the other day, which threw me a bit.'

'I'll call you Mike,' I said.

He smiled.

'So can I buy you a drink, CamillaMandy?'

Reader: They say that you fall in love when you least expect it. Of course, I said he could buy me a drink. Maybe it was the way he'd asked about what I'd prefer to be called, or perhaps it was more instinctive. Mike said that, from the get-go, he knew he'd found the person he would spend the rest of his life with. And I knew that I'd found someone special – a keeper – the real deal. Our relationship was intense and a whole lot of fun. We laughed a lot. We brought out the best in each other. But I had doubts. Part of me wondered if relationships were sustainable. How did you make them work? My own parents hadn't stayed together, nor the parents of most of my friends. So, although we both felt strongly about each other, I said we should take things slowly. Still, a year or so after we'd been together, I told Mike about my fondness for the name Grace and my childhood best friend Jess and her zillions and zillions of baby names.

He laughed and said he didn't want zillions of kids, just a manageable number.

'Say, a football team,' he said, smiling.

The circumstances of my birth were different from those of my brother and sister. They were born in London, and their births were straightforward. I was a little more awkward. I was born in Luton and Dunstable Hospital, and I announced my arrival into the world bottom first. I was breech until I was successfully turned by the midwife, much to everyone's relief. After my birth, as is the custom, in the days and weeks later, like all babies I would be named.

Our parents or caregivers stamp this new identity on us because, as the US psychologist Jean Twenge explains, 'Choosing a name is an early, crucial parenting behaviour, as names are the first transference of culture from one generation to the next. For the parent, naming a child reflects the cultural and social influences of the time.'

If we follow Twenge's point of view, my mother's cultural and social influences at the time her children were born were rooted in her colonial upbringing in Jamaica. Growing up, she read English textbooks and followed the British school curriculum. When she read books about Africa, they were about boys and girls with strange-sounding names who lived in mud huts.

By contrast, Sanni's cultural and social influences were rooted in Nigeria's Yoruba naming traditions. According to Dr Ebunlomo Walker, the Executive Director for Integrated Community Welfare in Nigeria, the birth of a baby is such a joyous occasion among Nigerians that wider family members are often involved in the naming process too.

'It's a shared practice,' she explained when we talked over Zoom. 'A baby's birth is a recognition of another member coming into the community, so it's not only the mother and father who name the child. It's not uncommon for grandparents or even for uncles and aunts to be involved in the auspicious practice of naming a child.' Except that for Sanni naming me and my siblings wasn't a shared experience. He was a lone wolf. He named at will, going ahead without my mother's consent like a Mafia boss in his own fiefdom.

Naming a baby is a serious endeavour.

How could it be anything *but* serious? Babies are soft, creamy and dreamy. They are innocent, the best kind of humanity. We love kissing their fat cheeks, making funny faces, crawling on the floor, singing 'The Wheels on the Bus', and *we love* naming them. A baby's sense of identity and self-concept are developed through a family's repeated use of a child's name. The more a baby's name is repeated, the more that child will understand the name their parents or caregivers insist on calling them is *their* name. Language and speech therapists think most babies begin to recognise their first name between seven and nine months. At this age, they start to recognise the pattern of sounds, rhythm and intonation of their name being spoken, before they start to get to grips with the name's syllables. And then it happens. The baby is ready to let their name rip and announce to the world: this is me.

In most countries the naming of a baby is enshrined in law. Under the UK's 1953 Births and Deaths Registration Act, newborn babies must be registered with a given name and surname within 42 days of birth. In Nigeria bestowing a name is in accordance with the belief that a baby who is not named within seven to nine days after birth will not outlive the parent of the same sex. Traditionally a Yoruba boy is named on the ninth day, and a girl on the seventh. In Australia parents have a whopping 60 days to register their baby's name. So does having longer to decide make parents more likely to go down the uncommon-baby-name route? Do parents think, *we've got nothing to lose? Let's go for it, honey. Let's live a little.*

In 2008 a New Zealand couple did just that. They named their child *Talula Does the Hula from Hawaii* and the child, unsurprisingly, took her parents to court because she wanted to change her name to something less wacky. The judge agreed and criticised the parents for giving their child such a bizarre name in the first place. In his statement the judge said the name made a fool of the child and set her up with a social disability and handicap.

To deter parents from going down the wacky-baby-name route, some countries have taken matters into their own hands. In Germany the national civil registration office must approve the name you call your child. Certain names, like Hitler, for example, are banned. Iceland has a registry of approved baby names that parents can choose from. If the name isn't on the list, citizens can petition the Icelandic Naming Committee to approve their choice of name. In Australia, under the Births, Deaths and Marriages Registration Act, a registrar can refuse to register a baby name if it is obscene, offensive or ridiculous. In 2023, journalist Kirsten Drysdale decided to test just how rigorously this was enforced by submitting the most outrageous baby name she could think of for her third child, which was 'Methamphetamine Rules'. Drysdale assumed the name would be rejected. It wasn't, and when she queried this a spokesperson the NSW Registry of Birth, Death and Marriages admitted that the 'unusual name' had 'unfortunately slipped through'.

In the UK and the US there are no such rules. You can call your child anything you want and in the US there is growing evidence to suggest parents actively pursue uniqueness and individualism.

But does the pursuit of uniqueness come at a price?

In 1948 professors at Harvard University studied freshly graduated young men to determine whether personal names had any bearing on academic success. Their study concluded that men with unusual names were more likely to have flunked out or to have shown symptoms of psychological neurosis than those with more common names. In short, the rarer the name, the greater the psychological impact on its bearer. The pursuit of the uncommon baby name didn't impress the US child development expert Lee Salk. Rather amusingly, he said, 'Parents who give their kids weird names are weird themselves.'

When I told people I was writing this book, friends contacted me, desperate to offload their baby-name stories. One friend who lives in New York told me that for her, choosing the right baby name was a huge responsibility. She felt that giving her child the right kind of name was key to ensuring their future prospects. Given that over the last few years in the US baby-name consultants and influencers seem to have become the must-have accessory for well-heeled parents, perhaps her anxiety was valid. Baby names are *the* ultimate form of parental or caregiver self-expression, so it is perhaps not surprising to learn that choosing a baby's name is one of the most stressful acts a new parent is expected to perform – no wonder our parents or caregivers are keen to bestow meaningful and memorable names on their offspring. One friend told me she thinks choosing a baby name is a nightmare because you want everyone to think your child is the most amazing and interesting person they've ever met, so their name must reflect that. She felt there was a massive unspoken pressure to choose the right name. But even if you *do* select the so-called right name – who says everyone will like it? In a recent survey of 2,000 grandparents in Australia, one in five admitted they hate their grandchild's name. Twenty-eight per cent said the name was ugly, 17 per cent too weird, and 11 per cent too old-fashioned. The results also found that 2 per cent of grandparents became alienated from their children because of their grandchild's name. Such feelings aren't unique to the grandparents in this survey. Family rifts over baby names occur more frequently than we might think.

After many years of trying, a friend of mine and her husband eventually conceived twin girls, who they named Acacia and Charity. Although both sets of parents liked their children's names, not everyone in the family agreed. My friend's brother-in-law certainly didn't. He couldn't understand why anyone wanted to name one of his twin nieces after a tree and the other a name best suited to, in his opinion, 'some kind of hippy'. He said their names had the wrong 'vibe'. He was so affronted by his brother's decision that he refused to talk to his younger brother or his wife, and his baby-name sulk lasted for years. But despite the brother's aversion to the names, by naming one of their babies after a plant my friend and her husband were following a centuries-old trend. Daisy, Hazel, Holly and Ivy were popular botanical girls' names in the nineteenth century. In the sixteenth century, virtue names like Grace, Faith, Hope and Charity were popular names to remind children of their duty to God.

In Nigeria twins are seen as a blessing and good fortune,

and perhaps because of this, they are named on the eighth day, not on the seventh or ninth day, as is customary in the country. There is even a self-proclaimed capital of twins, Igbo-Ora, in southwestern Nigeria, and there is no chance of family rifts when it comes to naming there. Irrespective of gender, the older twin is always called Taiwo, meaning 'the one that tests the world', and the younger is called Kehinde, meaning 'the one that came after'.

But if we follow the point of view of my friend's brother, who took offence at the uniqueness of his niece's name, does that mean a 'good baby name' has to be common, simple, easy to spell, and roll effortlessly off the tongue? And who decides? Someone else's great baby name is another person's lousy baby name. So what are parents supposed to do? Do they lick their fingers and flick through hoards of baby-name books for inspiration? Do they name their child after a much-loved grandparent, or is such a name deemed too old-fashioned? Would a derivative of that name be more suitable? And what happens if the child grows up and hates the shortened form and wants to be called by their grandparent's name? Or what about a baby-name mash-up like Saran, a mixture of Sarah and Anne? Or do those holding the power of naming ditch the baby-name books and the mash-ups and call the baby after themselves? The singer Jason Derulo named his baby Jason King Derulo. And let's not forget the ex-boxer and entrepreneur George Foreman. He named every one of his four sons George. Perhaps it takes a particular kind of father to name his son after himself or, as in the case of the former Chancellor of the Exchequer, Nigel Lawson, his daughter, who he named Nigella.

My childhood best friend Jess didn't name her babies after the members of Abba, despite her youthful ambitions to do so.

In the early 2000s, in one of those chance encounters that remind you of the passage of time, we bumped into each other at King's Cross Station, where we were both queuing for train tickets.

'Jess?' I said to the mousey-haired, no longer blonde woman who turned from the ticket counter, holding hands with a cherubic young girl of around seven.

'Mandy,' she said, her eyes crinkling at the corners. 'I didn't recognise you. How are you?' I didn't correct her and say, 'It's Camilla. I'm not called Mandy any more.' There was no time to explain the history and evolution of my name. I had a train to catch.

Instead we hugged. I was genuinely pleased to see her. We reminisced about the 'old days' and she introduced me to her daughter, who stuck out her hand and said in a confident voice, 'My name is Nicole.'

'Pleased to meet you, Nicole,' I said, smiling.

'We just loved the name,' Jess explained. 'My husband chose it.'

We chatted, exchanged numbers and promised to keep in touch but, of course, we didn't. Our intense childhood friendship was rooted in the past, not the future. But years later, while researching this book, I was reminded of the encounter and Nicole's name sparked interest. I read an article that said in the mid-90s, Nicole was the 36th most popular girls' name in Britain. Some 12,000 babies were christened Nicole, and this was attributed to a television advert. Some of you might remember it – a pretty young French girl floating around the countryside in her Renault Clio was called Nicole, and this inoffensive and breezy advert spiked a baby-name trend. I did the maths. Jess's daughter was born in the 90s, and I wondered if she called her daughter Nicole because of that advert.

Each year in the UK the ONS (Office for National Statistics) releases lists of the most popular boys' and girls' names. The lists reveal what's hot and what's not in the baby-naming world, and the results are analysed and pored over by media outlets, baby-naming experts, the 'let's start a family' general public and baby-name fanatics. They want to know whether Amelia or Jack will take the top spot, whether Archie is a short-lived fad or a new baby-name force to be reckoned with and if world events affect naming choices. The data suggests they do. During the first lockdown in 2020, a couple from India named their twin boys Covid and Corona, and a father from Uttar Pradesh named his newborn son Sanitiser. But a unique or cool baby name one year can be colder than a Popsicle the next. Trends change. And is the gender categorisation for boys' and girls' names outdated? What constitutes a boy's name and a girl's name?

Patricia, an artist, writer and lawyer from the US, explained how she longed to be called Richard for her Confirmation name. 'I picked Richard, supposedly after St Richard of Chichester, but honestly, I just really liked the name, and he was a saint.' But there was a problem. Patricia was told she couldn't choose Richard.

'The nuns said there was no way in heaven or hell I could have a male saint's name! I must choose a female saint,' Patricia said. 'So I reluctantly picked Elizabeth, but all these years I've harboured a bit of resentment that I wasn't allowed to take the name Richard.'

Patricia was on to something. In the Middle Ages, women often had what we now regard as men's names, partly because of the small number of female saints. So, in the mid-1500s, Richard was, in fact, a common name for boys and girls. Other names commonly used for boys and girls included Philip, Nicholas and Alexander. However, when the Church authorities recorded names, they did so in Latin, and, following the rules of Latin grammar, the names were written with feminine endings. So, Philip became Philippa, Nicholas became Nicola and Alexander became Alexandra, hence our modern misconception that feminised names were in use in those days.

For some, the blurring of lines between male and female given names can be problematic. The song 'A Boy Named Sue', recorded by Johnny Cash, talks about a boy whose absent father gave his son the first name Sue. The late broadcaster and writer Clive James changed his name from Vivian to Clive. The wrestler Big Daddy, famous in the 80s, was born Shirley Crabtree and in interviews, Crabtree alluded to the difficulties of growing up with a 'girl's name'. So what is it like to grow up with a name that blurs the lines between genders? In 2005, a US study found that boys in a Florida school with names more commonly given to girls were more likely to misbehave, display behavioural problems and attain lower test scores. But even so, over the last decade or so there's been a palpable shift. When I interviewed Pamela Redmond, the co-creator of Nameberry, the world's largest website about baby names, she explained, 'The biggest change we've seen in the past decade is the rise of gender-neutral names.' Redmond added, 'Another recent development is teens changing their names to reflect their changing gender identity as more people identify as non-binary or gender-queer and adopt they/them pronouns. Names that reflect this gender neutrality will become more and more appealing and more widely used.'

So what makes a good baby name? Redmond's advice is simple. 'What defines a good baby name is a name that's right for you, a name you love, and that's very individual,' she said. When naming her own children, Redmond explained what was important to her when she chose a baby name:

A name with personal significance, either via family connection or meaning.

A name with deep roots and history.

A name with a congenial rhythm and initials – you really cannot give your baby initials like A.S.S.!

A name that is uncommon but is still widely known and in step with modern styles.

A name you love in an instinctive emotional way – real love!

And that's what Mike and I did. A year or so into our relationship we didn't take things slowly any more. There was no need. When I was with him, my heart beat fiercely. In those early days, we discussed baby names, and even drew up a list.

Grace

Nesta

Marley

Garland

Ben

Of course, the list changed over the years, but they were *our* baby names.

Norfolk, March 2015

It is a Saturday, and I am standing outside my mother's bungalow, clutching a bag of okra, but this bungalow is not nestled in the streets of Bedfordshire. It is not in Luton, the town of my childhood, that was voted (unfairly, in my opinion) 'the crappiest town in Britain'. You see, after 40-plus years living among Luton's mixed, vibrant, diverse and sizeable Caribbean community, my mother and John have moved to – drum roll, please – Norfolk, 15 miles away from my new home town of Swaffham.

'Well, at least you'll up the ethnic minority count,' I told her a few weeks before the big move.

She shrugged.

'But it's—' I sighed. 'Norfolk is – different, Mum.'

'You and Mike moved from London to Norfolk. It can't be *that* different,' she said. 'And we'll be nearer to you. Who knows, your brother and sister might move to Norfolk. Wouldn't that be nice?'

'Mmm-hmm,' I replied, but in my head, I thought there

was no way Dunni and Abdul would ever move out of Luton. If you cut them, they would bleed Luton Airport.

But in one respect my mother was right. Mike and I were early move-out-of-the-city pioneers. We'd left London over 11 years ago and sometimes I wondered what the locals made of us, an interracial couple of out-of-towners. Some friends still couldn't understand why we'd moved. How could we leave the swinging metropolis of London to live in the middle of a market town surrounded by farmland and folk with broad Norfolk accents? One friend was blunt.

'Why are you moving?' she asked, and then she affected a Norfolk accent. 'Don't go. You'll be the only Black in the village.'

'That's not the accent,' I said, laughing. 'Why do people think someone from Norfolk sounds similar to the West Country?'

But who knew then that, when my mother and John visited us in Swaffham on weekends to help renovate our first floor into a yoga studio, they were hatching their own move-out-of-Luton-to-Norfolk plan?

I grip the bag of okra but, before I ring the doorbell, I take a deep breath to prepare myself for the visit. I gee myself up. Whenever I visit my mother, I revert to wearing that ill-fitting pair of jeans. I am still Mandy in her eyes. No wonder this so-called cousin, Teju, was confused. It's been three months since he called, and I haven't got any further than writing *Hello Teju*.

I press the doorbell, and moments later my mother flings open the front door in one of her Demis Roussos 70s-style, brightly coloured kaftans. Her hair is tied up in a tight bun, and close up she looks exactly the same as she did twenty years ago. It's like she's ageing backwards. When she was younger, she was often mistaken for the Hollywood actor Diahann Carroll from the 80s TV show *Dynasty,* but just recently she was asked by a neighbour if she was the newsreader Moira Stuart. Flattered by the compliment, Moira Stuart being a good few years younger than my mother, she said she was tempted to reply, 'Yes, I am!'

My mother takes the bag, thanks me for buying her okra, and ushers me inside. But even with a bagful of her favourite vegetable, I can sense she is preoccupied and, dare I say, not in the best of moods.

We sit in the spotlessly clean living room, but it is different. Everything has been moved around because, in addition to cleaning, my mother takes an almost pathological pleasure in rearranging her furniture.

John is in his reclining easy chair, an electric oversized slipper warming his feet. He is snoring, his mouth open like a fish, until he stirs and rubs his eyes.

'Hello, Mandy,' he says. 'You all right?' And then he closes his eyes because he is not what you'd call a conversationalist.

My mother asks if I want a cup of tea, and a few minutes later she comes back into the living room carrying a tray of hot drinks, napkins and a plate of rich tea biscuits.

The three of us slurp our tea, dunk biscuits in dainty china cups, and indulge in idle chit-chat about her new church. My mother was a late convert to religion. She started attending a church in Luton, but, since the move to Norfolk, her religious zeal has shifted into fifth gear. Last Christmas, she gave me a Bible as a present, and now she sends WhatsApp messages telling me to *Stay blessed*, accompanied by two emojis, a smiling face and hands in prayer position.

In a clipped voice, she asks how my classes are going, and this is the moment I realise something is wrong, very wrong. My mother *never* asks about my work. She can't understand why I teach yoga when I could be in an office holding down a proper nine-to-five job. I was the only person in the family to go to university and, in her eyes, I blew it to prance around in a studio in leggings like Jane Fonda.

'So,' she says, smoothing her hands down the fabric of her kaftan, 'have you got any news?'

I shake my head and then remember a sign I saw in the local shop in Swaffham about a lost cat.

'It was bizarre,' I said. 'And I'm quoting here, but it said it was a "very distinctive ginger cat with a huge head".'

She laughs, but it's not a genuine laugh.

'Are you sure?' she asks. 'Nothing else?'

'No.'

'Nothing else?' she asks again.

'Nope.'

She glances at John, and he picks up the remote control.

'I don't know why I pay for a television licence when there's nothing but baking or dancing on the telly,' he says.

'So,' she says, biting her bottom lip, 'you've had your chance. I know all about your hot-shot doctor Nigerian cousin.'

I start to say something, but she raises her hand like a tech bro giving a TED Talk and silences me.

'Your brother told me about this Teju person,' she says, her mouth pinched at the corners.

Perhaps sensing the atmosphere, John gets up, puts the remote control on the chair, and mumbles that he's going to the garage, which, in reality, means he is going to watch his model railway twirl around a track.

We watch him leave, and my mother says Teju is doing the dirty work for Sanni, and I mustn't fall for it. But I am furious. Why did my brother tell her about Teju? He promised he wouldn't. The last time I spoke to Abdul, he was jetting off to the States on business, and he said of course he wouldn't tell our mother about Teju or Sanni. But behind my back, he broke the bloody pact.

Blindsided, I squirm in my seat and bow my head as though preparing for the guillotine. What is it about parents that turns you into a bumbling child again? It is unsettling how we fall back into patterns. I feel like I am regressing. I am not 45. I am 14 again.

My mother leans back in her chair, and for the next few minutes it's like watching a just-popped champagne bottle. She fizzes with rage. She says you can't trust Nigerians, and in her opinion Teju is part of a secret cartel of Nigerian internet scammers.

'Maybe he's not your cousin. Did he ask for money?'

'No, of course he didn't,' I say.

'Good,' she replies. 'I read in the paper that half of all calls to landlines these days are from scammers.'

'He isn't a scammer, Mum.'

'How do you know that, love?' she asked. 'He could be. You're not going to contact this Teju person, are you?'

Why is it so difficult to say what I think? Why can't I say, 'Mum, you know what, maybe I will contact him. He sounds like a nice guy, and I'm curious about my Nigerian heritage. I understand how you feel about Sanni, but this isn't about you. It's about me.'

'No,' I say quietly because, in truth, I'm not certain if I do want to contact him.

My response pacifies her, but inside a rage builds in my chest at my feeble answer and at Abdul breaking our pact. These days, people deal with their anger by booking a couple of sessions in a rage room and smashing their way through their fury, but I make do with chewing the inside of my cheek.

I think about Abdul and try to reason with myself. He is much older than me, and his animosity towards Sanni comes from a different perspective, so perhaps his memories feel significant and deep-rooted. But mine are too, and I didn't break the bloody pact.

'I wonder who will win Miss World,' my mother says, her mood lifted.

'What?'

'Miss World,' she says. 'How many times do you think Jamaica has won Miss World?'

I shrug. 'I don't know—'

'Don't lecture me about feminism,' she says, interrupting. 'Miss World is a bit of fun. Go on, Mandy. Guess.'

'Once,' I reply, sighing.

'We've won three times, and I bet we'll win again in four years. We Jamaicans are unstoppable, love.'

And my mother was right: guess which Caribbean country won Miss World four years later?

A few weeks go by, and I am true to my word. I don't contact Teju.

When I interact with Abdul at family gatherings, I fold my arms in front of my chest when he says, 'Mum *needed* to know.'

I take comfort in teaching my regular yoga classes, and I don't get annoyed by the usual suspects who never say thank you at the end of the session.

I clean the fridge, which is pound for pound the best cleaning activity to take your mind off cousins or Sanni – but not forever. One wet Friday night when the torrential rain outside seems to come down sideways, Mike is whisking eggs in a bowl.

'Fancy an omelette?' he says.

'I'm going to message Teju,' I say. 'I'll write him an email, and I'm going to send it this time.'

He stops whisking.

'I've been waiting for you to say that,' he says.

'Have you?'

He nods.

'You could meet him in London. There's a nice cafe near Warren Street Station,' he says, vigorously whisking the eggs.

'You're over-whisking the eggs,' I say.

He smiles and places the fork on the counter, while I stand by the kitchen door thinking about the questions that have churned in my mind over the last couple of months. And then, once I've worked out what I want to say, I grab my phone, and retrieve the scrap of paper I wrote Teju's contact details on and compose a message.

Subject: Hello & Some Questions.

Dear Teju,

I hope this email finds you well!

I'm sorry it's taken so long to contact you. I intended to message you a few weeks ago, but I talked myself out of it. To be honest, I've gone through a myriad of emotions about sending you this message. But here it is.

It's far too soon to even consider contacting Sanni. Perhaps I never will. Instead, I thought, if that's okay, you could act as a go-between and ask him the question that's been whirling around my head. I'm struggling to understand why it's only now, suddenly, that he has reached out. What prompted him to ask you to find me? When he returned to Nigeria, he had plenty of opportunities. He knew where we lived at the time. Forty years without so much as a birthday card or a letter is a very long time. To be frank, I'm confused.

Thanks, Teju. I hope you don't mind asking him. And yes, let's meet up. Perhaps we could meet in London? It's not too far from Oxford or Norfolk.

One last thing. I'd appreciate it if you didn't pass on my contact details to him.

I look forward to hearing from you.

Very best wishes,

Camilla

After silently counting from one to three, the enormity of my email hits. My thumb hovers over the button and then, finally, I press send.

Mike slips his hands around my waist.

'I feel like the letter J is stamped on my forehead,' I say.

'Why J?'

'Judas,' I reply. 'I can't shake the feeling that I'm being disloyal to my mum. Contacting Teju is prising open the can of Sanni. It's not fair on her. I'm dredging up the past.'

'She'll understand you want to know more about your family.'

I throw him a look that indicates Are you nuts? Of course she won't understand. But that's Mike. He would say that. He sees the good in people.

'Oh God. . .' I trail off.

'What?'

'What if I meet Teju and he's a weirdo?'

He laughs and starts to say something, but he is interrupted by the ping of my phone.

'That was quick,' he says. 'He's obviously been waiting for your email.'

Before I pick up my phone, a bolt rushes through me. What if he's changed his mind? What if he doesn't want to act as a go-between?

Licking my lips, I read his message.

RE: Hello & Some Questions

Dear Camilla,

Nice to hear from you.

I am well. I hope you and yours are fine too.

I note your request not to pass on your contact details to your father. Of course I won't. Please give me a few days before I pass on your question to Uncle Rimi. In the meantime, I would very much like to meet up. I'll send you some potential dates. London is fine; it works well for me, and the weekend is best.

All my good wishes,

Teju

I put down my phone, wondering how I should respond. If this was a text message, this is one of those messages that require a thumbs-up, a smiley face or hands in a prayer position. But I am not an emoji fan. I have never used an emoji, much to the amusement of my family. I am, however, an enthusiastic user of the exclamation mark.

RE: Hello & Some Questions

That's great!! Thank you very much.

I hope you don't mind, but I've thought of another question. I'm curious about my name. Where does Camilla come from? Is it a popular name in Nigeria? It's no problem if you don't know. I just thought I'd ask.

I'll think about a suitable place to meet in London.

All best wishes,

Camilla

And this is how it begins.

Five

Carlton Long

A good name will wear out; a bad one may be turned; a nickname lasts forever.

—Johann Georg Ritter von Zimmermann

As the winter of 1982 was coming to an end, I was 12 years old, on the cusp of becoming a teenager. My once-inseparable friendship with Jess had fizzled out, and I had acquired a new best friend. Her name was Lisa. She was loud and expressive, and we shared a love of books, drama lessons and mimicry. Lisa's 'nickname' for me was Mand, so it wasn't a nickname strictly speaking, while mine for her was Rik, in honour of one of our favourite characters from the 80s television show *The Young Ones.* When I think back to those early years at secondary school, Lisa and I were in the minority. None of my other friendship groups bestowed nicknames on each other. We may have studied and read about various early rulers of England and Great Britain in our history textbooks who had nicknames like Alfred the Great, Edward the Martyr, Ethelred the Unready and Richard the Lionheart, but, around the corridors of my all-girls comprehensive secondary school, nicknames just weren't popular.

However, if you strolled a couple of metres outside to the boys' school next door, things were different. They threw nicknames around like confetti.

After school, languishing at the entrance of the boys' school, chewing gum in our bottle-green uniforms, we'd hear a cacophony of nicknames and so-called 'banter' between the pimple-faced, half-man-half-boys. The gentle, sometimes not-so-gentle interactions between them were, in the main, a playful and teasing exchange. As they loitered around the front gates, we'd hear them call one another Big Ears, Tall Tim, Brains or other nicknames I won't repeat as they're a tad too fruity for this book. Looking back now, some of their nicknames would be described as derogatory name-calling, but the notable point is the gender discrepancy: nicknames were far more widely used by the boys than the girls.

The word 'nickname' originates from the Old English *ekename*, meaning an additional (or supplementary) name. Before middle names and surnames were commonly used in Europe, nicknames were a useful tool to distinguish other people who shared the same given name. The easiest way to do this was to bestow a nickname on someone that described or implied something specific about them.

A nickname is generally given to you by someone else. Some are tokens of genuine trust, affection and familiarity, and they are a common feature in many cultures. In Thailand, babies are not always named immediately after birth, and it is common for children to be given a nickname before their official name is decided. In Filipino culture someone's legal first name isn't always the name Filipinos use in their day-to-day lives. Many go by nicknames like 'Baby', commonly given to the youngest child in a family, or 'Jun', which is a shortened form of Junior. In Nigerian Yoruba culture, nicknames are used rather uniquely. It is taboo for a new bride to call any member of her husband's family by his or her personal name. Instead, they observe the person's various physiological traits and give them a nickname based on these quirks. We can only hope the nicknames the bride chooses are taken in good spirit.

There are various types of nicknames.

Some can be used as a political tool, a sort of trademark, or as something the public will affectionately remember the person by. In Australia the prime minister, Anthony Albanese, is known by certain sections of the media and by his supporters as 'Albo'. In the 50s in the US, '*I like Ike*,' based on the nickname of Dwight Eisenhower, was one of the most memorable campaign slogans in American history. Perhaps it was so successful it was responsible for Eisenhower winning the presidency in a landslide. In hip-hop a rapper's nickname is tied up with their persona and identity and can be as significant as their music. For example, the rapper and record producer Snoop Dogg was given the nickname Snoop by his mother because of the 1970s television show *Peanuts.* He watched the show religiously, so much so that his mother thought he started to resemble one of the characters, Snoop. So Calvin Cordozar Broadus Jr became Snoop Dogg. The concept of a personal nickname is interesting when we consider the use of nicknames in prisons. In this often intimidating environment, a nickname can instil fear. How would you feel about sharing a cell with someone called Psycho, Satan or Killer Fred? Other nicknames, like Scarface, Jack the Ripper, Doctor Death and the Butcher of Bosnia, are notorious and etched within our minds because of the heinous nature of the individuals they describe. Of course, some nicknames are ironic – the person called Shorty who is, in fact, tall, or the person called Numbers who is terrible at maths. And what about the nicknames bestowed on people without their knowledge?

A few years ago, Mike and I attended a Christmas party. It was a merry affair – jugs of cinnamon-infused mulled wine and plenty of kisses under the mistletoe. Over the course of the evening, I was introduced to Ian. We chatted for a while. He seemed perfectly pleasant, if a tad tipsy. When he left, my friend sidled up to me.

'Sorry about Ian,' she said in an apologetic voice. 'He can be morose, can't he? We call him "The Atmosphere Hoover" because he sucks the life out of the room.'

At the time I thought her description and nickname were a little harsh but when I was growing up my mother, like my friend, had a penchant for bestowing nicknames behind someone's back.

In the early 80s, appointments to the doctor became a regular feature in my life. My mother accompanied me, and she was reverential to the toupee-wearing Dr Wilson in his consulting room. She nodded in agreement when he told her the chronic pain and vomiting I experienced every month was something all women went through.

'They are a part of life,' he explained with an impish smile.

'But it hurts,' I said.

'Can you describe the pain from one to ten, Mandy?' he said. 'Ten being the highest.'

I raised my eyes up at the ceiling. Today I would ask the doctor, why did I have this pain? What was it trying to tell me? But I was too young and intimidated by this man in a smart suit and bow tie to ask anything. Instead, glancing at my mother, I said, '100.'

'Keep on taking the paracetamols, Mandy,' he replied. 'The pain won't last forever.'

My mother thanked him.

But later, as we walked the quick route back to Bradley Road so she could get back to work and I could get back to school, she said, 'Dr Bad Breath is right, love. Every woman has monthly pain. It will settle down in time.'

I remember giggling at Dr Wilson's nickname, but it is in

the world of sports not medicine that nicknames come into their own. The American sports scene heaves with nicknames, and over the years there's been a steady roll call coined by the media or the sports stars themselves. But is a sports nickname different from a regular nickname? And what makes a good sporting nickname? There is a reason: the late boxer, Marvin Hagler, gave himself the nickname 'Marvelous'. Interestingly, Hagler loved it so much he officially changed his name to Marvelous Marvin in 1982. The boxing world is chock-a-block with nicknames. It is the kind of sport where nicknames thrive, and they thrived on Bradley Road too.

Before my growth spurt, Dunni and Abdul called me Titch and Lippy the Lion because of my full lips. I was called Four Eyes, of course, and Mr Magoo, the short-sighted cartoon character who didn't wear glasses so was constantly getting into scrapes. I retaliated by shortening Abdul's middle name, Babatunde. I gave him the nickname Babs, after the actor Barbara Windsor, and Dunni, Adam, after the lead singer from the group Adam and the Ants. One night, she attempted to draw his distinctive white stripe across her nose with white face powder. It failed miserably, but the nickname Adam stuck for a few weeks. Surprisingly, we kids didn't give my mother an official nickname, although I secretly nicknamed her The Hulk because you wouldn't like her when she was angry.

John called my mother a shortened version of her given name. She was 'Carms', but I don't recall her bestowing a nickname on him. They didn't call one another Mummy and Daddy, like the parents of one of my friends. I went to her house in a leafy part of Luton, and her mother asked if I'd like to stay for tea. I nodded enthusiastically, even though tea meant three custard cream biscuits, a shiny Granny Smith apple and a glass of lemon cordial. While we had tea, my friend's father turned to his wife and said, 'Would you like another biscuit, Mummy?' And she replied. 'Not yet, Daddy, perhaps later,' and some part of me recognised this was weird. Super weird.

In the summer of 1983, I sat with Dunni, my mother and John in the back room, watching the satirical consumer affairs programme *That's Life!* on the television.

Abdul was out, making his way home from one of his Soul Weekenders. Soul Weekenders were massive in the 1980s. Groups of teenagers descended on seaside towns like Caister-on-Sea, in Great Yarmouth and jigged about to music all night long. Even now, Abdul talks about those weekends as though they were some kind of religious experience. And I suppose to Abdul they were, and part of me was jealous. I was desperate to explore the world beyond school, Bury Park and the Luton Arndale Shopping Centre. Still, who needed Soul Weekenders when you had *That's Life!* and Esther Rantzen? At 13, I thought Esther was a sophisticated name. It sounded grown-up, and one of my favourite film stars was called Esther. Sure, her films were a bit niche. They revolved around swimming, but that didn't matter. Like Judy Garland's, Esther Williams's movies were colourful and hopeful, just like her name.

One of the television presenters on *That's Life!* made a throwaway quip about having a nickname, and my mother stretched out her legs and told us she used to have a nickname in Jamaica.

My stomach lurched.

When she talked about Jamaica, I hoped she'd reminisce about the positive experiences of her childhood, but more often than not it was the traumatic, so I steadied myself for my mother's emotional fallout.

'I was small and skinny in those days,' she explained. 'So the family I lived with called me Dot.'

'You were marga, Carmen,' John said, chuckling at one of the jokes on the television.

'What's marga?' I asked.

My mother said it was Jamaican slang to describe her small stature.

'It means skinny,' Dunni explained.

'Don't you go saying "marga" at school,' my mother said. 'It's "skinny", not "marga".'

John shook his head.

'Marga is fine,' he said. 'What's wrong with saying marga?'

'The family I lived with called me Dot,' my mother continued. 'I didn't know my name was Carmen until I was in primary school. A teacher called out my name on the register, but I didn't raise my hand because I didn't know it was me. I thought I was Dot.'

Dunni and John chuckled at a man on *That's Life!* trying to squeeze himself into a dustbin.

'I suppose my mother didn't know any better,' my mother sighed. 'It wasn't my mum's fault. She didn't know her so-called best friend and her family treated me worse than a dog.'

She blinked away a tear forming, and I bit my bottom lip, thinking, should I impersonate Shirley Bassey to cheer her up?

'She didn't know I was treated like a slave and—'

John interrupted her and, as a man of few words, his interruption was timely. 'Red Stripe is going back home,' he announced.

'Since when?' she asked, sniffing.

'He tells me he's going back to Jamaica in the summer,' John replied. 'He says he's built a big house over in Mandeville. You know how Red Stripe loves to boast.'

'Who's Red Stripe?' I asked, tearing my eyes away from the screen.

'Mr Thomas,' John said. 'The short, dark-skinned man who lives on Humberstone Road.'

'Why is he called Red Stripe?' I asked.

'He likes his drink,' she said. 'Red Stripe is a Jamaican drink.'

'So we call him Red Stripe,' John said, turning down the volume on the television. 'We Jamaicans use too many nicknames. If you kids ever go to Jamaica, they'll probably give you a nickname. But it's a bit of fun, isn't it, Carmen? They don't mean anything by it.'

He was right about Jamaicans and their penchant for nicknames. Most of my mother's and John's Caribbean friends and acquaintances had a nickname, and they were funny, tongue-in-cheek and often related to physical attributes or an aspect of their personality. One of their friends was nicknamed Tina Turner because she was a dead ringer for the late singer, and another was called Count Dracula due to his elongated and pointy teeth.

'If your mum goes to Jamaica, they'll nickname her "Mrs British",' John said, laughing. 'They won't think she's a Jamaican, not with that accent.'

My mother rolled her eyes at his comment and said, 'One day, I was beaten so badly by the people who were supposed to be looking after me,' she paused. 'And I found out my mother had sent me money and clothes from Panama – but they kept them. They spent the money on themselves. I—'

'Sanni's nickname is Carlton Long,' I said, interrupting her.

She laughed, and I was glad the conversation had shifted from the traumatic to something more light-hearted.

'Remember the time Sanni asked you to go to the shops and buy his Carlton Long cigarettes?' Dunni said.

'Amanda, go to the shop and buy me 20 Carlton Long cigarettes,' I said, mimicking Sanni's Nigerian accent and his peculiar pronunciation of my name.

'You told him if he wanted his cigarettes, he should go to the shop himself,' Dunni quipped. 'And you were only about six years old.'

'That's my girl,' my mother said, grinning. 'You told him, didn't you, love? Good for you, Mandy.'

We all laughed.

London, April 2015

Mike lurks outside the cafe in Warren Street like an M15 agent and, like an M15 agent, he is under strict orders. We have a code. If I adjust my black beret, it means Teju *is* a weirdo, and on that command he will rush in, grab my hand and whisk me off to the nearest pub for a pint of Guinness and a debrief. But if I scratch my nose, then it's okay. Teju is *not* a weirdo, and all is well in the long-lost-cousin world.

I'd arranged to meet Teju at three, and it's a few minutes past, so I stare at the door, checking out every person of colour.

Here's what I know about my cousin:

I know his name. He knows mine, so there will be no awkward informality. I know he is in his early 60s, and he told me he'd be wearing glasses and carrying a blue rucksack.

I gaze at the entrance, and I lock eyes with a tall man carrying a light blue rucksack and think, Is this Teju?

I acknowledge this man with a lopsided grin but, on closer inspection, the person I am grinning at has a beard and facial piercings. How can he be Teju? Teju is a doctor, not a Dalston hipster. It's not him.

Low-level jazz burbles away on a set of speakers, and I am reminded how much I miss London. Living in Swaffham is like being at a party and finding out you are the only guest. Visiting London for the afternoon is like being at a party with multiple gatecrashers. I miss the city. I miss seeing people who look like me. I miss restaurants and buzzy cafes like this one. I miss the sounds of life – car horns and people walking home late at night. But for all the talk of missing London, I can't go back. It's been almost 11 years since we moved out of

London. I am committed to this new rural rhythm and the house we're painstakingly bringing back to life, but every so often this craving for city life creeps up on me.

I glance up and notice someone who could be Teju. He looks like he's been spun in the washing machine. He's one of those people in life who wear clothes badly. They seem to wear him.

The man smiles and waves, so I wave too and think, whoa, wait a minute, Jesus Christ, I think it's Teju because he is the image of Abdul. Their likeness overwhelms me. I see the blood connections back through the generations to a cousin I never knew existed. Abdul and Teju are around the same height and share the same 'let's have a second helping of pudding' build. Thinking about Abdul, his and Dunni's absence hits me. We are back on speaking terms after Abdul broke the 'don't tell Mum agreement', but I have learned my lesson. I didn't tell them I was meeting Teju in London, and why should I? They have no interest in opening the long-lost-cousin can. But even so, I miss their presence, support and the feeling that someone else is on my side and I'm not in this alone.

'Camilla?' the person asks, narrowing his eyes.

'Guilty as charged,' I reply, swallowing.

We shake hands. His grip is firm, a positive sign.

He slips off his jacket and sits opposite me.

'How's your day been?' he asks, placing his briefcase on the floor.

I am tempted to be honest (he is a GP) and say, well, it's a few days before my period, and I feel lousy.

'Yeah, I've had a good day,' I say instead, choosing the safer response. 'I thought you'd be carrying a blue rucksack.'

'I know,' he replies cheerfully, taking a pair of thin silver-framed spectacles from his pocket. 'I was rushed for time, so I grabbed the only available bag.' He grins. 'It's a bit battered, isn't it?'

We pick up menus and scan the sizeable list of food and

drink options. I order a double-shot Americano coffee, and a slice of lemon drizzle cake with a side of crème fraîche, as does Teju, from a bored-looking waitress with a tattoo of a Robin Redbreast on her forearm.

Once she leaves, I glance over at the next table. Two stressed-looking parents are on their phones, heads bowed, not talking, and their child, a young boy of around nine years old, is also on his phone, captivated. His posture is hunched. The yoga teacher in me wants to go up to him, put my hand on this young boy's back and say, stand straight. And get off your phone. You'll be as stiff as a starched collar in 50 years. The boy looks up and catches my gaze, so I avert my eyes. Growing up, I envied this kind of family – a mum, dad and their kids on a family outing.

'Did you drive or take the train?' Teju asks.

'Train,' I reply. 'What about you?'

He says he took the train too. 'I'm glad to meet you, Camilla,' he says, smiling. 'All the family in Nigeria are pleased we are finally meeting. It was difficult for all of us to comprehend Uncle Rimi's behaviour when he lived in the UK. To be honest, I'm embarrassed he didn't get in touch with you sooner. I'm sorry I didn't either.'

'Out of sight, out of mind,' I reply, but I regret my flippancy.

I am keen to make a good impression despite the circumstances. I don't want Teju telling this new Nigerian family of mine that I was a disappointment or one of those people with zero conversation skills. And I dressed with care to put together a suitable meet-the-cousin outfit – a plaid shirt I picked up at a charity shop in Norfolk and a pair of oversized denim dungarees, which now, in hindsight, I think was the wrong choice. I worry I'm giving off a country and western kind of vibe.

Our drinks arrive. I share a witty anecdote about the last time I was in London, but as I reach over to pick up my cup it slips out of my hand, and hot coffee spills across the table and drips onto the floor.

Teju grabs a napkin.

I grab a napkin.

The sullen, tattooed waitress comes over, napkin in hand, and asks in a monotone voice if I'd like another coffee.

I nod, and there is a long pause as Teju and I eat our slices of cake.

Say something, I say to myself. Mention the weather, music, cake, make small talk, for goodness' sake. I *like* talking. I am nosey. I like being around people, but not today. Today, my finely honed conversation skills have deserted me.

'I'm glad you came, but it's a shame your brother and sister couldn't make it,' he says, narrowing his eyes. 'You look like your dad.'

'What?'

'Uncle Rimi,' he repeats, grinning. 'You look like him. You have his ears.'

My hand automatically flies up to my right ear lobe, and I twist it in my fingers as though I'm handling playdough.

'Could we not talk about him? I'm here to get to know you, not him.'

He says, of course, and tells me instead about his journey from Oxford, and then his eyes light up as he talks about his wife Hannah and their three children.

'Two live in London,' he explains. 'The other, our youngest, is in Nigeria. She's doing a placement at an NGO.'

I ask how long he's lived in the UK.

'Too long,' he replies, chuckling. 'But I go back to Nigeria pretty frequently. All being well, I'll visit this year or next for a long trip.'

There is another long pause.

'I have something,' he says, reaching into his briefcase and pulling out a photograph.

'Uncle Rimi wanted you to have this,' he says, handing over the photo.

And voilà, here he is – the man I haven't seen in 40 years. Growing up, there were no photographs of Sanni so, as a child, I created a fantasy. I imagined him as a combination of Will Smith and, for some inexplicable reason, the actor Gary Coleman from the television show *Diff'rent Strokes,* but here he is and, of course, he looks nothing like either of them.

Teju says it's a recent photo, and he's right. I turn over the back, and it says *I am 81 years old.*

I start to say something, but as I open my mouth I catch Mike peering through the steamed-up windows of the cafe, and he's gesticulating wildly. Teju stares at Mike too, and I think, shit, shit, shit, what's the bloody code? Is it touch the beret for weirdo, or is it scratch my nose or forehead? To cover all bases, I place the photograph back on the table, adjust my beret, scratch my nose, pick up my coffee cup, rub my forehead, and think, what the hell is the flipping code?

Teju asks if I'm okay, and I mumble I am just nervous.

Seconds later, a message pings through on my phone: Mike, asking if I'm all right because he can't understand the bloody code.

I apologise to Teju and bang out a hasty, exclamation-ridden response to Mike.

> *Teju is lovely and not a weirdo, but my head is in BITS!! I am currently staring at a photograph of Sanni. Arghhhh!!!!!!*

I put away my phone and stare at the smiling man in the photo with the hat and grey goatee beard. 'Does he still smoke?' I ask, not taking my eyes off the grinning man in the photograph, which is at odds with how I remember him.

Teju says he gave up all his bad habits, including smoking, years ago.

He sips his coffee and casually mentions other long-lost family members in Nigeria. He says there were four brothers, but only Uncle Rimi and his sister are still alive. Then he mentions other cousins, who all have grand-sounding jobs in Nigeria and the US in corporate finance, medicine, law and politics. And I wonder what these high-flyers will think of me, their woo-woo yoga-loving-teaching cousin.

'I'm the only cousin who lives in the UK,' he explains. 'I suppose that's why Uncle Rimi asked me to find you.'

'He couldn't be bothered to do it himself?' I ask.

He doesn't answer my question, instead saying, 'Our aunt in Nigeria sends her regards. Aunty Ayo is quite a character, you know. She's football-mad and supports Arsenal. But let's not hold that against her.' He smiles. 'Do you remember her? She said she met you once a long time ago.'

I nod and place Sanni's photo on the table.

'It was one of the few occasions he met the terms of his visitation rights,' I say. 'I can count on one hand the number of times he did.'

Shortly after my parents divorced, I met Aunty Ayo. I was seven or thereabouts. Sanni turned up for his weekend visit, and we drove to London. We went to Hyde Park, and his sister, who was visiting from Nigeria, tagged along. To my young eyes, she was like a hurricane – a colourful hurricane. She wore sunglasses, bright-coloured Nigerian clothing and a head wrap, which I recall whispering to Dunni 'looked like an enormous mountain'. I was embarrassed to be seen with this aunt. I couldn't understand why she didn't wear jeans and a T-shirt, like my mother, or clothes that faded into the background. I looked at her Nigerian clothes and her exuberance with the eyes of a wary outsider.

'She was certainly forthright and formidable,' I say to Teju, 'and she insisted on calling me by my middle name the whole weekend. I was Adebisi, not Mandy.'

He smiles and takes a bite of his cake.

'Aunty Ayo is like her mother, our grandmother,' he says

proudly. 'Her name was Asiata and, although she didn't know it then, she was a real trailblazer. She was a wealthy businesswoman, and she was involved in the Aba riots in Nigeria in 1929.'

I've never heard of the Aba riots. I may have studied history at university, but who owns the history? African history took up a meagre 20 minutes of a three-year course.

'Our grandmother spoiled your father,' he says. 'Uncle Rimi grew up with a sense of entitlement. I know he came to London with an allowance from his mother. I suppose, at some point, the money ran out, and of course there was the Biafra war in Nigeria.'

I am keen to learn more about the rather fabulous-sounding Asiata but I don't say anything.

I sip my coffee, hoping the questions whizzing around my head will begin to calm down soon.

'In your message you said you were curious about your name,' he continues. 'Adebisi means the crown has given birth to more.' He pauses. 'Camilla is an Arabic name. It's often spelt with a K. KAMILLAH or KAMILAT.'

'I didn't know that – I . . .' I trail off, blindsided by the information. 'So why wasn't it spelt like that on my birth certificate?'

Teju shrugs.

'Maybe the person who registered your name made a mistake, and your dad – sorry, I mean Uncle Rimi – decided it would be easier to use the English spelling.'

'Oh,' I say quietly.

'I thought you might like to know the meaning of your siblings' Yoruba names,' he says in a helpful tone. 'Adunni means sweet, like honey, and precious. Your brother's middle name Babatunde is interesting. When he was born, Uncle Rimi must have thought your brother resembled our grandfather, because Babatunde means a father has returned.'

'What does Camilla mean?' I ask quietly.

'To be whole or complete and perfect,' he replies.

Hearing this perception of my name hits me in the solar plexus. I chew the inside of my cheek to prevent me from crying and completely losing it.

'Your father lives in Abuja,' he explains between chews. 'It's not as glamorous as Lagos, but it's a pleasant city. Perhaps a little too pleasant for some. My kids think Abuja is a bit dull. They prefer Lagos. I get the feeling you'd like the bright lights of Lagos, too.'

'What happened when he went back to Nigeria?' I ask, regaining my composure.

Teju clears his throat.

'The family looked after him. He stayed with one of our cousins in Lagos for a while and then in his late 60s, they thought he should get married and – so, well . . .'

'Well – what?'

'Well, I'm afraid the marriage didn't last long. She – left him. She said she couldn't tolerate his behaviour.' He sighs. 'Uncle Rimi can be incredibly selfish.'

I don't say anything.

'Did I mention on the phone your father is obsessed with politics? He reads the newspaper religiously, you know. The last time we spoke, he said he was fascinated by Brexit. He's quite a fan of David Cameron,' he says.

I think, typical. Sanni is a Tory; of course he is.

'Uncle Rimi said you used to accompany him to the shops,' he says. 'He said you'd go together.'

This implication that we were this happy 'let's walk to the shop together' father-daughter unit annoys the hell out of me. We never walked to the shops. I went alone, or with my brother or sister, on the hunt for his bloody 20 Carlton Long cigarettes.

'Did he ever tell you about the time my mother asked him for money to buy food for us kids?' I ask.

He shakes his head. 'No,' he replies. 'He didn't.'

'My mother had left nursing by then. Money was tight. So she asked him,' I said. 'Do you know what he did? He chucked two and sixpence on the floor, and my mother bent down on her knees, searching the floor for coins.'

Teju listens as I recount all the stories I managed to tease out from my mother about Sanni: the parties, drinking, late nights, his frequent absences, his reluctance to provide for our basic needs, the menial jobs he worked in, then left, complaining they were beneath him. By the time I finish talking about Sanni, I am exhausted.

We sit in silence.

'I'm so sorry, Camilla,' Teju says, removing his glasses.

In a faltering voice, I gesture to the unsmiling waitress and ask Teju if he'd like another coffee.

He says he will have fizzy water and lemon because he's drunk his caffeine quota for the day.

I ask the waitress for another double shot of coffee, and Teju apologises for Sanni's behaviour again.

'Sanni should be saying sorry,' I say.

'I know this wasn't in the script, so to speak,' he says, apologetically 'but I have something for you. It's from Uncle Rimi. Perhaps he felt he needed to answer your questions fully. At least, I hope so.'

He reaches into his briefcase and places a yellow-tinged envelope on the table right in front of me. It reads: *To my beloved daughter, AMANDA*.

Six

Sorry, Can You Spell That for Me?

If they can say Tchaikovsky and Michelangelo and Dostoevsky, then they can learn to say Uzoamaka.

—Uzoamaka Aduba

Throughout secondary school, the name Mandy remained fully embedded in my records. My mother never changed Camilla to Mandy by deed poll. There was no time, money or inclination for that, and back then there were perks to being called Mandy. Although my secondary school was a diverse melting pot of children whose parents came to the UK from the Commonwealth, names were routinely mispronounced. My name wasn't. Mandy was the kind of name a teacher didn't trip their tongue over. It was a pronunciation-friendly name; by that, I mean it didn't scream 'foreigner' or stand out as different. It fitted in.

Dunni's name did stand out as different, and, growing up, her name was routinely mispronounced. She'd come home complaining of yet another teacher at her sixth-form college butchering her name.

One Friday evening, when I was around 13, I was chopping onions while my mother rubbed spices and garlic into a bowl of meat. Dunni, who was 17 by then, stood at the kitchen door, biting her bottom lip.

'The teacher called me Donny, Mum,' she said, pouting. 'Like the singer Donny Osmond.'

'Never mind, love. You'll be leaving soon and getting a job,' my mother said.

'But it's embarrassing. Everyone laughed, and someone at the back of the class started whistling "Love Me for a Reason" by the Osmonds,' she whined. 'What are you laughing at, Amanda?' she said, glaring at me.

Over the ensuing months, the mispronunciation of Dunni's name continued.

One of her teachers insisted on calling her 'Dunny', which, years later, Dunni learned was Australian slang for the toilet. Another called her 'Dengue', like the fever.

You see, back then, if a teacher couldn't pronounce a student's name, they had various options.

They made a 'funny' quip about the student's name.

They abbreviated the student's name.

They ignored the student's name.

They butchered the student's name.

They called the student a randomly made-up name.

One morning, in my science class, a supply teacher, who looked like the kind of person who didn't smile easily, hollered out the names on the register.

'Julie Brown.'

'Yes, sir.'

'Paula Cook.'

'Yes, sir.'

'Jackie Deakin.'

'Yes, sir.'

'Bridget Harrison.'

'Yes, sir.'

'Priti Patel.'

'Yes, sir.'

'Chin-chin–chiny–kat…'

Silence.

'Chin-chin–chiny–kat…' he spluttered, eyes peering around the room.

Longer silence punctuated by hands over mouths suppressing giggles.

'Oh, for goodness' sake,' he shouted. 'Cindy P.'

A quiet voice from the back of the classroom raised a tentative hand and replied, 'Yes, sir,' but that wasn't the name of the unassuming person who sat in front of me. Her name was Chinthaka, and her parents came from Sri Lanka. Who was Cindy P? But what else was Chinthaka supposed to do? Kick up a fuss? Report him? And why didn't I kick up a fuss? I was a class monitor, voted for by my classmates – not the teachers, I hasten to add – so why didn't I stand up and say something? There is general agreement that the mispronunciation of a name affects us all but significantly affects Black and Brown people. When a name is mispronounced, it intensifies feelings of not belonging or that a person's heritage and identity are being mocked.

Rita Kohli, an assistant professor at the University of California Riverside, has researched how mispronouncing a student's name can have a profoundly negative effect, especially on students of colour. Kohli says, 'We've found a lot of people feeling embarrassed – ashamed of their name, wanting to withdraw from raising their hand in class, and sitting on the edge of their seat during roll call so they can say their name before someone else messes it up.'

Names are such an important part of our identity. They are wrapped in our sense of self, so now I wonder how my classmate Chinthaka felt hearing herself referred to as 'Cindy'. Did she, too, feel embarrassed and ashamed of her name? I'll never know. I wish I'd asked her at the time. If you're reading this, Chinthaka, I apologise for my placidity. You did not choose to Anglicise your name; the teacher did. Of course, Anglicising names is not a new phenomenon, but shouldn't the person whose name it is decide? Surely it should be *their* choice, not the choice of the name caller.

But maybe you're thinking, what's the big deal about a mispronunciation? Why the outrage? Some people are more adept at pronouncing people's names than others. And that's true. Some people are. That's a fact of life. But if a mispronunciation is laced with malice and undertones of racism, it feels like a wasp hovering around your upper arm. The wasp attacks, and it stings.

Days after Dunni told us about her teachers mispronouncing her name, my mother asked in a breezy voice, 'What do you want to do when you grow up, Mandy?'

At the time, my mother and I were in the posh adults-only front room on Bradley Road. It was a Saturday morning, and I was helping her dust the already spotlessly clean ornaments and furniture.

Before I answered, I mulled the question over in my head for a moment or two.

I had a hazy career plan that involved books. But what? One thing I knew for sure was that I didn't want a regular nine-to-five job in an office – mainly because that would require a boss who understood women's monthlies. How else could I explain time off, hot-water bottles and paracetamols?

'Come on, love,' she asked impatiently. 'What do you want to do?'

A career in books seemed so distant and abstract that I chose what I believed to be the safer option. I was an avid film buff, creative, and a member of an after-school drama club. My ear for mimicry made my mother, Dunni and Abdul and my school friends laugh. So, in a theatrical voice, I said, 'Mother, I think I want to be in showbiz.'

She put down the brown feather duster on the settee and shook her head with such force that I was concerned about concussion.

'I didn't come to the UK to work hard and make sacrifices for you to end up in showbiz,' she said. 'That's not a career. Look at the films you love watching. All the Black characters get killed off first. No, love. Forget the showbiz. What about law? You're good at asking questions and arguing.'

She was right about arguing. At 13, with hormones raging through my body, I was going through a fold-your-arms-in-front-of-your-chest argumentative stage.

My mother picked up her duster and vigorously wiped the top of the sofa.

'There are loads of people in showbiz,' I said. 'Josette Simon, Mona Hammond, Carmen Munroe, Floella Benjamin, Br—'

'Forget the showbiz, Mandy,' she advised. 'And remember, never write your middle name on your job application. They won't be able to pronounce Adebisi. Look at your poor sister. At least your surname doesn't sound too Nigerian. Can you imagine if it did?'

'What's wrong with showbiz?'

'The best thing we can do is assimilate, love,' she continued. 'So don't write that Nigerian name Sanni gave you. Initialise it. If you don't, they'll read your name on your lawyer application and chuck you in the not-one-of-us pile.'

I opened my mouth to answer, then I thought about what she'd said. Phrases like 'unconscious bias' and 'job discrimination' weren't widely used back then, but I understood the subtext. If I wanted to succeed, I needed a name people could pronounce. I realised life might be easier if you had a name that wasn't perceived as difficult, unfamiliar or unpronounceable, and studies show that name pronunciation impacts prospects the most in the workplace.

From 1982 to 1986, St George's Medical School in London was so inundated for applications that they struggled to shortlist candidates. So, to make life easier and more efficient, they wrote a computer program to do this job for them. However, the computer program had an inbuilt bias against women and applicants with non-English-sounding surnames. The medical school thought a computer programme would make the admissions process fairer – but it did the opposite.

Another study conducted in 2023 by Vassar College and Hamilton College in the US looked at the hypothesis that having a difficult-to-pronounce name may lead to worse job-market outcomes. Their study analysed over 1,600 job candidates in the US to discover if having a name that was hard to pronounce impacted employability. It did. Their study found that individuals whose names took longer to pronounce had a decreased likelihood of getting an academic job or a callback. In short, potential employers were attracted to names that rolled off the tongue. They used the term 'name fluency'. So it seems some employers prefer names to be as easy as slipping on flip-flops, and that maybe Carmen was right. The candidate with the so-called tricky name might well be thrown into the 'not-one-of-us pile', and the person with the easier-to-pronounce name gets the job.

When I first met Teju, he told me that Sanni had come to the UK to study (in his case, engineering). I wondered about Sanni's name. I wondered if his teachers or employers shortened his name. Did they Anglicise his name? Did they mispronounce it? For Dr Ayokunmi Ojebode from Nottingham University's Institute for Name Studies, the peculiarity of a Yoruba name is that when it is mispronounced it loses its value and significance. When we spoke over Zoom, he explained that 'Yoruba is a tonal language. For example, my name Ayokunmi means "joy has been added to me", but with the wrong tone it could have varied meanings,' he said. 'My name was given to me to complement my father's appreciation of a second male child, so the pronunciation of my name is important to me.'

In China, names are selected with care. Bearing in mind the thought and consideration behind a name, it's interesting to consider the large number of Chinese-speaking students studying in the UK who choose to Anglicise their names. In 2018, Simon Cotterill, from Birmingham City University, studied Chinese speakers from three UK universities. His survey concluded that a whopping 255 respondents out of 330 used an English name in the classroom. The survey found 71 per cent of Chinese-speaking students who used English names said they did so because English names were easier for teachers to remember, while 60 per cent chose an English-sounding name because they were easier for teachers to pronounce. But why do international students from other countries with so-called difficult-to-pronounce names not take English-sounding names at quite the same rate as the Chinese? Is it that some Chinese speakers see changing their names as a way to emulate names associated with the Western world? Or to show that they have achieved something by living in the West? Or is it a mark of respect for the country where they're living? And let's not forget, perhaps some Chinese speakers *enjoy* conjuring up English-sounding names. It's part of the experience of being a student abroad. A friend who taught English as a Foreign Language to mainly Chinese-speaking students in London explained that many of her students took immense pleasure in choosing their new English monikers. Some picked fun names; others chose names that reflected their love for a favourite singer or actor. And for her, it was easier to navigate an English name than a hard-to-pronounce Chinese name. She was grateful they picked names like Sasha, Angelina or J-Lo.

But I couldn't help thinking wouldn't it be something if my friend had asked her Chinese-speaking students for their Chinese names and she made an effort to pronounce their names correctly? How would that make the student feel? And what about the large number of international students who do call themselves an English-sounding name in the classroom but, on graduation, use their birth names? I have heard multiple stories of many a butchered name on that most important of days that proved memorable for all the wrong reasons. Plus, given the enormous revenue international students bring to universities, shouldn't greater effort be made on graduation to pronounce a name correctly? Some higher education establishments in the UK are working towards this – correcting decades of mispronunciation of names in the classroom and the staffroom. Many, like the University of Warwick, have introduced audio name badges to avoid mispronunciation or name avoidance for both students and staff. It's a shame audio name badges weren't available on a cold tranquil day in January 2021, when a masked Joe Biden and his wife, Jill, watched as Kamala Harris made history. She was the first Black and South Asian woman sworn in as Vice President. It was a significant moment. But there's a but. As she was sworn in, the Supreme Court Justice mispronounced her name. She called her 'Kuh-mah-luh' instead of 'Comma-luh'. Given that Kamala Harris wrote a memoir that included a section on how to pronounce her name the mispronunciation of her name at such a historic event was an unfortunate moment. In 2020, during a Georgia campaign rally for President Donald Trump, the Republican senator David Perdue appeared to mock the first name of the vice presidential nominee Harris. More recently, on the campaign trail for the 2024 presidency against Harris, Trump said he 'couldn't care less' if he mispronounces her name. Unfortunately, US political figures don't cover themselves in glory regarding name pronunciation. In a 2022 Diwali celebration at the White House,

President Joe Biden introduced the then UK prime minister, not as Rishi Sunak, but 'Rashi Sunook'.

But let me raise my hand. I want to be honest and transparent with you. I am no name pronunciation saint. In the past, if I've been faced with an unfamiliar name, I, too, have resorted to not directly saying it, or butchered it. Years ago, I attended a yoga workshop in London. As a yoga teacher, being taught by someone else is pleasurable. The spotlight is on them. You can sit back and not be centre stage, and this particular workshop wasn't in the style of yoga I practised. It was called 'Unlocking the Secrets of the Pelvis', which sounded mildly pornographic. But I was late. I ran into the studio and apologised to the teacher for my lateness, and she flicked away a stray wisp of auburn hair and gave me a faraway smile.

'Namaste,' she said, placing her hands in a prayer position.

I didn't reciprocate this greeting. I wasn't the kind of teacher who casually bandied around 'namaste'.

'The train was delayed,' I explained.

'That's fine,' she said. 'Everyone is getting to know one another.'

This sounded odd. What did she mean? We were practising yoga. We were there to learn and improve our yoga and 'unlock the secrets of the pelvis', not to better understand our colleagues on some kind of CEOs' awayday. Nevertheless, I went along with the idea. Like I said, she was running the show.

She gestured to a table of blank labels for attendees to fill out. So I picked up a black Sharpie pen, wrote my name on a sticky label, stuck it on my chest, and joined a throng of yoga teachers. The 50 or so women looked like they were on a break from filming a wellness advert. They were sleek and skinny and looked like they survived on a diet of kale, the overrated vegetable of the food world.

I'd started practising yoga in earnest in the early 90s, but now the yoga scene was completely different. It was a slick operation that was slowly retreating up its own backside, and this group of yoga students were a serious bunch. And here I was in London, the only person of colour in the room.

There was a flicker of hope. A tall woman in ebony-coloured leggings and a seen-better-days T-shirt stood out among the other participants' carefully considered and expensive yoga bling.

I smiled, narrowed my eyes and read her name tag.

It said *AOIFE,* but there was a problem. I didn't have a clue how to pronounce it. Nevertheless, I gave it my best shot, and gobbledegook spewed forth from my mouth.

Embarrassed, I apologised.

'I should have asked before I made a complete idiot of myself,' I said. 'How do you pronounce your name?'

Thankfully, she smiled good-naturedly, and in her soft Irish accent she pronounced her name in such a way that the uninformed like me could easily understand.

'It's pronounced Eefa,' she explained.

I gave it another go, and she smiled, so I guess my attempt was satisfactory.

I don't remember what else I said to Aoife but I remember I learned an invaluable lesson in that yoga workshop. If you can't pronounce someone's name, ask. Trust me, they will appreciate it.

London, April 2015

The train from London to Norfolk whizzes past commuter-belt towns and garden cities, and Mike won't shut up.

'So Teju's all right?' he asks again.

'Yeah, he's all right,' I reply in an annoyed tone. 'I like him. I said we'd visit him in Oxford in the summer. We had a nice afternoon. What else do you want me to say?'

The man in the opposite seat crams a sad-looking burger into his mouth, slurps a soft drink from a straw and burps.

'You're just – a bit quiet,' Mike says.

'Mmm,' I reply, without detailing the excruciating last moments of my encounter with my cousin.

Teju gave me Sanni's letter, and I lost the plot. It was discombobulating, and so were the four double-shot coffees. They had been a bad idea, leading to heart palpitations, profuse sweating and verbal diarrhoea. Did Teju *really* need to know the difference between particular styles of yoga? No, he didn't. He isn't a downward-dog kind of guy.

'Aren't you going to read the letter?' Michael asks now. 'Aren't you curious to find out what your dad says?'

I shrug and think, of course I am bloody curious. The letter Teju gave me is in my bag, but, whenever I think about opening the envelope, something stops me: Fear, guilt and a reluctance to step into Sanni's letter-writing orbit.

'I'll read it later,' I say unconvincingly.

The man opposite screws up his burger wrapper, tosses it onto the floor, and grins at me as if to say, 'Who needs a bin?'

I glare back at him and stop myself from venting my frustrations at this man. I hold my tongue.

The train is approaching Letchworth Garden City and, as it stops, the carriage empties a little, but the burping litter man doesn't leave.

I tell myself it is only a letter. Read the damn thing! Read it!

I lean forward, retrieve the letter from my bag and wonder if the people sitting in the seat behind me can hear my heart pumping.

Tearing open the envelope, I clear my throat, mindful of the burping burger man in the seat opposite, who I'm sure is listening.

'Dear Amanda,' I say, reading the letter to Mike in a low voice. 'I hope you are having a fulfilled 2015. I am very sorry for the pain I have caused you over the years. I am writing this letter with a heavy feeling of sadness. I know I wronged you all. What I did was very wrong. I shouldn't have left the way I did. I should have said goodbye to you kids. Please tell your brother and sister I am very, very sorry. By the way, how is your mother? Please send my regards to her, your husband and your children.' I pause and lick my lips. 'I would very much like you to call me. I want to talk to you. My number is at the top of this letter. Or you can write to me. I would like that very much. You can see my address at the bottom. I hope you will you come to Nigeria. Greetings from all of us here. The family are very excited to meet you. Love always, your loving Dad.'

I fold the poor excuse for a letter in half and place it back in the envelope.

'Will you write back?' Mike asks over the broad Norfolk accent of the man opposite, who is now talking loudly on his phone. 'A letter is a good way of explaining how you feel.'

Mike's encouragement is annoying. I am tired of his positivity, relentless cheeriness and concept of happy families. He comes from a family with a dad, cousins, uncles and aunts, where Christmas meant his mum, Shirley, cooked for twenty or more. I didn't come from such a family. Before John came onto the scene, there were four people at our Christmas table, five if you include sitting through the Queen's speech.

'I can't remember the last time I wrote a letter,' he says. 'I th—'

'Will you shut up,' I snap. 'I don't want anything to do with Sanni. I'm not going to call or write a letter.'

He sighs, takes out his phone and says there's no need to shout.

'Why?' I say, raising my voice. 'Why can't I shout?'

'Because we are on a train,' he hisses.

'So what?' I yell and give him a look that says, I am done with this conversation.

Mike says he realises it's been an emotional day.

I respond by feigning tiredness, but I hear him mumbling

under his breath. He says I shouldn't bottle things up, which makes me even more furious. Shifting further to the window to ensure our knees do not touch, I think about Abdul and Dunni. They are playing the same 'we're not interested' tune – why am I off the beat? What's wrong with me?

A few minutes after seven, the train pulls into Downham Market Station. Mike and I get up from our seats and stand by the train door but, because of our earlier argument, there is an atmosphere between us. The train door slides open, he strolls ahead and places his hands deep into his pockets.

I languish behind, head bowed, thinking about Sanni's letter.

Dear Amanda,

The family are keen to meet you. I am sorry. How are your children? How is your mother? I am sorry. I am very, very sorry. You can write to me. Amanda. Amanda. Amanda. Please write.

Walking quickly to catch Mike up, it is me, not him, who waves the white flag.

'I'm sorry for being tetchy,' I say, slipping my hand into his. 'Do you know if we have any writing paper at home?'

Thirty-five minutes later, I sit at my desk gazing at a blank white page. I am unsure how to begin. The deal is, I should grab a pen and write, but write what? What do I say? The thing is, years ago, I was a passionate letter writer. They were a lifeline. In this very same office, at the back of the cupboard, there is a groaning box stuffed full of my letters, written to my mother and Mike. But in fairness, I came late to the letter-writing party. I wasn't one of those kids at secondary school with a childhood pen pal in the Dordogne.

And now, here I am, trying to write a letter to Sanni. This letter will exist in *his* hands. He will open it and feel my presence, but do I want Sanni to feel my presence?

What should I say? How should I start? Dear Dad? Dear Sanni?

Chewing the top of my Biro, I decide a neutral approach is best.

18 April 2015

Hi there,

I write.

I hope you are well.

Thank you for your brief letter. It was a shock hearing from you. I made it clear to Teju that I didn't want any contact and that Teju should be the intermediary between us. But thank you for taking the time to write.

I stop, and think about that last sentence. Was I *really* glad he took the time to write? I wasn't, so I cross it out, but now my letter looks like a bored teenager's doodles on a notebook. So I tear off another piece of writing paper and start again.

18 April 2015

Hi there,

I hope you are well.

Thank you for your brief letter. To be honest, it was a surprise. I made it clear to Teju that I didn't want any contact and that Teju should be the intermediary between us.

Can I ask something? Could you not call me Amanda? Mum told me it was you who chose the name Camilla. So why can't you use it now?

And then I think, of course, he can't call me Camilla. My mother was victorious in their naming tug-of-war, and Mandy was her chosen name, so perhaps that's why Amanda became his. Amanda was his defiant compromise.

> *I read your letter with interest, hoping you'd reply to the question I asked Teju. I'm curious to know why you've contacted me now, after so long. Perhaps you will answer in your own time.*

'How's it going?' Mike shouts from the landing.

'Fine,' I yell and start again, but what to say?

> *So, about me.*
>
> *Well, I am married, my husband is called Michael, and we have—*

I stop mid-sentence.

What the hell am I doing? I am my mother's daughter, for God's sake. What is there to say? And then I think, but wait a minute, shouldn't I continue? Isn't writing this letter one of those critical moments in life where you can change things for the better? Isn't this the eureka 'I've seen the light' moment? This is the turning point to make amends. This is the moment to heal the past for a brighter future. That's the Hollywood happy ending. And who doesn't love a happy ending?

Picking up my pen again, my thoughts drift. I wonder what my mother is doing. Maybe she's watching one of her favourite food programmes or playing Solitaire on her iPad, and what am I doing? I'm playing 'Let's Write a Jolly Letter to this long-lost person who's become a stranger to me.'

I stand up and close the window. The wind outside is rattling and annoying, and writing this letter is rattling and annoying. It is a futile endeavour – a waste of time. I am Team Mum, not Team Sanni.

Seven

Not a Camilla

A person's name is to him or her the sweetest and most important sound in any language.

—Dale Carnegie

By 1989 life was different. Abdul was an electrical engineer. Dunni worked in London as a medical secretary, and they'd both left home, although they didn't exactly tread far – they still lived in Luton, Abdul in a flat and Dunni in a house share with a friend. Bradley Road was a house of memories. It was sold to a new family, and a few days before the removal van came to take our belongings I wrote in pencil, *Mandy Camilla A. Sanni lived here,* on a corner of skirting board in my bedroom. I was sad to leave but, at the same time, I knew my mother had found her 'dream house', a detached bungalow in Luton on a road of identical 60s designed bungalows, close to my old secondary school.

On a physical level I was different too. I'd ditched my oversized glasses for contact lenses. My hair was no longer pressed with the dreaded pressing comb but chemically straightened. Instead of mimicry, I devoured culturally savvy magazines like *The Face* and *ID,* In my mind, I was in the wrong place and at the wrong time. I belonged in 1970s New York, dancing the night away at Studio 54, because at that age, like most teenagers, I was obsessed with America. I wondered why my mother had not boarded a ship bound for Ellis Island. If she had, we could have lived in Boston, not Bradley Road.

America was the land of the brave, the land of the free, the land of good-looking people who were polished like silver. Americans had Jheri curls or flickable-straight hair, sturdy white teeth and cool-sounding names. How could we folks across the pond compete with names like Chip, Courtney, Montel, Arsenio and Oprah? I mean, come on. Oprah Winfrey sounded like a precious stone. In comparison, UK names were like a cosy cardigan knitted by your grandmother.

I was 19 years old in 1989, and my fascination with America came to a fruition. Before I started university, I got a job teaching drama at a summer camp in the US. It was a summer of firsts – my first-ever plane trip. My first taste of life outside of Luton; and, perhaps most importantly, it was the first time I considered using my real name. I thought, here I am, about to leave Luton; for a six-week stint on a summer camp in Hartford, Connecticut, and no one knows me. This is my opportunity for a summer reinvention. Why can't I be Camilla, not Mandy? But something stopped me. I wasn't ready to fully commit to this new identity, at least not yet, and when I met my campmates I was glad I didn't.

The other teachers at the camp were the living embodiment of their names. Before I was introduced to Brad, the tennis coach, I conjured up a mental picture of what I thought Brad looked like. I imagined him supremely confident, tanned, athletic, Ivy-League-educated, and perhaps slightly arrogant. And I was right. Brad lived up to his name. He was all of those things, maybe more arrogant than I imagined. But you get the drift. Brad's name suited him. He looked like a Brad and this got me thinking. Did I look like a Camilla? Jump-forward to 2017, and a group of researchers in Jerusalem coined the term 'face–name match'. They wanted to find out whether a name matched someone's face, and, on that summer camp, I wondered the same thing, too.

I met my campmates, and I shied away from introducing myself as Camilla. After carrying the name Mandy for 19 years, uncertainty about using a different name now crept in. I realise this was partly due to a lack of confidence and to self-doubt. I wasn't sure I *looked* like a Camilla. I wasn't sure this name suited me. The doubts about my real name had gone up a notch by the late 80s. There were rumblings about another Camilla. It was a newsworthy name. This other Camilla was called Camilla Parker Bowles. At that age, I'd not come across anyone who shared the same name as me, and there she was, smiling from the newsstands, mousey-haired and outdoorsy. Looking at this Camilla, I questioned the name on my birth certificate. I thought, you know what? Perhaps Mandy wasn't so bad after all.

The summer camp was predominantly made up of American teachers. Three teachers, like me, were recruited from the UK, and they were White and came from the Home Counties. The only other Black teacher on the camp was LaTonya, a twenty-something African-American who lit up a room with her kilowatt charisma. She was from New York and was the kind of girl who turned heads, but she didn't take herself too seriously. I liked her, and I was intrigued by her name. I knew someone called Tonya in Luton, but I'd not come across a *La*Tonya before.

One morning the two of us sat outside the drama theatre, and she casually mentioned that all her siblings' names started with the letter L.

'My younger sister is called Lakshana,' she explained. 'And my brother is called La'Shawn.'

'What are your parents called?' I asked.

'Loretta and Luke.'

I laughed.

'Seriously. I'm not messing with you, and our surname is Washington,' she smiled. 'That's got to be *the* Blackest surname in America.'

And LaTonya was right. If we tumble forward a couple of decades or so, a 2000 US census showed over 160,000 people had the surname Washington, and 90 per cent of those counted were African-American. After the Civil War and the horrors of slavery, Blacks in the US were allowed the dignity of a surname, and many chose the surname of the first US president, George Washington, to establish their freedom and identities.

But it wasn't until after the summer camp that LaTonya's name became a source of interest.

I was invited to dinner by Cory, one of the other drama teachers. Cory was blond and blue-eyed, smoked copious amounts of marijuana, and was convinced he was going to be *the* next big thing. He lived in a house not far from the summer camp, but I ummed and ahed about whether I should go. To be frank, I was summer-camped out, but I went along, lured by the promise of beer and a barbecue.

Cory's house was white and significant on a wide, tree-lined road, with Stars and Stripes flags billowing in the wind among a sea of other white and significant properties. There were white picket fences and expensive cars parked on driveways, and as someone who as a kid gorged on *Dallas*, the television show about an oil-rich family from Texas, I was curious to step inside an actual American home.

Cory's dad, Pete, was in charge of the barbecue, and he wore a brown apron over a rotund belly with the words *Big*

Chef on the front. He was an amiable guy. His job for the evening was turning steaks on the barbecue grill. But these were no ordinary steaks. They were not the kind of steaks I ate at the Beefeater restaurant in Luton. These steaks were the size of my forearm. As the meat sizzled, I made small talk with Cory's mother, who tossed a salad in a large wooden bowl.

She was called Patty, and she was petite and perky.

'I just love the way you speak. It's brilliant,' she said, attempting an impersonation of my accent.

I was too polite to say her attempt was not dissimilar to Dick Van Dyke's dodgy British accent in the film *Mary Poppins.* How could I? I was their guest.

'Go on. Say "brilliant",' Patty whined. 'I just *love* the way you English folk say "brilliant". Have you heard the way Mandy says "brilliant", honey?'

'Say "brilliant",' Cory's father shouted from the barbecue.

'It's a shame LaTonya couldn't make it,' I said quickly. 'You'd like her. She's fun.'

'I'm guessing LaTonya is Black.' Patty smirked. 'I don't think I've heard of a LaTonya who is White. Those folks sure like their funny-sounding names.'

Everyone giggled except me. I didn't know it back then, but Blacks and Whites in the US chose relatively similar given names for their children up until the 1960s. However, that pattern changed dramatically as most Blacks (particularly those living in racially isolated neighbourhoods) adopted increasingly distinctive names. This re-evaluation of African-American names coincided with the rise of the Black Power and Civil Rights movements, which, for many, was an opportunity to choose names that reflected their African identity or were distinctive and creative. In one study using data that covered every child born in the US state of California since the 1960s and 1970s, two American academics, Fryer and Levitt, found there were marked differences between the naming choices of Blacks and Whites. Some given names (such as Shanice and Precious) were found to be relatively popular among Blacks for girls but virtually unheard of for White girls; some boys' forenames (such as Connor and Jake) were found to be distinctively White. So, if LaTonya was labelled as an African-American-sounding name, what did that mean for all the other people whose names hint at their race, religion, gender or ethnicity?

In the landmark 2004 study 'Are Emily and Greg More Employable than Lakisha and Jamal?', two American academics set out to measure racial discrimination in the job market. Fictitious résumés were sent out to help-wanted ads. Each résumé was assigned either a very African-American name, for example, Lakisha Washington or Jamal Jones, or a very White-sounding name like Emily Walsh or Brendan Baker. Their study discovered applicants with White-sounding names were more likely to get callbacks for an interview than applicants with African-American-sounding names. One of the academics from the study said, 'For us, the most surprising and disheartening result is seeing that applicants with African-American names were not rewarded for having better résumés.' Despite this study being conducted in 2004, unfortunately subsequent studies show there's been very little improvement. In our modern, open and inclusive worldview, we like to imagine we've moved on, and a name will not hinder someone's chance of employment. However, in a recent study by the GEMM survey (Growth, Equal Opportunities, Migration and Markets) based in Europe, researchers applied for thousands of real jobs in Britain, Norway, Germany and the Netherlands. The ethnic ancestry of applicants was indicated through the applicants' names but was identical in terms of education and skills to White-sounding names. The results were damning. They found countries with a long history of immigration from the Commonwealth or former colonies had the highest rates of discrimination. White-sounding names got the most responses from prospective employers, whereas names that sounded Asian, Middle Eastern or African had the fewest. In 2017, social scientists at Bristol University sent out two identical CVs in terms of experience but submitted them with different names, Adam and Mohamed. Adam received 12 positive responses and four inquiries from headhunters, but Mohamed only won four positive responses and two inquiries. The person who led the study explained the results. 'What we've identified very clearly is the Muslim-sounding person's CV is only likely to get an interview in one out of three cases.' Of course, name-blind recruitment can help. But other indicators on their résumé can hint at their race or religion, like a scholarship for minorities or attendance at a traditionally Black college, like Howard University. So, what does name discrimination in the job market do? It forces applicants to take matters into their own hands.

Let's take the surname Iqbal. It's a popular last name in the Punjab region in India and Pakistan, but, for Shahid Iqbal, based in the UK, it wasn't a popular name in the job market. He sent out multiple job applications but on each occasion he was informed that the position had been filled. So he took drastic action. Shahid Iqbal used a completely different given name and surname. He started applying for jobs using the name Richard Brown. And something strange happened. Under this new name, he managed to secure interviews, and, realising his name was key to his success, he went on to set up his own business under the 'White, British-sounding name', Richard Brown.

Some might shrug this off as an isolated incident, but it is not.

The British-Asian comedian Romesh Ranganathan's parents were so worried about the discrimination he might face in the job market that they gave him 'Jonathan' as a first name (Romesh is his middle name).

Other job applicants resort to a practice called 'résumé whitening' and, according to Dr Sonia Kang, whitening a name for your résumé or CV is fairly widespread. When I interviewed her, she explained the meaning behind the term. 'Résumé whitening is the practice of removing or downplaying cues that may reveal a candidate's minority status from their résumé – for example, names, experiences, and educational institutions,' she said. 'A candidate with a stereotypically Black-sounding name like DeAndre may downplay his race by listing his name as Andrew. Résumé whitening makes it harder to tell that a candidate is not White and/or makes a candidate appear more "mainstream" in the hope they will increase their chances of being selected for a job interview or job offer.'

As part of her study identifying the prevalence of name discrimination in the US, Kang interviewed 59 Asian and African-American candidates between the ages of 18 and 25. Thirty-six per cent of those interviewed admitted to 'whitening' their résumés, and 64 per cent said they knew of someone who did.

Ethiopians make up one of the largest African immigrant groups in the US, and in 2020 the Ethiopian-American academic Dr Hewan Girma conducted a study about their experiences. Girma analysed how first-generation Ethiopian-American immigrants living in the US negotiated different layers of identity around naming. Her study examined the names first-generation immigrants gave to their children and the relevance participants attached to their first names. Some parents actively encouraged using traditional Ethiopian given names for their children. However, the majority of Ethiopian-American parents didn't want their children to feel put on the spot or singled out because of a foreign-sounding name. To solve the problem, parents gave their children easy-to-pronounce Biblical names. They chose names like Michael, Abigail, Christian and Ruth. Or they opted for not overly ethnic-sounding Ethiopian names that were short, had two syllables (just like my mother and her fondness for two-syllable

Mandy), or names that were easy to pronounce, such as Bona and Senay. One father in Girma's study said, 'Imagine my kid in kindergarten having to explain his name and other kids making fun of him. No! I don't want that for him. I want him to fit in and not be different.'

Years ago, at a wedding, I sat near two people I didn't know who, in animated voices, were discussing their jobs. At a certain point, though, the work chat turned to names, so of course I tuned in. One of the women explained that at the start of her career in the tech industry, she routinely initialised her given name on job applications.

'Why?' I asked, intrigued.

'In the macho world of tech, an initialised name obscured my gender,' she explained. 'I got way more interviews for jobs too.'

As depressing as this statement was, when we consider gender in the job market, there is growing evidence to suggest that, if a woman adopts a more gender-neutral name on a job application or blurs her gender, the response is greater. In a 2016 post on Linkedin after finding no employment success using her real name Erin McKelvey, on job applications, Erin tweaked her given name to the more masculine-sounding Mack, and this resulted in a 70 per cent improved response rate. In a 2016 study carried out in Australia and New Zealand, two identical applications were sent out to employers, but they used a male name, Simon Cook, on one application and a female name, Susan Campbell, on the other. The results found recruiters were more likely to hire Simon over Susan.

Reading and researching about name discrimination made me consider the experiences of my mother and Sanni when it came to securing employment or housing. Before they married, my mother's given name and surname weren't visibly different from any White-British person in the UK in the

50s and 60s. Carmen Francis (my mother's surname before marriage) might have been the person who worked in the tea shop on the high street in Watford or in one of the offices on Carnaby Street. In many respects my mother was fortunate. She arrived in London in 1959, boarded with a friend in west London and then secured student nurses' accommodation in Wembley. From the snippets of information I gleaned from Teju about Sanni, he came to the UK with an allowance and stayed with well-to-do family friends. Because of this, they didn't experience the well-known racist message embedded in the national psyche of England to the same degree as others. The *no blacks, no dogs, no Irish* signs, displayed in the the front windows of properties for let. However, some of my mother's friends were not so lucky. Flicking through newspaper advertisements for vacant accommodation, newly arrived immigrants circled the details of prospective rooms to let. One of my mother's friends told me she came across a suitable-sounding accommodation, called the number and gave her name.

'It's Vanessa Clarke,' she said over a crackling telephone line.

In a welcoming voice, the landlady invited Vanessa to view the room. But of course, Vanessa Clarke, who turned up in her finest attire – hat, gloves and a well-ironed frock – was not the person the landlady expected.

'Sorry, pet,' the landlady said. 'The room has gone. Better luck next time.'

Except next time, the exact same scenario happened again and again.

Now, of course, we like to hope, with legislation and laws governing discrimination, that name discrimination in housing is in the past. It isn't. There are many incidents of name discrimination in housing or simply booking a room for the night. The shared experiences on social media under the hashtag 'AirbnbwhileBlack' are a testament to this. To test the discrimination faced, in 2020 researchers at Harvard Business School sent out messages from fake accounts and used some names that sounded Black, others White. The study uncovered 'widespread discrimination' against Black guests by pretty much all of the hosts. Another recent study found that, across the US, housing providers were less likely to respond to applicants with African-American or Latino-sounding names, and, in a *Guardian* investigation in 2018, room seekers with the Muslim name Mohammed were less likely to receive a positive response than renters with the name David.

A couple of years ago, I read Mary Lassiter's book *Our Names Ourselves*. Written in the early 1980s, one chapter stood out. A fifteen-year-old girl, Catherine, who lived in the UK, explained how she loathed her name because it didn't suit her personality or colour.

'I'm not White. I'm Black, and so I would like a name that is given to Black people. I'm not against White; it's just that I like to know that my body, mind and name represent the real me.'

I reread this passage recently and wondered what an older and wiser Catherine thinks now. I'd imagine she's in her mid-50s, and I wonder whether she's changed her mind. Does she like being called Catherine? Or has she changed her name to something that sounds Black? What exactly is a Black British name? Is Mandy a Black British name? Is Camilla a Black British name? Not according to the person in Norfolk whose jaw hit the floor as I strolled into the room at a recent event and said my name was Camilla.

'Your name is misleading. I thought you'd be White,' she spluttered.

And not according to the person I met in my first week at university.

In September 1990, deep into freshers' week – the week of forced joy where you meet other fresh-faced students who, in a few days' time, you'll cross the corridor to avoid. Still, I got chatting with a bunch of students, downing glass after glass of double-shot vodkas and cranberry juice.

Their names were straight out of a Jilly Cooper novel and, as I prepared to introduce myself, I thought, Why not? – Here I am, this is me. Go for it!

'I'm Camilla,' I said, and an overriding sensation of pleasure hit me as I uttered my name for the first time. I felt less of a fraud and, looking back now, I realise why.

When I applied for the course and registered at the university a few days before, the official form asked for my full name. Because it was an official document, I wrote Camilla. But Mandy or Amanda was such a massive part of my psyche – so embedded in my DNA – that I am ashamed to admit I omitted my Nigerian middle name.

I wrote:

Full name: Camilla Amanda Sanni.

So, by introducing myself as Camilla, I thought I was making some kind of statement about who I was, thereby banishing the middle name registration debacle.

One of the girls gulped down her vodka and cranberry juice and eyed me up and down.

I was wearing a rather fetching vintage white jumpsuit from Camden Market, and I assumed she was admiring my sartorial choices.

'Camilla,' she slurred. 'You don't look like a Camilla. For starters, you're Coloured. All the Camillas I know are red-haired or pale-skinned with freckles, and they listen to Enya and wear tweed.'

The other girls laughed, and I smiled out of sheer embarrassment.

'Yeah, it's Camilla,' I replied quickly. 'But I don't really use it. Everyone calls me Mandy, so call me Mandy. That's my name.'

Can I mention at this point the person who made the comment about Enya and tweed was called Alexa? So, thank you, Jeff Bezos and Amazon.

Nine months later, I gave Camilla another shot.

It was June, and a friend from university invited me to her home town in Gloucestershire. The plan was to go to a secret 'event', AKA a rave, somewhere near Cheltenham, which turned out to be a disappointing field of about twenty people gurning and wearing Day-Glo.

The next day, mildly hungover, I trudged along with my friend and her mother to a local farming event. On a rainy Saturday morning, I watched men and women, young and old, gawp over livestock. I saw grown men in flat caps salivate over a shed full of tractors. I watched a sheep-shearing competition and in the afternoon, while my friend chatted to her mother's farming pals, I purchased an overpriced cup of cider, sat in a tent, and read an overhead banner swaying in the wind with the words *Somerset: the crème de la crème of the British countryside.*

A few moments later, a thin-as-a-pencil woman clutching a walking stick, with the demeanour of someone who has inhaled deeply of the good things in life, sidled up to me and asked if I was having a good time.

I told her I was because, in a strange way, I was enjoying myself.

'Where are you from, sweetie?' she asked.

'Luton.'

She made a sort of 'poor you' face.

'The weather's ghastly. I've got a feeling the blackberries will be late this year. And it's almost parasol mushroom season,' she said, giving me an absent-minded smile. 'Do you know how to spot an edible wild mushroom?'

I shook my head.

'They have a particular smell, milky, and a large pointy nipple. Are you from London?'

'Luton,' I said again.

'I was born in London,' she said wistfully. 'Chelsea. Golly, I do miss those days on the King's Road, with a glass or two of bub.'

She stuck out her hand and told me her first name, which was long and at least four syllables.

'What's your name, sweetie?' she asked, four gold bracelets jangling on her wrist.

'It's – Camilla,' I said in a quiet voice.

The woman placed a bejewelled hand to her mouth.

'Camille.'

'No, it's Camilla, not Camille.'

'No, it isn't,' she said, eyeing me up and down. 'You're not a Camilla.'

I told her I was indeed a Camilla.

She said I mustn't tell fibs.

'What's your *actual* name?'

'That is my name. I'm Camilla,' I hissed.

'That's what you call yourself?'

'Yes.'

'You don't look like a Camilla at all,' she said, shuffling away.

I watched her leave, clutching my now-flat cider, and I thought, you know what? Maybe she was right. Maybe my mother was right.

Everyone knows you as Mandy. You can't change it. That's your name.

Oxford, June 2015

We are, the sat nav informs us, seven minutes away, so I message Teju to let him know.

It is a Sunday, and, although I used enthusiastic exclamation marks in my text to Teju, I am tired. I'm not sleeping well, which is unlike me. I am an exemplary sleeper, I could fall asleep on a swing, but since I received Sanni's letter two months ago I am failing to perform a basic human function. I've forgotten how to sleep. There are three-in-the-morning wake-ups: churning thoughts, an overwhelming sense of guilt about contacting Teju, the image of Sanni's smiling photo and his letter. The letter I still haven't replied to.

Since meeting Teju in April, plenty of emails and texts have shuttled back and forth between us. We've spoken on the phone, and this will be our second meeting. But it's still an odd feeling having a cousin. It feels strange saying 'my cousin' and here I am in Oxford, meeting *my cousin*.

'Maybe I should have worn another dress,' I say to Mike. 'Something cooler. It's so hot. I wish I'd worn a pair of shorts.'

He stops the car at a set of traffic lights as a couple, hand in hand, both shirtless, strut past the vehicle, their biceps pumped like tyres.

'You look great,' he says, smiling. 'And shorts? I can count on one hand the times you've worn shorts.'

'I'm not drinking coffee,' I say, drumming my fingers against my thigh. 'Honestly, if Teju mentions caffeine, I'm not going there. Not after last time. I'll have a peppermint tea or something instead. What do you think Hannah will be like?'

'I don't know, but I hope Hannah and Teju are brilliant cooks. I'm starving,' he says.

When we last spoke, Teju asked all the usual 'new people for dinner' questions. I told him we were easy guests, and he said, 'Good, because we're preparing a Nigerian feast in honour of your visit.'

I wasn't what you'd call a connoisseur of Nigerian cuisine. Sanni was never around much and, if he was around, my mother did most of the cooking. She was an excellent cook; food was her way of showing love. The sole occasion we ate Nigerian food was at Sanni's apartment, so the memory stands out. I must have been around seven years old at the time.

They'd been divorced for a while and Sanni, unbelievably, turned up for one of his weekend visits. I don't recall the day, although it was likely a Saturday because we'd spent the morning shopping in Marks & Spencer. He'd brought us gifts. Perhaps they were gifts of guilt for his shoddy absences. By then, he lived in a flat in east London. It was on the top floor, and now, when I look back, that flat screamed, 'Bachelor pad!' Frantic music played in the background and, to my young ears, it sounded nothing like the crooners Mum liked. Sanni's music wasn't Rod Stewart or Barry White or Johnny Mathis. This music was relentless and loud and attacked the auditory senses. Over the sound of drums, horns and singing, Dunni, Abdul and I sat with straight backs on our best behaviour in the dining room. Our visits to Sanni's flat were awkward. How were we expected to build a relationship with someone we now only saw sporadically and who had been largely absent in our earlier childhood? Plus, it was a sunny day. I wished I was playing in the park with my friends, and not listening to this wild and crazy music Sanni said was called 'Nigerian High Life'.

'I don't like his cooking,' I whispered to Dunni and, to be honest, at that age I was a fussy eater. The chips had to be crispy. I wasn't keen on vegetables and, even if I liked the dish, I would usually leave mounds of food on my plate, which Abdul would then tuck into.

'When he's not looking, put the food in a tissue,' Dunni advised.

'I'm not doing that,' Abdul said. 'I'm hungry, and it smells good.'

'I wish we were having Mum's Saturday soup,' I told my sister.

A few moments later, Sanni came out of the kitchen carrying bowl after bowl of steaming food. But nothing looked familiar. Where was the Saturday soup, corned beef hash, fish in white sauce, fish fingers, spam, chips, rice and peas, chicken and my mother's tasty dumplings? What was this food? There was rice, so at least that was familiar, but nothing else looked like my mother's cooking.

'What's that?' I asked, pointing to a bowl of what looked like mashed potatoes.

'Garri,' Sanni replied. 'It's good for you. It will make you strong.'

My sister looked at the bowl of garri and said she wasn't hungry.

I pointed to another dish that reminded me of freshly mown grass.

'And what's that?' I asked in a tentative voice.

'Greens,' Sanni replied. 'You'll be like Popeye. They are good for your muscles.'

I raised my eyebrows towards my brother to make the first move. He had an appetite like a Labrador and ate anything.

'Ah, that's right, son. Good,' Sanni said as Abdul placed a hearty pile onto his plate. 'Eat up.'

The two chewed with abandon while my sister and I looked at the patterned tablecloth.

Eventually, Dunni took a mouthful of the food on her plate as the music in the background screeched to a crescendo.

'Come on, Amanda,' Sanni said. 'Eat up. Next time, we'll have yam. I'll make you soup. Pepper soup – you'll like that. Or how about I make jollof rice? Nigerian jollof is the best there is.'

'I don't want "jolly off rice",' I said, pushing food around my plate. 'Can we have soup next time? Mum makes the best soups. She puts dumplings in her soup. Can we have Jamaican dumplings in pepper soup?'

Dunni giggled.

'Eat your food, Amanda!' he barked.

I placed morsels of food into my mouth and chewed with all the speed of a three-toed sloth.

'Good?' Sanni asked.

'Mmm-hmm,' I replied, not telling him I willed myself to eat this food. As I chewed and swallowed, I pretended my mother had cooked this food, not him.

As per Teju's email instructions, Mike parks the car in front of a smart-looking Victorian semi-detached house with a black front door and two large, vibrant green plants in blue and white pots.

He turns off the engine while I lean over to the back seat and grab a bouquet of colourful flowers and two bottles of artisan Norfolk apple juice. There are no bottles of wine on the back seat. Hannah and Teju do not drink alcohol.

Smoothing down my dress, I ring the bell, and seconds later a smiling, petite blonde woman with sparkly blue eyes flings it open.

'Camilla. Mike,' she says. 'I'm Hannah. I hope the journey wasn't too awful. It's *so* hot. We shouldn't complain, I suppose. Come in. Come in.'

The hallway wall is filled with expressive art and photographs of presumably their children in varying stages of life – toddlers, teenagers, and then grinning university students with mortar-boards.

Hannah leads the way, chatting about Oxford in a friendly, inclusive tone.

Mike tells her we've visited the city before.

'My niece is studying medicine,' he explains.

'Oh, good for her,' Hannah says. 'Which college?'

'St Catherine's,' he replies.

'Ah, you made it,' Teju says, emerging from the kitchen and wiping his hands on a tea towel.

He smiles broadly, and I smile too, because I am genuinely pleased to see him. This is our second face-to-face meet-up, but our embrace isn't awkward. It's warm and friendly and, dare I say it, cousin-like.

The four of us stand in the hallway.

Hannah thanks Mike for the flowers and apple juice.

Mike thanks Teju for inviting us over, while I comment on the delicious smells wafting from the kitchen.

'That's nothing to do with me, I'm afraid.' Teju grins. 'That's down to Hannah and our surprise guest. She's just popped out to the shops. She'll be back in a moment.'

'Who's the guest?' I ask, following Teju into their sleek, well-equipped kitchen.

'Your cousin. My younger sister,' Teju replies. 'She lives in Nigeria, but she's staying with us for a few weeks. She wanted to surprise you. She's desperate to meet you.'

Of course, I don't say it, but I don't want to meet another cousin. I am still getting used to having one. I don't need to meet any more – at least not yet. One is plenty.

'Can I get you and Michael a drink?' Hannah asks.

There is no alcohol – only soft drinks – but after the long journey from Norfolk and the heat, I could murder a double gin and tonic or a large glass of cool, crisp white wine in one of those enormous balloon-shaped glasses.

Hannah opens a bottle of elderflower cordial, pours a large glassful over ice and hands me a drink.

'Ifemi is a great friend of Uncle Rimi,' Hannah explains.

'Oh yeah,' I reply, sipping the sweet liquid, wishing it was something more satisfying than bloody elderflower cordial.

Hannah wants to know if Norfolk is as flat as people say, but before I get the chance to respond we are interrupted by an unfamiliar voice shouting, 'Camilla!' from the hallway.

'Come on. Give me a hug,' the new arrival says, putting down two overflowing shopping bags.

Ifemi, my cousin, Teju's younger sister, gathers me into her bosom and presses the back of my head with her hands.

I pat her on the back, which is ridiculous. She is not a dog, elderly or ill. I'm not consoling her, but I don't know what else to do with my hands.

She releases me, and we stare at one another for a moment.

Ifemi's natural hair is long, and styled into two thick French plaits. She is younger than me but taller, and she is standing so close I can feel her breath on my skin.

'Uncle Rimi calls you Amanda,' she says with a smile. 'What do you prefer? I called you Camilla because Teju told me you liked Camilla.'

'I do. It's Camilla.'

'He's right,' she says, eyeing me up and down.

'About what?' I ask. 'Who's right?'

'Teju,' she says, grinning. 'You *do* have your dad's ears.'

Eight

Big in Japan

Life is for one generation; a good name is forever.
—Japanese Proverb

In March 2019, an 18-year-old high school student from Yamanashi prefecture, west of Tokyo, submitted an application to the family court requesting permission to change his given name. His parents had named him Ōji-sama, which translates as Prince. However, he felt the name was ostentatious and that his parents were influenced by a trend called 'kira-kira', which is considered by some people in Japan to be a glittery and unorthodox naming trend. Japanese naming conventions are, in the main, traditional, and, because the name Ōji-sama was unusual and drew a negative reaction from his friends, Ōji-sama was desperate to change it. The application process cost around 3,000 yen, which translates to about £15 or $20, and after a month-long wait, permission was granted. The family court agreed he could change his name from Ōji-sama to the more traditional-sounding Hajime. Once his new name became official, Hajime said it marked a transformation and the beginning of a new chapter in his life.

Two decades earlier, in the winter of 1994, I sat in a grey, grim windowless room in central London on a too-small plastic chair, explaining why I was the right candidate for the job.

I was 24, and my response was as bland as my outfit. I wore a demure blue skirt, a white blouse and sensible black shoes in the hope that my cobbled-together attire would scream potential teacher of English in Japan material and not, 'You were in a sweaty club on Wardour Street till late last night, with your hands in the air, cutting through laser lights.'

By then, I'd graduated from university, and I was back home, living with my mother and John in their bungalow in Luton. It was, I hoped a temporary arrangement. Mike was working in Manchester, and I sold advertising space for a cinema magazine. The sole perk of the job was watching films for free. Apart from that, selling advertisement space wasn't what I planned to do with my life.

There were two interviewers – a serious-looking Japanese woman who spoke faultless Received-Pronunciation-accented English and an older non-Japanese man. They cocked their heads to one side as I talked at length about *Shōgun* – the 1980s television series set in 1600s feudal Japan. On reflection, waxing lyrical about my love for a cheesy television show most likely sounded a bit daft. Still, in fairness, *Shōgun* was the catalyst for my youthful obsession with Japan.

Growing up, every Saturday night in 1984, Dunni, Abdul (if he wasn't dancing at one of his Soul Weekenders), my mother, John and I sat on the sofa and endured *Are You Being Served?*, the sitcom following staff and customers at a London department store. We'd sit through the programme's tongue-in-cheek references to Mrs Slocombe's pussy until, bang on eight o'clock, the music for *Shōgun* began. I'd put down whatever I was reading at the time and watch spellbound as

I was transported from Bradley Road in Luton to Japan, samurai swords, and 'dishy Richie', my mother's moniker for Richard Chamberlain, the show's main protagonist.

'I think *Shōgun* was why I picked up a few Japanese phrases,' I explained to the serious-looking interviewer. 'I used to yell "Ohayou Gozaimasu" like a town crier each morning and "Konbanwa" every evening.'

The woman's mouth formed a half-smile, while the other interviewer ran his hands through his curly mop of black hair and picked up my application form.

Filling out a form or any official document asks us a simple question:

NAME:

The form or document will leave a space for you to write your given name and surname. Most people won't even think about it. They'll write Bob, Trisha or Darren, followed by their middle name (if they have one) and surname, and move on to the next question.

But I was different.

Two weeks before the interview, I sat at my mother's kitchen table in Luton, mulling over how to answer the request on the application form.

NAME:

I swallowed, staring at this innocuous request for my name.

The hallway clock chimed. My hands felt sweaty and clammy, like I'd been at a fun fair and eaten candy floss. I swallowed harder this time and reread the single word on the form asking for my NAME. In the past, whenever any official form or document asked for my name, I wrote:

CAMILLA (but call me Mandy) or CAMILLA (Mandy). Mandy was my constant shadow, but it was time to step out of the shadows.

With a swish of my pen, I wrote CAMILLA. There were no open brackets, Mandy or close brackets. There was only

Camilla, and, inside, multiple fireworks exploded. This was the moment I shed my old Mandy skin, and, as I sat in my mother's kitchen, I'd figured out how I was going to make it work. If I got the job, I could be Camilla in Japan and Mandy in England. That way, there would be no confusion. The two names could lead separate lives and never meet.

'Camilla is a tricky name for Japanese people,' the unsmiling interviewer said, gazing at my application form. 'Do you have a nickname or a middle name your prospective students might use?'

'No,' I said a little too loudly. 'I'm Camilla. I realise it's a tricky name for Japanese people to pronounce, but that's my name. I don't have another name.'

'What does the A in your middle name stand for?' the smiley interviewer asked.

Now, this stumped me because, reader, I wasn't completely transparent on my application form. I took my mother's advice. I initialised my middle name.

'My middle name is even harder to pronounce,' I replied quickly. 'Camilla is best.'

The female interviewer looked unimpressed.

'In Japan, surnames are placed before given names,' the man explained.

I already knew this but, because the interview was going so badly, I feigned surprise at the revelation.

'If your application is successful, you'll soon get used to Japanese names,' he said. 'I don't do so much classroom teaching these days. I'm more senior management, but, when I used to teach at our language school in Tokyo, I once had three young ladies called Hiroko in my class, and there were two students called Keiko. Female names that end in "ko" are popular.'

'"Ko" means child. Did you know that?' the woman asked, glaring straight at me.

'No,' I replied, glad for the change of subject around my name.

And then, they both stood up and thanked me for coming.

I didn't get up. What now? What was my backup plan? Mike and I had been together for three years by then, and we had a loose plan. If I got the job, I would go to Japan, and he would follow, but what if I didn't get it? How long could I continue selling advertising space in a cinema magazine, living at home with my mother and John, living as Mandy? I possessed two names, and sometimes it felt like I was navigating two opposing personalities, and for the last twenty-four years Mandy was forging ahead.

In his book, *The Language of Names*, co-authored by his wife, Anne Bernays, Justin Kaplan explains how being known by two given names affected his self-esteem and sense of identity. Kaplan says, 'On my birth certificate I'm Justin, a name my mother favoured and my father barely tolerated. When she died (I was seven), he reimposed his own first choice, which had been Joseph, and when he died (I was twelve), I was left with a double first-name identity, as well as confusion in school and medical records. By the time I went to college, I had to define the situation this way. Joseph was the double orphan, alone, afraid, uncertain. Justin was an evolving, more confident and more competent person who had begun to see the possibility of finding his way to definition through love and work.'

And, like Kaplan, this was my chance to define myself.

'We'll be in contact to let you know if you've been successful,' the female interviewer said, discreetly catching a yawn with her hand.

'Thanks for coming, Camilla,' the man said, leading me to the door.

I walked into the crisp early-morning London sunshine. Yards from the interview building on the corner of Charing Cross Road was a red telephone box. In the 1990s, these iconic boxes were used for making calls, whereas today they house defibrillator machines or act as a mini library for books. But I was on such a high from the interviewer's last sentence that I ignored the rancid smell of urine and the sleazy stickers advertising dodgy massages. I loaded multiple coins into the box and, before Mike said hello or asked how the interview went, I blurted out a sentence in a rush of adrenalin.

'What?' he said. 'I didn't get a word of that.'

'There's no more Mandy,' I said, barely containing my excitement.

'What do you mean?'

'The interviewer just called me Camilla!' I said, in a garbled rush. 'But I don't think I got the job.'

Of course, this wasn't the first time someone had uttered 'Camilla', but in that moment in that stuffy room it meant something. It really meant something. And I didn't say it, but part of me wished Mike had heard it too. I wished he had been with me to witness the moment that my name came alive in someone else's mouth.

Back in Luton, one week later, a Next mail-order catalogue and an official-looking brown envelope dropped onto the jute *Welcome home* doormat at the bungalow.

The catalogue was addressed to my mother and the brown envelope was addressed to me: *Camilla A Sanni.*

I opened it, read the brief letter inside, and yelled so loudly I could have woken the dead.

In early April, three months after the interview in London, my mother wiped a tear forming in the corner of her eye as we said our goodbyes at Heathrow Airport.

She hugged me, a Carmen version of a hug, which was more like a gentle coming together of the top half of her body against mine.

'Make sure you call. Ask your headmaster or -mistress if you can use their phone,' she said, shouting to make herself heard over the Tannoy announcement for my flight.

'I don't have a headmaster, Mum; it's not like secondary school; it's a language school. They're different.'

'Well – make sure you write,' she said, wiping her eyes.

I promised I'd write and call, and many years later, when my mother recalled the moment I turned and gave a final wave from the departure gates, she said she'd never seen me look so happy.

And I was happy.

Not only was I fleeing Celine Dion's 'The Power of Love', which in 1994 was all over the airwaves, but I was also fleeing Luton, Bradley Road, Mum and John's bungalow, the Arndale Centre and Bury Park. I was fleeing Mandy, but, at the same time, Camilla wasn't some kind of reinvention.

I was reclaiming my name.

To reclaim means to take back something that was previously lost or taken away, and that's what I was doing. I was reclaiming Camilla and now, if I think back to that day, I refer to it as my *Stars in Their Eyes* moment. Some of you might remember the show. It was a talent competition with an infamous catchphrase. Members of the public impersonated singers, but, before they walked through the door and transformed themselves into their chosen performers, they said to Matthew Kelly, the host, 'Tonight, Matthew, I'm going to be . . .' And this might be Whitney Houston, Elton John or any other singer popular at that time. There was no host called Matthew as I walked through the airport departure gate doors and, ironically, I discovered years later that the presenter of the show wasn't called Matthew at all. His name was David. Still, as I walked through the gates and greeted the other rookie teachers bound for a year's contract teaching English in Tokyo, I stuck out my hand and said, 'Hi, I'm Camilla,' and it was a pivotal moment. My name was no longer hidden in my mother's bottom drawer.

Years ago I read an article in the *Guardian* newspaper about the given name Trevor. The article discussed how, after years of rejecting Trevor for its middle-of-the-road blandness and connotations of geekiness and dim wits, Trevor Cunningham set up a website called Trevors Together, celebrating the name. Once I finished the article, intrigued, I emailed Trevor straight away. We arranged a time to talk. And we did talk. We spoke for a long time – so long that, by the time we finished, my piping-hot cup of coffee was now cold and untouched.

'I feel like I'm home at last,' Trevor said. 'This is me. This is who I am. I'm Trevor. I reclaimed my name. It's part of my identity.'

'But you haven't reclaimed your name,' I replied. 'You've always been called Trevor, so how can you say you've reclaimed it?'

He explained that he'd reclaimed his name because, after many years of hating it, he'd finally accepted who he was and what he was called.

'I *like* being a Trevor,' he said in a matter-of-fact voice. 'I *love* being called Trevor.'

We said our goodbyes, and afterwards I thought about what Trevor had said. Had he *really* reclaimed his name? I continued to mull it over for a few days and concluded that of course he had. Trevor took back something that was his, even though his route to reclaiming his name differed from mine. I realised then that there are various routes to reclaiming a name. In their 2020 'Reclaim Her Name' campaign, the Women's Prize for Fiction chose 25 books from authors who wrote under male pseudonyms and rereleased them under their female names. For decades, the legacy of colonialism in Canada meant indigenous people were forced to use their European colonial names on all official documents. This forced assimilation meant traditional indigenous names that carried deep cultural meaning were not recognised. However, in 2021, the Canadian federal government implemented a new policy allowing indigenous people to reclaim the dignity of their indigenous names. In response to the new policy, a statement by the Canadian government said, 'A person's name is fundamental to who they are.' Reclaiming this sense of who you are can be as simple as changing how it is spelt, like the actor Thandiwe Newton, who, a few years ago, chose to use the original Zulu spelling of her name, not the name she'd used professionally for decades, Thandie. In an interview she explained, 'That's my name. It's always been my name. I'm taking back what's mine.'

I recently interviewed Ayo Akinwolere, the first Black male presenter of the iconic children's television show *Blue Peter*. Ayo explained how he, like Thandiwe Newton, reclaimed his given name after personally and professionally being known by another name. 'The whole time I was on *Blue Peter*, I was known by my Catholic middle name, Andy or Andrew,' he explained. 'But when I left the show, I didn't feel like my authentic self. The name Andrew didn't represent who I was. It was only when I started to ask questions about my name's meaning and heritage that I knew I couldn't use the name Andy any more. I thought, here I am, standing with some profile in the public eye and being called Andy. Ayo means "joy", so in the Nigerian naming ceremony, when the elder of the family gave me that name, it meant that I would be a giver of joy. The name Andrew represented none of that.'

Years ago, I came across a letter I wrote to my mother. I wrote plenty of letters to her from Japan, and in one of her marathon tidying-up sessions she bequeathed them all to me – and there were bundles of them. Tied up with industrial-strength twine.

I don't recall sitting down to write this particular letter, but

I do remember I could never dash off a letter to my mother in a few minutes. Writing to her took time. It was a purposeful action, and, in the mid-90s, writing letters to family and friends was an essential part of life. There was the phone and the fax machine (remember those?), but the humble letter was my preferred choice of communication. I knew I wouldn't be able to describe the hustle and bustle of Shibuya or the next moment venturing into a tranquil garden or Shinto temple in quite the same way over the phone. Only in a letter could I explain the feeling of walking into 7-Eleven, picking up a tuna onigiri and hearing 'Irasshaimase!' (Welcome to the store!) and thinking, wow, that doesn't happen in Woolworths! Or sitting on a toilet, pressing a button and, in the blink of an eye, the toilet performed all manner of unexpected thrills – warm seat, hot air and water jets. In those days the number of *gaijin* (the term Japanese people use for foreigners) was minimal. Since then, the number has risen steadily. It is estimated now that over 3.3 million foreigners live in Japan. But in the early 90s, there were few of us, the exchange rate was favourable, and there was a high demand for English teachers.

This particular letter to my mother was written in the summer of 1994. By then, I'd been living in Tokyo for three months.

Dear Mum,

How are you?

Can you let Dunni know I received the photo? She looks amazing. Pregnancy suits her. I can't believe I'm going to be an aunt!

It's true, Mum. The Japanese do have 'a bit of a thing' about Jamaica. It's a popular holiday destination. You wouldn't believe the number of reggae bars there are in Tokyo, and dreadlocks and a fondness for over-tanning. It's quite a sight seeing a dreadlocked, over-tanned

Japanese person strumming a guitar, singing Bob Marley's 'Redemption Song'!

Please don't worry about the sento-baths. No one bats an eyelid. We're all naked. Communal bathing is part of the culture. I realise I'm a novelty, but the Japanese ladies in the bath are too polite to stare.

The teaching is going well. One of my colleagues, who is American and speaks fluent Japanese, has helped me settle in. My students don't call me Mandy. I'm Camilla. That's the name I use out here, Mum, Camilla. I'm not Mandy, and they use honorific titles, so I'm Camilla-sensei (Sensei means teacher) or Sanni-sensei or Sanni-san (San means Miss).

I'll call soon.

Ja mata ne (It means 'See you then')

Camilla

By the way, I'm thinking of starting yoga. Who knows it might help my monthlies.

Reading this letter, now, it's telling that I didn't mention my work colleague, Otis, by name. I suppose, in many ways, he was my secret. Otis was in his early sixties. He was from Texas, an ex-Vietnam vet with a grey-haired afro and side parting, who spoke fluent Japanese and Mandarin. I didn't tell my mother that, if the two of us went out for a beer or met up for a coffee, people presumed he was my dad. This amused Otis. He'd smile and, in his distinctive Southern drawl, he'd say, 'Guess what? The waitress referred to me as your *otou-san*.'

And I'd grin, too, but secretly, I liked the assumption. I liked the idea that people thought Otis was my dad. He didn't have any children of his own, and part of me, a big part, wished he was my *otou-san*. What's also striking about this letter, indeed all the letters I wrote to my mother in Japan, is the ending.

Every letter I wrote to her ended ended in the same way. I underlined my newly reclaimed name.

Lots of love, *Camilla*

See you soon, *Camilla*

Talk soon, *Camilla*

Why can't you call me *Camilla?*

Or, we'd talk on the phone and, although I couldn't underline my name, my God, I tried to make my mother call me by my name:

Carmen: How are you, love? You looked skinny in that last photo, Mandy.

Me: It's Camilla, Mum. I don't use Mandy any more. There's no more Mandy.

Carmen: How is the food, love? Do you need me to send any more rice?

Me: They have loads of rice in Japan. It's the rice capital of the world. I don't need rice.

Carmen: But is it *proper* rice?

Me: Rice is rice!

Carmen: Okay, Mandy, I'll write to you. Take care, love.

Me: It's *Camilla.*

Carmen: You left as Mandy, and now you want us to call you something else. It's not right, love. It's confusing. What will people think? You are Mandy. Everyone knows you as Mandy.

My mother was right. I might have called myself Camilla in Japan, but Mandy was firmly embedded in people's consciousness. When Mike moved to Tokyo six months after I arrived as one of the only people there who knew me before my name was reclaimed, even *he* struggled to get it right – so much so, our friends in Japan presumed he had two girlfriends.

'Mandy – oops, I mean Camilla,' he stuttered in those early few months, and I'd have to explain to the person we happened to be with that, for the whole time we'd dated, Mike knew me as Mandy, and he, along with everyone else who knew me as Mandy, was still getting used to the change.

Otis found this dual naming amusing.

'That's cool, Mandy – oops, I mean, Camilla,' he said, grinning.

It became his catchphrase for me for a while, so much so that it is inscribed on one of my most treasured items from that time. Otis and I shared a love of books. We swapped books regularly and one afternoon, after I'd finished teaching my class, he pressed a dog-eared book into my hand.

'It's a gift. Keep it,' he said.

The book was *The Good Earth* by Pearl S Buck, and the pages were frayed even then, so I knew it was one of those novels Otis read and reread.

He told me it was set in China in the 1930s.

'It's about the importance of the land,' he explained. 'Actually, I think it's about more than that. It's about our human connection to the earth and ourselves. It's about finding simplicity. Anyway, read it. Tell me what you think. You might like it, or you might not.'

I thanked him, opened the first page, and saw that he'd written inside the cover in his large, sloping handwriting.

To my dearest, Mandy – oops, I mean Camilla.
Peace and progress, all my love, Otis.

★

In the following years, I have retold the story I am about to tell many times. Each time I retell it, someone says, 'Now that's a story to tell the grandkids.'

So here it is.

It was a Saturday night, and a bunch of musicians from the US were wooing an enthusiastic crowd of revellers. Mike and

I were with a couple of friends, but not Otis. He wasn't a club kind of guy; more of a misfit who was cerebral and bookish. Most of my friends in Tokyo were certainly bookish, but they were fun-seeking, club-dwelling, nocturnal types.

The air was cloudy with nicotine smoke. I sipped my beer, mindful of the late hour. It was a few minutes past 11.30, and at the time we were renting a no-bigger-than-a-postage-stamp traditional tatami-mat-floor apartment in Ikuta, a suburb an hour from Shinjuku. How we travelled back home was always an issue. We lived in one of the most populous, neon-lit, futuristic cities on earth, with a fiendishly punctual and clean transport system, but there was no 24-hour subway. So our options were either cycling home (not the most sensible after a few beers) or flagging down a taxi. And it was a school night. I had a class the following day at 9 a.m., and they were a tricky group of beginners. I listened to the music at the club, but I was preoccupied, not fully engaged, mulling over my lesson plan, wondering if it was stimulating enough or too difficult.

I didn't notice the smart-looking Japanese man standing beside me until he asked in American-accented English if I was enjoying myself.

I glanced at my watch and replied that I was, thinking it couldn't be a lame chat-up line, not with Mike's arm resting on my shoulder.

'Can you sing?' the man asked, shouting over the robust sounds of the saxophonist on stage.

'What?' I replied, craning my neck to hear what he said.

'Can you sing?' he asked again. 'You look like you can sing.'

At the time, I thought, what *exactly* does a singer look like? Does he think I can sing because I'm Black? Does he presume I'm a great dancer too? Or maybe it was my outfit. Back then, I was playing around with a more androgynous look, but it was still distinctively feminine – buzz cut, gold hoop earrings, lipstick and an oversized trouser suit I had bought in the sale from a cute little shop near my apartment.

The man asked again if I could sing, and all the occasions I'd burst into song in the past flashed into my head.

There were the 80s Abba songs with Jess.

At secondary school, I sang a medley of Paul Young, the 80s mullet-haired pop star and fellow Lutonian, for our school's annual charity day.

At my sister-in-law's wedding, I broke into song with a few of the other champagne-addled guests.

Karaoke.

In the shower.

And that was about the sum of my singing career to date.

'Call me,' he said, slipping a crisp *meishi* (business card) into my fingers.

'But I teach English. I do a bit of voice acting now and then, but I'm not a singer. I teach English,' I explained.

He grinned and asked for my name.

'Camilla,' I replied. 'But I'm not a singer.'

'Ah – but you *could* be a singer, Camilla-san,' he replied. 'Call me. I'll be waiting for your call.'

Oxford, June 2015

After dinner, the four of us take photographs in Hannah and Teju's too-hot living room in front of a squishy-looking sofa and vibrant scatter cushions.

Hannah says she'll use Ifemi's camera phone, and I am ushered into the middle, where I stand sweating like a sentinel between my two grinning cousins.

'Say cheese,' Hannah says encouragingly.

'Say cousin,' Ifemi quips.

Say traitor, I think. That's what I am, because this 'happy families Nigerian cousin thing' is getting way out of hand.

'Let's take a selfie,' Ifemi blurts. 'Come on, Camilla.'

Ifemi brandishes her sparkly purple phone in the air like a light sabre, and I take a selfie of the two of us with my phone.

After we finish, I stuff my phone in my pocket and try to ignore the paddling pool of sweat forming between my breasts. Oblivious to any notion of personal space, Ifemi plonks herself right next to me, so close our thighs touch.

'When I get back to Nigeria, I'll show the photos to Uncle Rimi,' she says, as though I will be thrilled by this revelation. 'It's a shame your brother and sister aren't here. If they were, we would have the full pack of cards. Never mind. Photographs are fine for now until you come to Nigeria and visit your father in person.'

'It's a bit too soon for trips to Nigeria,' I reply, wiping my brow. 'That's—'

'Camilla,' she interrupts. 'When I last spoke to Uncle Rimi, he wondered why he hadn't received a reply to his letter. He said he wrote to you, but he's not heard back. Why haven't you replied to your father's letter?'

'You know I love my job, but I'd be lying if I said I wasn't looking forward to retirement,' Teju says.

'I'm not sure if retirement will suit you,' Hannah says, playing along with the abrupt change of subject. 'You like being busy. We both do. Who fancies a coffee?'

'If you don't want to write to Uncle Rimi, why don't you call him? Or better still, come to Nigeria. He'd like that very much. You can both come,' Ifemi says, smiling at Mike.

And, annoyingly, he grins back and Ifemi rambles on about Uncle Rimi as though he were a Nigerian version of *Uncle Buck*, the jovial 80s film with a ridiculously loveable central character whose family initially disapprove of his wayward lifestyle, but who are eventually won round. Well, I am sorry to report that Sanni is no bloody Uncle Buck. Coming to Oxford wasn't supposed to be about Sanni. It was supposed to be about getting to know Teju and Hannah. And what is it about this guy? Why does no one speak badly about him? The only person who's been vaguely critical is Teju. When we'd met in London, he had admitted Sanni could be selfish. But since then, Teju has been reverential in his tone. Both he and Ifemi act as though Sanni is Santa Claus – cuddly, wise and ho ho ho.

Mike, perhaps sensing my growing discomfort, tells Hannah he'd love a coffee if there's one going.

'Anyone else?' she asks.

'Not for me,' I say quickly. 'But let me help,' and I attempt to get up, but Ifemi places her hand on my knee, so I remain seated in the too-hot room, on its too-squishy sofa with my too-direct Nigerian cousin.

'Did you know?' Ifemi says, pausing to raise her hand to tell Hannah she'd like coffee, too. 'There was a poll a few years back, and we Nigerians were voted one of the world's most optimistic and happy nations.'

'Is that so?' I say. 'Can I open a window?'

Teju gets up and prises open the latch at the top of the window to open it, but I feel no respite or suggestion of a breeze, just warm air.

'It's true, isn't it, Doc?' she says, grinning at her use of Teju's nickname. 'And Nigerians are among the most educated too. I can't remember the statistics, but we Nigerians have a certificate in something.'

Teju smiles and asks if I'm all right.

'I'm fine, just a bit hot,' I reply.

'Nigerian culture is everywhere,' Ifemi says.

She's right about that. Even in sleepy Swaffham, you'll hear the pulsating sound of Burna Boy or some other Nigerian artist blaring out of some youngster's car window.

'The best time to visit Nigeria is – any time.' Ifemi grins. 'In fact, more people should visit Nigeria. When you come, Camilla—'

'Where's the toilet?' I ask, standing up.

'Are you okay, Camilla?' Teju asks again, before telling me where it is.

I nod, but I am so distracted, overheating and out of sorts, I barely listen to his directions.

Once I find the bathroom, I don't need the toilet. What I require is a moment of respite. I turn on the tap, splash cold water onto my face, and wonder why I didn't wear my glasses. My contact lenses make me feel like I've been through a sandstorm. I take them out, blink a few times, and slip them back in again.

It's not that I dislike Ifemi. I like her. She's fun, and part of me likes her forthrightness. What I don't like is this overwhelming pressure. This coaxing of all things Uncle bloody Rimi. That wasn't the plan. And it's my fault. I am out of my depth. I'm not comfortable with this 'other Nigerian family' that only I am party to. It's lonely. Other than Mike and certain friends, there is no one to share in this odd feeling of having 'another family' when I already have a family, and they want nothing to do with the Nigerian branch.

Standing in front of Teju and Hannah's square white sink, I make a decision. I take out my phone from my pocket and compose an identical message to Dunni and Abdul.

Hi,

This is a quick message.

So, a curveball. I'm in Oxford, visiting our cousin Teju, and I've met another cousin! Talk about being in the cousins' deep end.

Let me know if you fancy meeting Teju, too. I could cook dinner.

I'll call when I get back.

Camilla x

Before I send it, I add:

I received a letter from Sanni. I didn't expect it. I haven't written back.

But, knowing how incendiary mentioning Sanni's letter might be, I delete it and write:

I'm going to tell Mum I've been in contact with Teju and about coming to Oxford. That way, everything is out in the open. But let me tell her, okay?

I press send and go back downstairs.

The door to the living room is closed, and I don't open it straight away. I stand outside, listening to Mike explain the intricacies of his job.

'Acupuncture doesn't hurt,' I hear him say good-naturedly. 'The needles sound scary, but you feel no more than a pinprick.'

Hannah says a couple of her friends swear by acupuncture.

'What made you decide to become an acupuncturist?' she asks.

Mike says that he has always been fascinated by East Asian health traditions, but he doesn't mention the other reason. He studied acupuncture to help me. Mike was at his wits' end seeing me doubled up in pain every month.

'When you come to Nigeria, can you do this acupuncture on Uncle Rimi, Mike? He has aches and pains. Maybe you can help him,' Ifemi says.

Taking a deep breath, I open the door.

'Camilla,' Ifemi shrieks. 'There you are. We thought we'd lost you. We were talking about your dad.'

'Oh,' I say.

'When you come to Nigeria, Mike says he will help Uncle Rimi,' Ifemi says, dazzling him with a smile.

'Whoa, wait a minute, I didn't say that exactly,' he replies giving me a concerned stare.

I don't make eye contact; instead, I focus on the task ahead.

'Any chance of that coffee?' I say to Hannah.

Nine

The Tricky Middle

Luck is my middle name. Mind you, my first name is Bad.
—Terry Pratchett

For a long time, my middle name was an irrelevant nuisance. This thing that lurked between my name and surname was a source of embarrassment and other people's amusement. One incident stands out from when I was growing up. I was nine years old or thereabouts, and I exchanged middle names with my primary school friend. His name in the middle was bright and breezy; he was called Paul or Mark or something like that, and, with a certain amount of pride, he told me he was named after his granddad, who'd died in World War 2. How could I follow that? All I knew about my middle name was that it was different, and it didn't slip out of your mouth like Louise or Anne.

'What's yours?' he asked.

'Adebisi,' I whispered.

'What?' he replied, making a face as though I'd uttered a rude word, not a middle name.

'Adebisi,' I repeated, but louder this time.

He laughed, and I mean laughed. He doubled over, clutching his stomach, and, for the following few days, he and a handful of other classmates thought it would be funny to replace the letter B in Adebisi with the letter P. This new name spread like the plague for a few weeks. And you know what? After all these years, I still remember those kids' contorted faces poking fun at my middle name. After that, I felt no burning desire to divulge this *thing* that lurked in the middle until I reached the age where official forms, most notably job applications, requested your full name – first, middle and last.

So, in my teens and twenties, with my mother's encouragement, I became an enthusiastic middle-name initialiser. It was the perfect dumping ground for a foreign-sounding name. Why write Adebisi when the letter A had endless middle-name possibilities? And I reasoned there was something mysterious and fashionable about initialising it. Now, of course, I realise I was hiding an integral part of who I was.

The practice of initialising middle names started in the nineteenth century, and it was so popular in *Who's Who* and similar registers in the 1940s, 65 per cent of the elite initialised their middle names. It was regarded as a sought-after status symbol. It was prestigious, and, if we consider the kind of people who enjoy a healthy dollop of prestige, we don't have to look far. Among politicians, most notably American politicians, the initialised middle name has graced the Oval Office numerous times. So, what is it about the initialised middle name? Perhaps, like me, you initialise your name to hide something. Or, perhaps in our increasingly busy lives, it is easier to initialise. Why write your middle name if K for Kimberley will do? But does choosing to use a middle initial signify greater intelligence? In 2014, a study set out to answer this question, and the results were illuminating. The study found a person with an initialised middle name *was* perceived as smarter, more eloquent and more qualified than someone without an initial. Interestingly, the study found that, the more initials someone had, the more intelligent they were perceived to be. For example, David F P R Mitchell signalled a higher perceived status than plain old David Mitchell. When I spoke to one of the study's authors, he advised using middle initials in contexts where 'intellectual expertise mattered', he explained. 'However, in other areas like sports, physical labour or down the pub, using middle initials might be awkward and perhaps counterproductive,' he advised.

But as a young journalist at the *New York Times,* the writer Nicholas D Kristof believed the middle initial added a bit of authority and gravitas, especially when you're a 25-year-old *Times* reporter covering global economics and hoping to be taken seriously. However, Kristof has subsequently dropped it. He now considers middle initials priggish.

And Pamela Redmond, from Nameberry, agrees. When I asked her if she thought there might be a comeback for the initialised middle name, she replied, 'I don't see a comeback as any more likely than that of the clip-on tie.'

But I'm not sure I agree. Who knows? Trends change. There may well be an initialised middle-name resurgence, and let's not forget that there is a practical element. Plenty of actors, authors and academics use middle initials to differentiate themselves from someone else who has the same first and last name. So I guess it depends on the context; in that regard, the middle initial lives on.

So, from where do middle-names originate? In his book, *The Means of Naming,* Stephen Wilson suggests their use most likely started among the elite in Italy as early as the late thirteenth century and spread throughout Spain and France into the rest of the population. But England was different. England's upper classes didn't begin using middle names until some time later.

As the population grew, using middle names became increasingly necessary as a way to differentiate between other similarly named people. Imagine a smoke-filled room in the 1900s with multiple John Smiths and Mabel Bells. Middle names solved the problem. In America, middle names had started to catch on for everyone by the time of the Civil War in the 1860s, and by 1900 most Americans had middle names. By the 1900s they were so commonplace that the American enlistment form used in World War 1 was the first government form to provide space for writing a middle name. Among American men, using their mother's maiden name as a middle name was widespread. Five of the dozen American presidents who have held office in the years since 1945 have a middle name taken from their mother's maiden name. A middle name, then, can provide an opportunity to strengthen ties within the family. But who knows whether or not this deceased relative you are named after held unsavoury opinions on issues close to your heart? Given such unknowns, a person's attitude to their middle name may depend on their relationship with the person they were named after. It's worth mentioning here, too, that in some cultures, in China, for example, using the name of a deceased family member is frowned upon and, in others, you shouldn't use the name of a living relative, as it is very bad luck. Although in the Ashkenazi Jewish community, naming a child after a relative who has died is considered a way of honouring the dead.

For many people, middle names are convenient. They provide an opportunity to shift identities. If you don't like your first name – why not use your middle name instead? My much-loved mother-in-law, Shirley, was named after the actor Shirley Temple, but Shirley was her middle name. Her given name was Margaret.

In his memoir, *Knife*, the author Salman Rushdie relives the horrific and brutal attempt on his life, and, with his considerable wit and style, he also explains the circumstances of meeting his wife, the poet and novelist Rachel Eliza Griffiths. She preferred to be known by her middle name, and, ironically, Rushdie is also is a middle-name user. He is more commonly known as Salman, but Ahmed is his given name.

In interviews and in his memoirs, Barack Obama has spoken openly about the evolution of his given name. In the days after Obama first mused publicly about running for president, the Republican strategist Ed Rogers said, 'Count me down as somebody who underestimates Barack *Hussein* Obama.' By emphasising Obama's middle name, Rogers capitalised on the reaction he knew would be likely among some American voters and many within the Republican Party, Obama's middle name seeming the perfect political tool. In their eyes, it marked Obama as a foreigner and un-American. But Obama defied the middle-name critics in unbeatable style. Taking the presidential oath, he used his full name, Barack Hussein Obama, and in 2012, when he addressed guests at an Alfred E Smith (note the middle-name initial) memorial dinner in New York City, he mentioned the so-called controversy around his middle name. 'It's not about the disagreements Governor Romney and I may have,' Obama said. 'It's what we have in common, beginning with our unusual names. Actually, Mitt is his middle name. I wish I could use my middle name,' he deadpanned.

A middle name is also the perfect opportunity to include a fun name in the mix. And there is a fun element to a middle name. Matthew Barratt, the CEO of the UK Deed Poll Service, explained that Danger was among the UK's most popular 'fun' middle names in the past few years. 'It was mainly from male applicants,' he said. 'However, since Covid, we've noticed a decline in Danger's popularity. People no longer want to change their name to a fun name, and the cost-of-living crisis has also rendered such frivolity.'

In some ways, that's the beauty of a middle name. You can

stick anything in the middle. Weird. Wacky. Experimental. Playful. Serious. Plentiful. Perhaps that's why they've become a little excessively used in recent years, as some folks get truly carried away. They forget there is limited space on official forms to accommodate more than one or perhaps two, at a push, middle names, but three? That's just greedy.

Who can forget the 1980s British royal wedding middle-name kerfuffle? I remember watching the extravagant royal nuptials on the television with my mother. As a Diana fan, she gasped and gawped in awe at Princess Diana's elaborate white dress. And then, like the millions of people watching, she shook her head in commiseration as saying her vows Diana tripped over her husband-to-be Charles's extravagant and numerous middle names.

My university degree certificate sits in a large box of memorabilia in a cupboard in my office in Swaffham. Unlike some of the contents of this box, it is rarely taken out because, whenever I am forced to do so, part of me hangs my head in shame. For most people, the day they graduate evokes fond memories. Beaming parents. Celebratory drinks after the ceremony, buzzing anticipation as they mark this new chapter ahead. But when I think about my graduation, I am confronted with my past, and it's not an edifying memory. I registered my name as Camilla Amanda Sanni at university. At the time, I was too bound up in name shame to recognise such decisions have consequences. On this most formal of occasions, as the presiding officer bellowed out my name, I stood up, adjusted my gown and wonky mortarboard, and walked towards this marker of educational attainment – my certificate; it was too late to shout out, 'That's not me! I've made a terrible mistake. My name is Camilla Adebisi, not Camilla Amanda.' But it was too late. The certificate was already written:

Bachelor of Arts awarded to Camilla Amanda Sanni.

On the plus side, if there is a plus side, I should be thankful my certificate doesn't read *Mandy Camilla* or, worse still, *Mandy Amanda,* but what the heck was I thinking? Names matter, and so on the rare occasions I take out my university certificate, it's a reminder of a time I was ashamed to be wholly me.

Like me, plenty of people do not wish to be associated with their middle name.

In 2021, the then Labour leader, Sir Keir Starmer, revealed to a live audience that his middle name was Rodney. And what did the audience do? They broke out into laughter. Flustered by and self-conscious as a result of the audience's reaction, Starmer explained that he pretended he didn't have a middle name for many years. So much so that when he filled out his marriage certificate in 2007 he omitted it. As middle names go, Rodney is one of those names. Some people might say it's a tad old-fashioned and outdated and slightly naff. Plus, most people in the UK of a certain age will be familiar with the television show *Only Fools and Horses* and the catchphrase, 'Rodney, you plonker!' Perhaps Sir Keir, whose given name is a nod to the Labour Party's founder, Keir Hardie, thought his middle name didn't match its punch. If a punchy middle name is required, Sir Keir might turn to the Tory Party. In 2024, at the Conservative Party conference, gasps were heard around the auditorium as one of the prospective candidates for leader, Robert Jenrick, revealed his daughter's middle name was Thatcher, in homage to you know who.

★

What was meant to be a one-year contract teaching English in Japan swiftly turned into two, three, four and then five years. Living in Tokyo suited me. This homogeneous, overpopulated city felt like home; reflecting back, I wonder why. Was it because I finally reclaimed my name or because I released a CD? You see, I did make that call to the stranger who had approached me in the nightclub, and in 1998 my four-syllable middle name graced the cover of my debut album.

The men in grey suits from the record label asked if I would record under Camilla. I smiled politely and didn't hesitate.

'No,' I replied. 'I'd like to record under my middle name, Adebisi.'

There was no resistance to the name, only a nodding of heads, which now, looking back, was remarkable, given this was the 90s, and there were very few Black-British singers from the African diaspora with visible African given names or surnames in mainstream rock and pop. There was still a degree of caution around singers using their African names. In a recent interview the soul and folk singer Michael Kiwanuka, British-born, with Ugandan heritage, was initially encouraged by his record label to release music under a pseudonym for fear that his surname would cause audiences to assume he was a traditional African artist.

'Where does Adebisi come from?' one of the men in grey suits asked in American-tinged English.

'It's Nigerian,' I replied.

I sensed he was waiting for some long-winded explanation about its meaning or, perhaps, an anecdote about being named after someone, say, an aunt or a grandmother. But back then, I didn't know what Adebisi meant. Now, if he asked the same question, I'd reply differently. I'd say, Adebisi is a Yoruba name, and it's used as both a given name and a surname, and, as Teju explained, it means 'the crown has given birth to more'.

In 1998, I simply replied, 'It feels right to use Adebisi,' without explaining that, by using this name, I was exorcising demons and my own naivety.

I rarely listen to my CD now. It is hard listening to the lyrics you wrote as a 20-something. Does *anyone* enjoy revisiting work they created in their past? Plus, some of the lyrics were raw. I have to be in the right frame of mind to listen to it. But at the same time, I am proud of the music I made with a Canadian producer on a small subsidiary label linked to one of the record label's big guns. I remember strolling into Tower Records' flagship shop in Shibuya and seeing my album in a prominent position at the front of the store, next to the UK girl group Eternal. There was my CD, and next to it was a handwritten sign with an accompanying blurb in Japanese and English.

It read:

'Voodoo Spirit is a new album from Adebisi, an up-and-coming London artist. It's the perfect album for fans of the UK trip-hop scene!'

Back then, trip-hop was a still relatively popular and sellable genre. I suppose you'd call it 'chill out' music. It was easy on the ear, atmospheric, slow-tempo and moody. The men in grey suits from the record label called my album 'perfect dinner party music.' Looking back, I'm not sure if this was a compliment. But you know what? I felt like a fraud. I was a girl from Luton who got lucky because of a 'right time, right place – and you look like you can sing' moment. Sure, I carved out a 'career' of sorts. I performed a few gigs. I sat behind a table in a tiny record shop in Shimokitazawa, signing copies of my CD, trying to work out why the handful of eager 'fans' chose to buy my CD instead of some other UK trip-hop band like Portishead or Massive Attack. I was interviewed on the radio. I was on the guest list at bars, clubs and swanky new openings. I was able to reduce my English teaching hours, knowing full well singing was what surfers called a 'bomb', and I was riding a massive wave. And, reader, before you tap *Adebisi* into Spotify or some other music streaming service, I'm sorry to say you won't find my album. I've already checked, although I do know it was selling on eBay a few years ago for $18 – a bargain.

Not everyone was happy with the shiny CD I posted back to Luton, emblazoned with my middle name at the top.

'Why on earth did you call yourself that name, love?' my mother asked a week or so after she'd received her copy in the post.

'The line's bad,' I lied. 'I'll call you back another time,' and I put the receiver back in its cradle, and didn't call back for a few days.

Are you NUTS?, Amanda. Dunni wrote in one memorable letter. *You've called yourself Adebisi? Why the hell have you done that? PS, Thanks for the Hello Kitty stuff for the baby. She loves it!*

'Interesting choice,' my brother said, chuckling down the receiver. 'We can't understand why you didn't just call yourself Mandy. That's your name.'

Of course, their responses annoyed the hell out of me. We never spoke about it at the time, but perhaps they presumed, by calling my CD *Adebisi,* I was demonstrating some sort of misty-eyed loyalty to Sanni. Maybe they thought I was wavering, that I was no longer on Team Mum, and that wasn't the case. If anything, by the late 90s my bitterness towards Sanni was more entrenched. I didn't realise this then, but now I know that my anger towards him came from my close friendship with Otis. I resented Sanni. My relationship with Otis was supportive, and inspiring. I came away from conversations as though I'd been shaken and rattled, fizzing with confidence. This was how I imagined a father-and-daughter relationship had the potential to be. I gave Otis a signed copy of my CD. We were in the staffroom at the time, and he stared at the front cover, drinking in my middle name, and his response overwhelmed me.

'Don't worry, they are happy tears,' he said.

Norfolk, July 2015

Nothing is more grounding than a visit to the local Swaffham supermarket with my mother, and that's exactly what I need after my trip to Oxford.

I push a squeaking trolley around the fruit and vegetable aisle, making all the right noises about the increase in the price of lemons, but I am not fully engaged. I think about Oxford. I think about Ifemi. I wonder if I am the subject of Nigerian family gossip, given Sanni hasn't been shy about telling people I haven't replied to his letter. And I feel weird about that. Part of me, and it is entirely ridiculous, but part of me feels guilty. Sanni's an old man. He probably doesn't have much going on in his life, and I can't shake the image of him waiting by the door for a letter from his youngest daughter, wondering why I haven't replied.

Yet there are positives. My contact with Teju is out in the open.

A few days after I returned from Oxford, I called Dunni and Abdul to tell them about Ifemi, Hannah and my trip. But they weren't interested. They're not interested in getting to know Teju or any of the Nigerian branch of the family. Abdul said he was too busy with work, and he is busy. He's no longer a Soul Weekender kind of guy; he's an IT kind of guy, and what with a high-flying job, two kids and a wife, life is busy, busy, busy. And Dunni is busy too.

'You'd like Hannah and Ifemi,' I told her, pressing the receiver against my ear. 'Ifemi is a little abrasive, but I liked her.'

'Did you tell Mum you'd visited Teju in Oxford?' she asked, over the *EastEnders* theme tune blaring out from her television.

'Yes, but I'm not sure how well it went down,' I replied.

I told my mother about Teju, in what I thought to be an opportune moment. I visited her in the bungalow in Norfolk.

The sun was out, it was a warm day, and she wasn't ironing; that's been relegated to the third division over the years. She was gardening. She trimmed the ends from a robust-looking rosemary bush in the corner of her immaculate, not-a-pot-out-of-place back garden. After a brief chat about one of her neighbour's chickens, I thought I'd go for it.

'I went to see Teju in Oxford last week, Mum,' I said.

'Fine,' she replied, brandishing a pair of lethal-looking secateurs in the air.

'He sends his best regards to you,' I told her.

'Mm-hmm.'

'We ate jollof rice, but it was no match for your rice and peas.'

'That's nice, love.'

'We didn't stay long. I met Teju's wife. She's lovely. You'd like her. And I met another cousin. That *was* a surprise.'

'Fine,' she replied, attacking the top of the bush. 'I'm glad you had a fine time with your new Nigerian family.'

Of course, she didn't mean it. She wasn't glad I'd had a fine time. She wasn't fine, nor was the poor rosemary bush. She hacked it to death. By the time she finished snipping away, the once-glorious bush was a shadow of its former self. All that remained were a few sad twigs.

'No grapefruits again,' my mother says now, examining the empty supermarket tray. 'They didn't have any last week either.'

I pick up an apple and turn it in my hand for signs of bruises while my mother examines a fat garlic bulb.

'When I came to England, they didn't have garlic. It was difficult to find,' she says, popping the garlic in the trolley. 'Spices too. Now everyone cooks with garlic and spices. Even what's his name, the cockney cook?'

'Do you mean Jamie Oliver?' I quip.

'He cooks Jamaican food now, you know. Jerk chicken this. Curry goat that. We West Indians came to England, and they complained about our food. Now they can't get enough of our curries or the jerk,' she says.

Then something odd happens.

A brunette woman approaches us, pushing a trolley stacked high with toilet rolls, bottles of bleach and bags of organic carrots.

She grins.

I grin back, even though I have no idea who she is. Perhaps she's one of my ex-yoga students? Or a current student. We may have met before, or maybe she's just one of life's super-smiley people.

'Hello Carmel,' she says to my mother.

I think about interrupting and saying, 'Sorry – you're mistaken. That's not her name. You've got the wrong person,' but my mother responds with a warm smile, and the two women exchange pleasantries.

I am introduced as my mother's 'Swaffham daughter, Mandy' and, although I smile politely, I think, who the bloody hell is this Carmel person?

The two discuss the warm weather, their annoyance that the cereal aisle has moved to another section of the store and the lovely new Polish family who've joined their church.

Afterwards, the woman bids 'Carmel' goodbye and saunters off towards the meat counter.

'She called you Carmel, not Carmen,' I say once the woman's out of earshot.

'Yes, love.'

'But your name is *Carmen*.'

'Not any more,' she says, pushing the trolley ahead.

But I can't let that go. I mean, come on. How could I?

We load up my car, I start the engine and I ask again why her friend called her Carmel, not Carmen. She winds down the window, clicks on her seatbelt, and says triumphantly that Carmel *is* her real name.

'Since when?' I ask, trying and failing to keep the sarcasm out of my voice.

'There was a mix-up.'

'What do you mean, mix-up?'

She sighs deeply.

'My father registered my name, but the man at the registration office liked a drink,' she explains. 'Because my mum was Panamanian, she wanted to give me a Spanish name. She liked the name Carmen.' She pauses. 'Careful, there's a tractor ahead, love.'

I realise it is triggering for my mother to bring up the spectre of the person who left her as a baby with another family; little wonder she mentions a tractor. But I also want to know more about Carmel, so I gently steer her back to the subject – names.

'So, this registration guy liked a drink,' I say.

'The drunkard had too many white rums,' she says, shaking her head. 'He wrote down *Carmel*, not Carmen, but it didn't matter. Everyone called me Carmen or Dot. I was never called Carmel.'

I don't know what to say, so I say nothing. We drive past endless fields of rapeseed, and I press the accelerator hard, thinking about my name and my mother's name, wondering if she's being entirely serious. Perhaps this is all an elaborate joke. At my expense.

'I've decided I like Carmel,' she says, adjusting the strap of her seatbelt over her chest. 'And they are so similar. Carmen. Carmel. There's no difference, really.'

'So – let me get this straight. You now want to be called Carmel, not Carmen.'

'No, just Mum will do.' She grins. 'Everyone at church knows me as Carmel, and the more I tell people my name is Carmel the more I like it.'

The irony of this revelation is not lost on me but, again, my mouth stays firmly shut.

'Do you know what Sanni once told me?' she asks.

'No,' I say, still processing her name revelation but curious she's mentioned him.

'He said he liked the name Camilla because it sounded similar to Carmen.'

We sit in silence at a red light, and I am tempted to tell her everything. I want to offload the weight of Sanni, this stranger who is worming his way back into my life. But I don't. I chew my bottom lip and remain silent.

'Carmel, Carmen, Camilla,' my mother says in a sing-song voice. 'The Three Cs. It's like The Three Degrees. Do you remember them? I used to like their music.'

'Mum,' I say, 'I'm glad you mentioned Sanni. I – er—'

She starts to hum one of The Three Degrees' songs, and I know it's a tactic, her way of dealing with the difficult subject of Sanni, and I can't help myself. I hum along with her because, in truth, I find the subject of Sanni difficult too.

Ten

Chardonnay

We must first come into possession of our own names. For it is through our names that we first place ourselves in the world.
—Ralph Ellison

Some time in the 1940s, Eric Arthur Blair, more commonly known as George Orwell, wrote, 'England is the most class-ridden country under the sun.' This may explain why Orwell adopted a pen name to avoid being associated with a perceived class his original given name implied. And yet, seven decades later, and Orwell's statement is more relevant than ever.

In 2013, the controversial media personality and former reality-television contestant Katie Hopkins was a guest on ITV's cosy flagship daytime TV programme, *This Morning.* Hopkins explained that for her a name was a short way of working out what class a child belonged to. Once she found out their name, she weighed up whether or not she wanted her children to play with that child. Some names were a no-no. 'Lower-class' names like Charmaine, Chantelle, Chardonnay and Tyler were the kind of names she didn't want her children to associate with. Instead, she favoured children with 'good old-fashioned Victorian names' or those of Latin or Greek origin as playmates for her children.

Hopkins's remarks were widely condemned as snobbish and classist and, as someone who is not what you'd call a Hopkins fan, I shared the sentiment that she was ridiculous and her comments were equally ridiculous. And then I thought a little deeper about what she'd said. Class is one of those subjects the British feel awkward discussing. Because our names are such rich sources of information, whenever we hear one, perhaps it is inevitable some of us automatically attach a class-based stereotype to it.

A few years ago, I taught a yoga/movement workshop at a college in London for a group of performing-arts students and, for a rainy Friday afternoon, they were remarkably focused. Some were embarrassed they couldn't touch their toes. Others giggled as I instructed them to 'lift the buttocks' or 'grip the hips' but, for reasons unknown, 'tailbone' was the real humdinger. Uttering this word caused mass giggling hysteria. But I was teaching teenagers. What did I expect? Bodies are weird, and your body is super weird when you are 17. Still, despite their giggles, they enjoyed the class. There was a chorus of loud snores in relaxation and, at the end of class, there was a palpable sense of quiet introspection and reflection.

Afterwards, as I rolled up my mat, some expressed interest in attending another yoga class. One or two said they'd accompany their mum to yoga, which made me feel ancient, but even so, as I gathered up my belongings, I was pleased. I thought, job done. Big pat on the back.

On my way out of the drama studio, one of the teachers asked how it went.

I told him the group was lovely and they enjoyed the class.

'I did, too, to be honest,' I said. 'They were a lively and enthusiastic bunch.'

The teacher lowered his voice and leaned in towards me.

'Oh – God. Were Wayne and Jake a nightmare?' he asked.

I had taken a register at the beginning of the class, and those particular names didn't jump out as a nightmare.

'They're brothers,' he explained. 'Wayne and Jake. Chav name central.'

I bristled at the word 'chav'. I wasn't a fan of the term, which, at the time (the early 2000s), was bandied around liberally. In his excellent book, *Chavs: The Demonization of the Working Class*, Owen Jones addressed how the term 'chav' was widely used to deride the working-class. There were chav towns, and my home town of Luton was high on the list. There were chav haircuts. Chav alcoholic drinks. Chav ways of dressing. There was chav taste in music. But what was a chav? According to the Cambridge Dictionary, 'chav' is 'an insulting word for someone, usually a young person, whose way of dressing, speaking and behaving is thought to show their lack of education and low social class'. So by labelling Wayne and Jake as chavs, the teacher was deriding their names and associating them with a certain social class.

I didn't respond to the teacher. I made my excuses and left, but on the tube home I thought about what he'd said. I wondered if it was common for teachers to form an opinion of their students based on their names. Studies reveal some do. A 2014 study found almost half of UK teachers said they conjured up a mental picture of the student after reading the school register. Top of their 'troublesome' names were Callum, Crystal and Chardonnay. Another study by the economist Gregory Clark and his colleagues compared the names of students at Oxford University between 2008 and 2013 with the general population. He found there were more than three times as many Eleanors at Oxford than average, closely trailed by Peters, Simons, Annas and Katherines. But Shanes, Shannons,

Paiges and Jades had less luck. The number of Jades at Oxford was less than one thirtieth of the average rate.

Social class in relation to naming is not limited to the UK. A few years ago, I read an article in the *Guardian* about the case of Emmanuel Taché de la Pagerie. This grand-sounding name belonged to a newly elected MP for Marine Le Pen's far-right party in France. Born in the working-class suburb of Montreuil, he worked in fashion and broadcasting before entering politics and back then his name was plain old Emmanuel Taché. However, the new surname of his new chosen moniker, Taché de la Pagerie, was similar to the name Tascher de la Pagerie, and that name belongs to one of France's most aristocratic families. Although the male line died out in 1993, the three female surviving members of the family filed a complaint to protect the family name, arguing their historic name had been appropriated by this young man. According to the family lawyer, their aristocratic name was rare and noted. However, the spelling was different; it went back centuries and, being descendants of Napoleon Bonaparte's wife, this small elite family wanted to keep their grand and posh surname to themselves, thank you very much.

When it comes to first names in France, one name in particular divides opinion: Kevin. Surprisingly, in the early 1990s, the first name Kevin – sometimes spelt Kévin – was one of France's most popular boys' names. In 1991, more than 13,000 babies were given this Celtic-origin name. So, if a French male introduced themselves as Kevin today, you might be able to guess they were born some time in the 90s, they were probably in their early 30s, and maybe their parents were fans of the actors Kevin Costner or Kevin Bacon or the English footballer Kevin Keegan. You might even be able to guess their social class. For Kevin Fafournoux, a graphic designer from a family of public sector workers, the name Kevin is rooted in social class. 'Kevin in France is clearly seen as a name of working-class origin,' he says. 'Working-class families chose more American-sounding names – and that's what's being mocked.'

Baptiste Coulmont, a sociology professor based in France, agrees. Coulmont argues that, although working-class families in France in the past chose traditional names that were popular among the bourgeoisie, and those names trickled down to the rest of society, that changed in the 1980s and 1990s. Coulmont says, 'Working-class families began choosing their own names, often English-sounding, which had never been used by the Parisian bourgeois.' Studies show that, because of the name Kevin's so-called working-class origins, it comes with an attached bias. In 2015, a research institute monitoring social exclusion found that applicants named Kevin in France were between 10 and 30 per cent less likely to be hired than someone called Arthur, despite having equivalent qualifications and experience. Perhaps this explains why some 2,700 Kevins in France apply for a name change each year.

If the first name Kevin in France might be associated with stereotypical class connotations, the name Tracey, sometimes spelt Traci, Tracee or Tracy, is described by a close friend of mine as the ultimate 80s working-class moniker in the UK. And she should know – her name is Tracey, and there is something about Tracey.

In 2023, a discussion about workplace culture in relation to an incident on ITV's *This Morning* (there is something about this programme too) made the headlines. Production staff on the show denied using the term 'Tower Block Traceys' to describe viewers whenever ideas on the show were deemed as 'too highbrow', and the comment caused enough outrage to be discussed on a government committee.

Years ago, when I started writing the proposal for this book, I visited my mother at her bungalow in Norfolk.

It was summer. The sun was insistent, burning down, so the two of us sat in recliners in the back garden in a slip of shade. John was in the garage, hunched over his work desk, fixing one of his model train sets, whistling along to a song on the radio.

'How's the name book going?' my mother asked.

I told her it was fine, even though I wasn't 100 per cent sure she knew what I was writing about, but despite that, my as-yet embryonic book was a growing source of intrigue to her.

'So what it's about?' she said, shooing away an insect crawling on her forearm.

'Do you think Camilla sounds like I'm some sort of English aristocrat?' I asked her, swerving around her question.

She smirked.

'You said you couldn't yell "Camilla" at the primary school gates in Luton, but there was no reluctance in yelling "Mandy" and I wondered why not?'

'Camilla does sound a bit . . .' She paused. 'Do you remember *Upstairs Downstairs*?'

The show was a period drama set in the 1930s, and it followed the lives of a rich London family and their servants. I suppose now you'd compare it to *Downton Abbey* or *Bridgerton* or another of those television dramas about repressed British folk in period dress.

I told her I remembered the jaunty theme tune and not much else.

'Well, Camilla sounds like the lady of the manor from *Upstairs Downstairs*,' she said. 'Mandy is a bit more down to earth. It's the name of one of the girls downstairs.'

'I suppose so,' I replied. 'Camilla is definitely a posh name in the UK, but I don't think it's seen as particularly posh in other countries.'

'Mmm-hmm.'

'What about Carmel?' I asked with a heavy dose of sarcasm. 'Is that a well-to-do name?'

She rolled her eyes, but there was the faintest of grins, and I didn't tease her any further because the property porn programme *Escape to the Country* was on the telly, but I was surprised at her candour. She thought Camilla sounded posh and in some ways, given her tendency to lean towards that particular kind of West Indian aspiration to climb up the social ladder, I wondered why she didn't embrace the name. But she couldn't. Posh or not, for my mother, the association of Camilla with Sanni overrode everything.

A couple of years ago, I came across a discussion on the radio about names, so I stopped what I was doing, grabbed a coffee and listened in.

The programme was presented by the podcaster and presenter Jane Garvey. She and her panel of guests opened the discussion by talking about the name Jane. In Garvey's opinion, Jane was a little bit dull and if you were called Jane, you were more than likely White, female, middle-aged, and quite possibly lower-middle class.

Garvey and her guests then went on to talk about how certain names are perceived within the prism of class, and guess which name was highlighted as 'upper-class'? You guessed it, Camilla. Other names in the programme's canon of upper-class-sounding names were Tarquin and Rupert. In 2017 *Tatler*, the magazine of choice for a certain kind of reader, listed the most aristocratic and 'poshest baby names of all time'. At the top of *Tatler*'s boys' name list were names like Albert, Benjamin, Inigo and Youngblood (yes, Youngblood). But it was the girls' list that was the biggest surprise. At the top of the pile (it was in alphabetical order) was Amanda, the name I adopted as my middle name at university rather than Adebisi, and the name Sanni called me growing up.

There it was, sitting alongside names like Quintana, Xanthe and Jemima.

And what if a double-barrelled surname is added into the mix? In the UK, there can be a tendency to associate the hyphenation of someone's surname with wealth, influence, aristocrats or the upper echelons of society. People, myself included, tend to make presumptions about someone's class if they are faced with a double-barrelled surname, and a survey conducted in 2015 seemed to back this up. It revealed more than a quarter of young people in Britain thought it was easier to obtain a work placement if you had a double-barrelled surname. If, for example, I was called Camilla Clarkson-Rutherford, what would my name say about me? And by the same token, for people who don't know me but read my first name alone, what does Camilla say about my class?

Growing up, I didn't consider the class ramifications of being called Camilla; I wanted to reclaim what was mine and, posh or not, Camilla was my name. And it was a unique name. I'd never come across anyone called Camilla before. It might not be a big deal for most people. Let's say you are called Sally or Robert, then chances are you've come into contact with plenty of other Sallys and Roberts. But it was a *big deal* for me – a huge deal. I'd met plenty of Mandys and Amandas over the years. But I'd never met anyone called Camilla. The only person I'd come across called Camilla was in 1986. I went to the cinema in Luton with a friend to watch Spike Lee's *She's Gotta Have It.* At that age, I was a big Spike Lee fan, but I had an ulterior motive. I found out the leading actor in the movie was called Tracy Camilla Johns. I realised she wasn't a fully paid-up member of the Camilla club, given Camilla was her middle name. Still, it was close. She was *almost* a Camilla.

When I finally met another Camilla in real life, I suppose

it was fitting that I should do so in Tokyo on a spring Saturday afternoon in 1999 in Harajuku, a suburb synonymous with street fashion and Yoyogi Park.

I'd cycled from our apartment, which by then was a large, by Japanese standards, two-bedroom flat in the gloriously named Takadanobaba, a bohemian area of the city close to Shinjuku. I was meeting Otis and he was late, which was unusual; he was a stickler for punctuality. I was more than happy to wait, read my book and people-watch. The part restaurant, part cafe, part bar we were meeting in was *the* place to hang out in the 90s. It was French and pretentious and hugged a prominent position on the corner of a bustling tree-lined street.

As an avid eavesdropper (the book wasn't great), I listened to the conversation at the next table. I did that a lot in Japan, learning from conversations. The ladies beside me weren't Japanese. They were blonde, well-dressed and much older than me – perhaps in their late fifties – and they were dressed in expensive weekend wear.

I strained my ears and discovered that one of the women, the older of the two, was called Allegra. And what was striking about Allegra was her accent. She sounded like she'd swallowed a member of the British aristocracy.

Allegra chatted about holidaying in Singapore, and she asked her companion, Camilla, if she was considering returning to the same island in Malaysia for her holidays.

I almost choked on my iced coffee. It took an enormous effort not to stand up and say, '*Sorry to disturb your lunch, ladies, but I'm called Camilla too.*'

I didn't; wisely, I kept my mouth shut and thought, this person is called Camilla, and she looks and sounds nothing like me, but that's OK. Another Camilla existed and I was thrilled to be in close proximity to someone who shared my name. Now, of course, I have met other Camillas. Not many. At a push, I've encountered five Camillas, including Tokyo

Camilla. Three of those were Polish, and spelt their name with a K, and only one L. I met the other Camilla recently, and we spent a good hour or so dissecting our shared name.

Otis waved from the entrance to the restaurant.

'Sorry, I'm late, Miss Pop Star,' he said, sitting opposite me. 'Isn't Mike joining us?'

'Later,' I said, lowering my voice. 'The woman at the next table is called Camilla.'

'Is that news?' He grinned.

'I've never met anyone called Camilla before,' I said, trying and failing to keep the excitement out of my voice.

'I'm just fooling with you,' he said, removing his cycling helmet. 'I know it's a big deal.'

'I know it's silly, but it's—'

'I get it. I understand,' he said. 'How was the meditation retreat in Kyoto? Ten days meditating, no speaking, writing or gesturing, right?'

I glanced up at Camilla, gesturing for the bill.

'It was challenging, but it was good to clear my head of all this singing stuff,' I said. 'For the first few days, I thought about food nonstop and then, for some reason, Jack Nicholson. God knows why. I mean, he's a brilliant actor and all that, but talk about random.'

Otis said when he first started meditating he thought about random people too.

'Not Jack Nicholson, though.' He smiled, but it was a little forced. I sensed something was wrong.

'What's up?' I asked.

'Well – there's no easy way to say it, but I'm leaving Tokyo,' he replied. 'Not yet. My annoying face will be around for a while.'

At the next table, Camilla and Allegra stood up, and I watched them saunter out of the restaurant, talking in their high-pitched animated voices.

'So you got the lecturing job at the university?' I said to Otis, trying to sound upbeat.

'I got it,' he replied shyly.

I made all the right noises. I told Otis I was pleased for him, really chuffed he'd got the job, but inside, I flat-lined.

I asked him about the job, and his face lit up like a candle as he explained his new 'adventure' teaching at a university in South Korea. And I was pleased for him – genuinely pleased for him – but his leaving forced me to consider what I was doing in Japan. By then Mike and I had lived in Tokyo for five years, and we had a good life – a great life. But I was 29, Mike was 30, and, when you're hurtling towards your 30s, something starts to shift about what you are doing and where you are going. Singing wasn't a viable career option. Sure, I was asked to sing at the odd gig here and there, but I was not making a living as a singer, so I was back teaching English again. Mike was teaching English and studying Japanese acupuncture, and now Otis was leaving, along with a bunch of other close friends. Our gang of misfits, drifters and fun seekers was shrinking. And the truth was, I knew Mike was keen to go home too. Five years away from family and friends was a long time and, in the last year or so, we'd discussed leaving. Part of me resisted the pull. What did going home mean? But at the same time, I knew something was wrong: my health was unravelling. It wasn't normal to be doubled up in bed most months, and it certainly wasn't normal to gobble paracetamols at the rate I was doing just to be able to function. And there was another reason too. In Japan if anyone asked, - 'What's your name?' I'd got used to replying, 'It's Camilla.' If I went back home, I didn't know what I would say.

But we did go back home.

Four months after Otis left Japan, in the winter of 1999, Mike and I returned to the UK with a thud – quite literally.

Our exuberant pilot threw the plane onto the tarmac at Heathrow Airport as though he wanted to emphasise the point.

YOU ARE HOME. DEAL WITH IT.

It was snowing, and I tried to pretend everything was the same. Except it wasn't. Life was different. The UK had morphed into this alien place of lads' mags, ladettes, and celebrities spilling out of expensive cars in Louboutins. And my family were different too.

Abdul, now in his mid-30s, was a married father. My mother, still sprightly, was going to be 60 in the summer, and there she was, dressed in a patterned dress, waving from the arrivals gate. I waved back, weary from an eleven-hour flight, fat rucksack on my back, blinking at the harsh fluorescent airport lighting.

Abdul greeted Mike with a manly bear hug and then he turned to me.

'Welcome home, Mandy,' he said.

I opened my mouth to correct him, but my mother enveloped us in one of her not-quite-full hugs and commented on how thin we both looked.

'Some good home cooking will soon fatten you both up,' she said, patting Mike on the shoulder.

I gazed around the concourse at this strange new version of the UK. In the five years we'd been away, I'd returned home twice and left feeling like a stranger both times. Now, I was a *permanent* stranger.

'Welcome home, Mandy and Mike,' my mother said. 'Welcome home.'

'It's Camilla now, Mum,' I said but, to be honest, what stands out most when I look back on that time was I wasn't sure who I was.

Norfolk, September 2015

Working from home is both a blessing and a curse. On the plus side, my yoga studio is on the middle floor of our house, which means my daily commute is a flight of stairs. Nevertheless, sometimes I miss the old days, whizzing around London teaching classes everywhere, from church halls to any one of the many yoga studios that sprang up in the Noughties. I realise I am lucky, and I am thankful I have my own space, but here's the thing. There is no sense of privacy. The hundred-plus yoga students who strut through my door each week know which brand of toilet paper we use (the eco-type, in case you were wondering). They know which magazines we subscribe to and which books we read. They know whether I've washed towels or bed linen because the clothes swaying on the washing line are a dead giveaway. But because I don't have a commute, just a flight of stairs, after teaching my regular Thursday night class on a drizzly, grey autumn night I am able to make important decisions quickly. Over a post-class cup of herbal tea, I finally reply to Sanni's letter. I write the letter to Sanni that's whirled around my head for the last five months. The opening is calm enough. Then I go for the jugular. It is like I am writing a letter on behalf of my mother and siblings and, like a gunslinger taking aim, I pull the trigger and fire words as wounding bullets. I am not ashamed to admit that it is a foaming-at-the-mouth-fuelled message. It is the letter I needed to write.

The next day, bulging envelope in hand, I say 'good morning' to one or two familiar faces and stand in the queue at the post office, reading a sign on the noticeboard asking customers to be patient as they are short-staffed, and another that says: *We will not tolerate abuse.*

When it is my turn, I place the envelope on the weighing scales and, before I know it, my words to Sanni have been tossed into an overflowing mailbag.

I don't move.

'Anything else, love?' the woman behind the counter asks.

'No,' I reply, and I walk back home, my hands stuffed in my pockets, thinking perhaps my letter is a bit harsh. But it is too late. I can't press the rewind button and ask for it back. All I can do is wait for a reply.

So I wait.

Six weeks later, tapping my finger on the kitchen worktop, I ask Mike if he thinks the letter got lost in the post.

'Maybe there's been a postal strike in Nigeria,' I say. 'Or maybe he's not well?'

'You could always call Teju,' he says.

'It's too late,' I reply, glancing at the clock on the wall. 'Weren't you always told never to call someone after nine o'clock?'

He smiles and says Teju strikes him as the kind of guy who wouldn't mind a late call.

That's all the encouragement I need. My hand reaches for my phone like a greyhound out of a starting block.

'Camilla,' Teju says in a cheery tone. 'How are you?'

'Yeah – I'm good. You're not working, are you?'

'Yes, but I'd rather talk to you. You sound tired. Are you all right?'

I say I am fine and think, how can I casually ask if he's heard from Sanni? How can I say he hasn't replied to my letter, and now I'm anxious about what I've written? If I say this, I'll have to explain my rant of a letter and Teju will think badly of me. He'll think, how could I write such a venomous letter to good old Uncle Rimi?

'How's Ifemi?' I ask.

He says she's busy and thinking of expanding her shop.

'So you haven't heard from Sanni?' I ask in a breezy tone. 'He's not ill or anything, is he? I sent him a letter a good while ago, and he hasn't written back.'

'No one back home has mentioned he's been ill. I'm sure he's fine. I can check if you want. I'll call Ifemi.'

I say there's no need for that.

'I'm glad he's okay. I – just wondered, that's all. I thought he'd have replied by now,' and then I think it took me five months to reply to his letter; perhaps he's giving me a taste of my own medicine. He's making me wait.

'I know there is a family wedding in Lagos,' he says. 'Perhaps that explains the radio silence.'

'Maybe that's what it is,' I reply.

'Or you could always call him. Just be careful,' he says, chuckling. 'Nigerians have weird phone habits.'

I ask what he means, and he chuckles some more.

'The generator,' he explains. 'It's up and down, so calls can be frustrating.'

I tell him I've no intention of calling Sanni.

'Letters are fine for now,' I say.

Sanni's letter arrives four days later, on a Tuesday morning, before I am due to teach my beginners' class. Our postman knocks on the door and hands over a delivery and a sliver of an envelope. The front is addressed to *Amanda Camilla*, and in the corner it says *BY AIR*.

I shut the door, stomach backflipping, and tear open the envelope.

Dearest daughter,

Thank you very much for your interesting letter. My letter to you will be short because since I had my stroke last year, I have struggled to use my right hand so well. I don't know what happened between Carmen and me. That is why I keep apologising to you. We bothered one another. Sometimes this happens in marriages.

Do you remember I used to ask you to go to the shops

to buy my cigarettes? Do you remember we used to go to the VG shop on the estate? We used to hold hands, and I'd buy you sweets. Do you remember? How is Luton? I have fond memories of the town. I am sorry to learn about your women's problems. I hope your health will improve. I pray to God for the miracle of life for you and your husband.

I will save more till we meet or talk. Please write again.

My best regards to all the family.

Your only Dad,

PS Wishing your prime minister, David Cameron, the best of luck.

I feel sick. I need to lie down

What does he mean by my *interesting* letter? Why can't he say my angry, harsh or emotional letter? *Interesting* sounds like he's describing a film or an odd sandwich combo. It isn't the word you'd use to describe the first letter you've received from the daughter you haven't seen or heard from in decades.

I stand in the hallway, unsure what to do, clutching the piece of paper. I tell myself not to cry, to keep it together, to make a coffee, sit down for a few minutes, but I can't. The gate at the front of the house clicks, and then there's the sound of multiple footsteps crunching on the gravel path: the arrival of eager yoga students. Eighteen minutes early yoga students. I fold the letter in half and prepare to greet them with a faraway smile and the calm demeanour of a yogi. Not the emotionally addled daughter who's just received a letter from a man I struggle to call a father. And yet, the following day, I write back.

November 2015

Hello there,

I hope this letter finds you well.

Thank you for your letter. I do appreciate your apology and how much you've reflected on your behaviour.

You asked about Luton in your last letter. I'm not sure what the town is like now. I rarely visit. It still has a sizeable community of different races, faiths and religions. I must say that was a plus for me growing up, although I couldn't wait to get out! I used to call Luton 'the armpit of Bedfordshire'. But I am fond of it, too, I suppose. It holds memories.

I hope to visit Jamaica next year, my first trip. Nothing is set in stone; I'm just making tentative plans, but if I do visit, it will most likely be in the summer.

Do you remember I asked Teju a question? You've never answered it. No hurry. I just wondered if you'd thought about it at all.

Everyone is well here. I'm looking forward to Christmas. It's a chance to stop. Everyone is on an enforced break. I like that.

Mike sends his best regards.

All best wishes,

Camilla

December 2015

My dearest daughter,

Thank you for your letter, which I received with God's grace.

I am very happy we are in contact.

We are keen to host you here in Nigeria. You will be most welcome. When are you coming home? Abuja is a lively city. As a young man, I found great enjoyment in Lagos. You will enjoy it too.

I am very interested in this political situation in the UK.

This European question is most interesting. What do you think will happen?

How are your husband's and Carmen's health? Please give Dunni and Abdul my regards.

Your loving Dad.

PS I'm sorry this letter is short because the telephone works very well for me.

February 2016

Dearest daughter,

Happy New Year to you and your loved ones.

Thank you for your letter. I read your comments on this Brexit question with interest.

This letter will be short again. As you know, I find it difficult to write. The telephone would be better. Perhaps then we can talk, and I can answer your questions. If you don't want me to have your number, that is fine; you can call me. I am here most days. I'll be waiting for your call. You can call any time.

Your family here send their best regards. They pray for your continued health and hope to see you in Nigeria.

So, are you thinking of going to Jamaica? I pray your trip will be fruitful.

Your loving dad.

These letters started something between Sanni and me, but even now, years later, I struggle to pinpoint exactly what. Perhaps underlying it all was this feeling I couldn't shake. At night, lying in bed, one question played on repeat inside my head.

Could I trust him?

Eleven

Last Orders

My name is my identity and must not be lost.

—Lucy Stone

For years, Mike and I didn't agree with the institution of marriage. But as we got older, calling him my 'boyfriend' sounded like we were teenagers, and my 'partner' sounded like he was my business partner. So, after 13 years, we decided to cement our relationship in the traditional way. We got married and I 'sort of' took Mike's surname. I say 'sort of' because I dragged my feet. That's not to say I didn't like the surname Balshaw – I do – except I was genuinely fond of my existing name too, which might sound odd, given my relationship with Sanni, but it was the surname I'd carried around for decades. It was part of who I was, and I was reluctant to disassociate myself from it, which is why I only 'sort of' took Mike's surname. I am now officially both a Sanni and a Balshaw because, like many women, I simply haven't got around to changing my last name. I remain a Sanni on my passport, but on other official documents, like my driving licence, I am

Balshaw. Don't get me wrong; I enjoy being called 'Mrs Balshaw' and, by 'sort of' taking Mike's surname, I followed the cultural patronymic norm. However, not all countries do. In the Netherlands, married women are required by law to keep their surname at marriage. They can take their husband's surname under special circumstances, but they will always be identified in documents by their name before marriage. It is tradition in South Korea for women to keep their birth surnames, although, unlike the Netherlands, there is no law preventing women from taking their husband's name after marriage. In my case, choosing to become Mrs Balshaw and (sort of) using Mike's surname is the route most women in English-speaking countries take. A recent survey by the Pew Research Centre found that eight in ten American women take their husband's last name, although there is no legal requirement to do so. In the UK, around 94 per cent of women married to a man change their surnames after marriage, even though no law dictates that they should. In Japan, however, it is a legal requirement for married couples to use the same family name, and this nineteenth-century law has caused a huge amount of controversy. Although it was amended in 1947 to remove the requirement that only the man's surname can be chosen, in about 95 per cent of cases wives in Japan take their husbands' surnames. There is growing pressure to update this law.

The word 'surname' originates from the Old French word *surnom*. In Europe, inherited surnames became normal in bureaucratic written records from about the fifteenth century onwards, though at different times in different countries. By then, surnames were a necessity. As populations grew the pool of single names was becoming depleted and bureaucratically challenging. A second name was needed for convenience (how else would all that tax be collected?) and to lessen the administrative burden. In English-speaking countries, most last names can be classified into distinct surnaming categories. Some are locative, derived from places and place names, e.g. Starmer, Moore or Gatsby. Some are rooted in relationships, such as Cousins, while some are derived from nicknames, like Little, Goodfellow or Cameron. Other surnames, like Potter, Farmer or Smith, describe their holders' occupations, and, if we think about surnames and occupations, today, some researchers claim a person's last name can determine the type of job they go into. This is called an aptronym, or an apt surname, and the Olympic champion Usain Bolt is an example of someone whose name perfectly fits the owner and matches their job. He runs pretty fast, right? Or how about the yoga teacher I met years ago, called Catherine Bliss? Or the keen birdwatcher, face reddening, who told me she was called Elaine Starling. Or Hannah Willow, recently crowned Glasgow's first champion tree-hugger. Would Hannah or Elaine still love tree-hugging or birdwatching if their surnames were Brown? I posed this question to Brett Pelham, a professor of psychology at Montgomery College in the US, who has studied the strange phenomenon of apt surnames.

'Men named Carpenter do indeed gravitate toward carpentry,' he explained. 'And similarly, those with surnames like Baker, Barber, Butcher, Butler, Farmer or Painter also gravitate towards those careers. Most people like themselves, so it makes sense that they gravitate towards occupations that remind them of themselves.'

Maybe Pelham is right, or perhaps it's simply coincidence, who knows, but there is an argument someone's surname can hint at their personality too. I'll never forget a past yoga student of mine, called Mrs Sunshine, who more than lived up to her surname. She was the embodiment of joy. And it is not just surnames that can be apt. A few years ago, in a cafe, I overheard two friends talking. One of them commented on their daughter. It turned out her daughter was called Storm, and the woman said to her friend in an exasperated tone, 'Her name suits her. Because for the last 16 years of her life she's given me nothing but trouble.'

According to my father-in-law, Ken, the surname Balshaw is probably derived from a place name in Lancashire, but it's not a common surname. I frequently receive letters addressed to Mrs Belshaw or Mrs Belyshaw, or someone will ask how Balshaw is spelt. Ironically, the surname Sanni is also tricky. If I am on the phone, it is one of those surnames people can't quite seem to get right.

'No,' I'll say in a calm voice. 'It's not *F*. It is *S* for sugar. Or *S* for splendid. *Not* F for Freddy,' I'll explain.

'So that's S, not F?' the person on the phone will say.

'Yes, it is Sanni. There is no F,' I will repeat, trying to keep the exasperation out of my voice, until it finally dawns on the person, and they apologise and laugh awkwardly for mistaking Sanni for Fanni.

So why have I partly retained my name since marriage? Maybe I've grown accustomed to my last name languishing at the end of a register. As a Balshaw, I am near the top. Or is it because, as a Sanni, there is a direct link to my ethnic identity? But I am conflicted. Given our decades-long estrangement – why do I want to be associated with the person who gave me this name? And then there is the Anglo tradition of girls and women being the property of their fathers until marriage. I am, by the association of my surname, the 'property' of Sanni until I marry, and then I become the 'property' of Mike. I am uncomfortable with being anyone's property.

I have avoided using the term 'maiden name' to describe a woman's surname before marriage. I think it's an old-fashioned and outdated term, so I've limited its use. But regardless of the terminology, it is a woman's choice to keep, discard or modify the name that belonged to her before she was married. It is her decision, yet it is a decision loaded with controversy. Let's not forget that in the US, as recently as the 1970s, married women could not use their birth surname to vote, gain a passport or hold a bank account. This is why Lucy Stone's actions in 1855 are so remarkable. Stone, an abolitionist and suffragist, became the first known American woman to keep her surname when she married Henry Blackwell. However, her actions had consequences. Stone registered to vote in the Massachusetts state elections but was removed from the electoral rolls because she did not use her husband's surname. And there are plenty of other Lucy Stones who faced legal challenges if they tried to change their name. In 1974, a woman in Indiana took her husband's name in marriage but later tried to change it back to her birth surname with her husband's consent. But this was denied by the court in rather crude terminology.

> *... perhaps Mrs Hauptly's need was not for a change of name but for a competent psychiatrist... Namely, a sick and confused woman, unhappy and unsatisfied with her marriage, unable to determine what she wants to do with her life.*

Unfortunately women's retention of their names before marriage continues to raise eyebrows. In a recent article in the *Independent,* a wedding planner from Sydney explained that when she married her fiancé she intended to keep her Russian surname.

'We've been taking the surnames of our husbands, dads and granddads for far too long,' she explained. 'It's time for women to create their own names and identities.'

However, her decision polarised opinion and resulted in a slew of unsavoury online messages, mostly from other women. Some of the comments said that keeping her birth surname demonstrated she was 'keeping her husband on a tight leash', while others suggested she and her partner should divorce because she was violating a long-held tradition.

Why does a woman's decision to keep her name cause such a visceral reaction? One friend told me she didn't feel comfortable having the surname of her partner thrust upon her. Another agreed. She explained that taking her husband's surname supported the patriarchy. Conversely, another said taking her partner's surname was a marker of their commitment and love. So does that imply you are not showing sufficient commitment and love if you don't take your partner's surname? And what about the women who hate their surname and frankly can't wait to see the back of it? Years ago, someone told me about a young work colleague who had the same given name as her surname. My friend's work colleague was called Carol, and her surname was Carroll. According to my friend, Carol couldn't wait to get married, ditch her surname and take her new husband's last name. It is fairly uncommon to share a given name and surname, although I remember reading an article about the ex-Manchester United player Gary Neville's father. His name was Neville Neville, and at the time I thought this was some kind of early April Fool's joke. It turned out it wasn't. Neville Neville *was* Gary Neville's father's name.

The sociologist Norbert Elias says that our given names help to denote individuality (or 'I' identities), whereas surnames are important in signalling 'we' identities. For some couples, creativity and flexibility are the key to answering the thorny question of whether or not to take a partner's surname. Some couples decide to keep their birth surname and use it as a middle name following marriage, while for others the answer lies in meshing. The idea of meshing is simple. Couples fuse their surnames to reflect both partners' identities. For example, on marriage, Mr Pugh and Miss Griffin would morph into Mr and Mrs Puffin. So if Mike and I followed the meshing route, our combined surname might be Sanbal or Balsan, which, to be honest, sounds like the name for a newly launched alcoholic drink. But regardless, meshing is increasingly popular. It allows couples the freedom of a symbolic reinvention without any history tied to their new surname. It is a new start. Another popular idea is the practice of joining two names with a hyphen, otherwise known as the double-barrelled surname. But which couple's surname comes first? Do couples flip a coin? Or work it out over a few rounds of rock-paper-scissors? And what happens if a couple with a double-barrelled surname get married and have children? How will double-barrelled names work then? Can you imagine filling out forms or writing an email? The other option is the trend of creating a double surname without the hyphen. This is a popular option for civil partnerships and same-sex marriages.

And what about all the men out there who decide to take their wife's surname? It's uncommon, but a few men do just that. Recently a friend told me that her husband-to-be was considering taking her surname. However, she discovered that, while a woman only needs to provide a marriage certificate to do so, a man needs to fork out £30 for a deed poll!

A surname often acts as a geographical marker. If we hear a surname, it can hint at someone's nationality or ethnic origins. However, years ago, before I married Mike, after hearing my given name and surname on the telephone, the person calling asked if I was Italian. She was of Italian heritage herself, and according to her the surname Sanni, spelt with one N, not two, was a common surname in Italy.

Given her and Sanni's less-than-amicable divorce, my mother chose not to revert to her surname before marriage. This shocked me. I assumed she would jump at the opportunity to cut all ties with Sanni, so, when I asked her about her reluctance to change our surname, she surprised me with her candour. It was 2003, three weeks before Mike and my wedding party and four years since we had left Tokyo. By then we were living in London. I taught drama at a college and in the evenings I taught a couple of yoga classes. Mike was coming to the end of a three-year acupuncture course, and we were both slowly, and I mean slowly, acclimatising to life back in the UK. Over lunch in our flat in south London, my mother discussed the final last-minute logistics of our wedding party. Mike and I had chosen a venue in east London, we'd asked a couple of friends to DJ, and my mother asked if she should wear heels or flats.

'Definitely flats,' I said. 'You'll be dancing. I've asked my friend to play a couple of your favourite tunes. How high are the heels?'

She raised her right hand to indicate the distance between her thumb and index finger.

'Are you kidding?' I asked her but, by the look on her face, I knew she was 100 per cent serious.

And then the conversation veered away from footwear to Sanni, the man whose name wasn't on the guest list, which, looking back, was a glaring omission. But how could he be anything but an omission?

'When you divorced him, did you ever think about changing your surname back to your birth surname?' I asked.

She put down her knife and fork and shrugged.

'I thought about it, Mandy,' she said. 'But you kids were Sannis, so I thought it would be too complicated to change my surname.'

'It's Camilla, Mum.'

'Mm-mm,' she replied. 'I can't get used to calling you that name.'

'Try harder,' I said.

'Mm-mm,' she said again, and I didn't want an argument, so we resumed reviewing the names on our wedding-party guest list.

At the time, I didn't fully understand her reticence to revert to her old surname. Sure, it was a hassle, but, given her feelings towards Sanni, I was surprised. Now I'm more understanding. For a single mother in the 70s, there was a stigma around divorce. Plus, the divorce took a toll on her, and adding a change of surname into the mix was, I suspect, too time-consuming and exhausting. And she bided her time. When she married John in 1984, she took his surname, officially banishing the surname Sanni from her identity.

After lunch, I walked my mother back to the train station.

The train to Luton was delayed, and it started raining, so we took shelter under a canopy on the platform. As the rain drummed on the roof, I thought about telling her about the other name missing from our wedding-party list. But I didn't. The train chugged into the station. I waved her goodbye and ran back to my flat, dodging the downpour, thinking about Otis.

In 1999, a week before he left Tokyo to teach in South Korea, Otis cooked Mike and me a farewell meal in his tiny apartment in Waseda, a lively university district close to our apartment in Takadanobaba.

The three of us sat cross-legged at a traditional low table, devouring plate after plate of his restaurant-standard Japanese cooking.

We exchanged books.

I pressed a copy of Hanif Kureishi's semi-autobiographical novel, *The Buddha of Suburbia,* into Otis's hands. It was one of my favourite books at the time, mainly because the central character, 17-year-old Karim, like me at that age, was desperate to escape the suburbs and head for London to experience people, life and culture.

'It's a rebellious book,' I said. 'It had a huge effect on me. I think you'll like it, but it's a bit – er—'

'Sweary,' Mike quipped.

'I know you don't like profanities,' I said to Otis.

He smiled, gave Mike a book about Japanese shiatsu, and handed me a copy of *Beloved* by Toni Morrison. And Otis, being Otis, had a story to tell about the novel.

'I was at some party in New York,' he said, shaking his head at the memory. 'I got chatting to a lady. She said she was a librarian, so I asked her if she'd read any Toni Morrison and guess what she said?'

Mike and I shrugged.

'Is that Toni with a Y?' he replied.

I shook my head with disappointment.

'We need to figure out a way to keep in touch,' I told Otis. 'We'll probably move to London, but you don't know yet where you'll live in Korea.'

We decided the most sensible option was to give Otis my mother's home address in Luton.

'That way, we'll have a point of contact,' I explained.

I wrote her address and phone number in one of Otis's notebooks and handed it back to him.

'It doesn't matter if you write once a month or once a year; just write to me,' I said, and then I paused and thought, how can I tell him how much I'm going to miss him?

He got up and said he'd made a cake and, as he walked towards his no-bigger-than-a-fingernail kitchen, I whispered to Mike, 'He will write, won't he?'

'Of course he will,' he replied reassuringly.

When Otis came back, we made a huge fuss over his triple-layer chocolate cake, but, as I watched him take a knife and slice thick slabs of gooey sponge onto our plates, I knew Mike was wrong – I probably always knew.

Otis didn't write or call. I never heard from him again.

For a long time I was hurt. Deeply hurt. Feelings of rejection and abandonment bubbled and whispered in my ear and, during those first few years of navigating life back in the UK, I often thought about Otis. I thought about him when, a few months after I landed at Heathrow Airport, I enrolled on a writing course, but I cancelled my place at the last minute. I told myself not yet. Wait. It's not the right time. You'll know when you are ready. I wished I could have talked to Otis about not being ready, about what exactly I was waiting to be ready for. He was the person who encouraged me to write and, many years later, when I found the courage to write a short story that was published, he was the person I wanted to tell.

I'd be lying if I said not having Otis in my life didn't affect me. It did, and it took a long time, a very long time, to get over his decision. But now I understand why. Otis lived in the present. I believe people like him come into our lives briefly when you need them the most. They float in and out. They are the kind of once-in-a-lifetime people who you think you know but never do. They are unknowable. I knew very little about Otis, and it's inconceivable now to think this man who had such an influence on my life for almost five years never told me his surname. He was always Otis, or Otis-san, or Otis-sensei, and that was fitting. He didn't need a surname. For the few years I was fortunate enough to know this giant of a man, his given name was more than enough.

After years of marriage, couples may face questions and presumptions about whether they have children or when they will start having children.

In 2011, a few months after I'd moved from London to Swaffham, a friend organised a local cook to teach a group of six or so women how to make authentic Indian curries. It was fun. I learned some new techniques, which, as the daughter of Luton's number one curry connoisseur, AKA my mother Carmen, was eye-opening.

As we ground spices with a pestle and mortar, I talked about a meditation retreat I'd recently attended in Devon, and then the conversation turned to childbirth. I didn't know everyone in the group; some were local and others, like me, had moved to Norfolk from London or from further afield. One of the women made a comment about her labour. I don't recall what she said, but it was about the circumstances of her second child's birth.

'We're all mothers here,' she said, gazing at the group. 'Let's be frank with the childbirth horror stories.'

The rest of the women in the group nodded, and I calmly said I wasn't a mother.

'Oh, I'm sorry,' she said, making a clown's sad face with her mouth. 'But there's always IVF or adoption, isn't there?'

There is always IVF and adoption. I'd be rich if you gave me £100 for all the well-meaning people who've said that over the years.

I kept quiet. I bowed my head and ground those spices into a pulp. Who knew a pestle and mortar could be so cathartic?

I didn't explain that, after decades of chronic illness, I finally received a name for my condition. Deep into my 30s, I was diagnosed with endometriosis, the gynaecological condition where tissues similar to the womb's lining grow in other places, like the fallopian tubes and ovaries.

I didn't tell these women that the consultant shuffled my notes in his hand. Peered over his half-moon spectacles hanging from a chain and said, 'I'm afraid yours is a pretty severe case.'

I didn't tell them I wiped my eyes and cleared snot from my nose as the consultant said in a matter-of-fact voice that I probably wouldn't be able to have children.

I didn't say how, at that moment, I thought about Mike and how he'd joked that he wanted a football team of kids.

And that, long ago, we wrote a list of our favourite baby names.

Grace
Nesta
Marley
Garland
Ben
Ola
Tayo
Otis

I didn't explain I knew, then, sitting in that consultation room, that there wouldn't be any players.

Twelve

Wood and Water

Wi likkle but wi tallawah.

—*Jamaican proverb*

The summer I turned seven, a boy at school called me Kizzy.

'Kizzy, you are Kizzy, and you are my slave,' he said.

I told him to shut up and told him my name was Mandy, not Kizzy.

'It's Kizzy,' he said, but louder this time.

'I'm going to tell Miss you called me Kizzy,' I replied, glaring at him.

Hearing this, he sloped off, but at the time the name was regularly thrown around the playground in the 70s because of one programme.

Kizzy was a character in Alex Haley's seminal novel *Roots.* In 1977 the book was adapted for television and broadcast to a primetime audience. Every Sunday, my family, along with millions of others around the world, were gripped by this groundbreaking drama that depicted the brutality of the trans-atlantic slave trade. We watched as African men, women and children were chained by their necks and ankles, uprooted from their homes and thrust onto ships bound for plantations in America. Like most families, before *Roots* was on television, I knew nothing about enslaved people or that the inhabitants of those tall ships were also bound for coffee, sugar and cocoa plantations in the Caribbean.

In my family, like many immigrant households, back then, the transatlantic slave trade and its impact on the Caribbean and Africa wasn't discussed. My sole education came from *Roots.* I have a vivid memory of the opening scene. One of the author's African ancestors holds an infant in his arms and whispers the name he has chosen for the baby in the child's ear. It is a poignant moment. We know that, in time, the name whispered in the child's ear will be lost, and he will suffer the indignity of being named by his so-called 'master'. His African name will be beaten out of him and replaced with a new name: Toby.

Trevor Burnard, a Wilberforce Professor of Slavery and Emancipation at the University of Hull, has written about the callous, poisonous legacy of slavery in Jamaica and its impact on naming. In his paper *Slave Naming Patterns: Onomastics and the Taxonomy of Race in Eighteenth-Century Jamaica* Burnard discusses how enslaved people were named on plantations. 'Slaves recognised the humiliation implicit in the names that they were given,' he says. 'They were denoted by first name, sometimes accompanied by a modifier referring to age, occupation or ethnicity.'

According to Burnard, these names came from a small pool. 'On large plantations providing a new name for each slave was difficult,' he explains, 'partly because sales and amalgamations led to duplication and partly because slave owners' imaginations were limited.'

Burnard is also the author of a book about a White Jamaican plantation owner called Thomas Thistlewood. In his book

Mastery, Tyranny & Desire, Burnard reveals through Thistlewood's diaries the horrifying and sheer brutality of slavery in Jamaica and the casual physical and sexual violence that untold numbers of enslaved Jamaicans experienced. Thistlewood's diary also indicates that, in times of illness, enslaved people rejected their oppressors' names for them and turned to African names to heal and comfort. One of Thistlewood's diary excerpts reads, 'When Negroes are sick, their relations and friends usually gave them some very ugly New Name which they think may deter God Almighty from taking them, as they have such an ugly name.'

Before his and my mother's divorce, I don't recall Sanni mentioning the impact of slavery on Nigeria or Africa, even though it is estimated some 3 million Nigerians were affected. My mother sometimes talked about the Taino Indians, the indigenous tribe in Jamaica, who the Spanish wiped out in the late 1400s. Or she mentioned the islands' diversity or how she lived in Kingston, the capital, before she came to live in the UK.

'I'd go to drive-in movies and concert halls,' she said wistfully. 'I wanted to live in Kingston and work in one of the fancy offices, but in those days only White Jamaicans or light-skinned girls were allowed to work there.'

'Why?' I asked.

'It's too complicated,' she'd reply.

I was around eight at the time, so perhaps she thought I was too young to understand the complexities of colourism or colonialism. Or maybe she thought, Why dredge up a horrific trauma of the past? She was preoccupied with other matters, like putting food on the table and clothes on our backs. There was no time to discuss the brutality of slavery in the Caribbean. Like most Jamaicans, growing up, she wasn't taught about the slave trade in relation to her heritage and identity. My mother grew up with pictures of Queen Elizabeth II in the classroom. There was no rigorous examination of the past in her childhood. When I interviewed Diane Allen West, a Holness Fellow for Atlantic World History at the University of the West Indies in Jamaica, she suggested the reason for this contrast with America is that 'The US is tied to more recent vestiges of slavery and the civil rights generally – and also a history of segregation which reinforced the need for self-identity in ways that the Caribbean did not.'

Despite her usual batting away of questions about her past, when the final episode of *Roots* aired, my mother, Dunni, Abdul and I stared at the television, watching the credits roll in silence.

'My maiden name is a slave name,' my mother said quietly. 'Francis was most likely the name of the plantation owner in Jamaica,' and then she told us children to go to bed. 'That's enough *Roots.* It's way past your bedtime, Mandy.'

When I was older, I was able to process the relationship between names and oppression. As an adult, I understood how names can be lost and how they carry the weight of history. I understood the power of a name and how it can be used as a weapon to break someone's resolve and spirit. And, unfortunately, history is littered with examples. In 1930s Germany, the Nazis used names as a way of controlling and enforcing identification. This meant all Jews were forced to bear names that were selected from a list sanctioned by the Nazi government. There were 185 names for male children and 91 names for female children and, by 1939, Jews were required to adopt a second forename. For men, 'Israel' and for women, 'Sarah'. In prisons and concentration camps, names were removed and replaced with numbers. On the notorious Robben Island, Nelson Mandela became prisoner '46664', and in Auschwitz Primo Levi became '174517'. The celebrated Zimbabwean author Yvonne Vera's novel *Butterfly Burning* is an example of how names in the Ndebele language were slowly abandoned for English ones. More recently, a few years ago, I watched a play in London. *The Convert* was written by the Zimbabwean-American playwright and actor Danai Gurira. Set in the nineteenth century in Southern Africa, Mashonaland, renamed Southern Rhodesia, then later Zimbabwe, the narrative confronts the links between Christianity and colonialism, but what was more striking to me was how names were used to strip away any trace of Zimbabwean identity. Throughout the play, Zimbabwean names were changed to English names, and I was reminded then of how names can be so easily weaponised to negative effect and how the weaponising of a name can also be the trigger for regaining control of the narrative. In the US, honouring African ancestry was part of the 60s Black Pride movement. So, in 1964, when Cassius Clay, later Muhammad Ali, expressed contempt for his name as a slave name, rejecting it altogether and reclaiming his African name, other notable African-Americans followed suit. However, according to the journalist, memoirist and novelist Jill Lord, there was some unease within the African-American community around doing this. Lord changed her name to Itabari Njeri to reflect her African identity, but some within the Black community struggled with her choice of name.

'You're one of those Black people who changed their names,' someone remarked to Itabari at a party. 'Well, I still got the old enslaver's Irish name.' The man who made this comment used the surname O'Hare. So who is right here? The person who changes their name to reflect their culture and heritage or the person who doesn't? In my opinion, it is about choice. Names have been hard fought over for some communities and, because of that, the need to reclaim something taken away is too strong an emotion to ignore.

Watching *Roots* as a young person was the catalyst for change for Kwame Kwei-Armah, the former artistic director of the

Young Vic in London. Kwei-Armah was born in the UK and given the name Ian Roberts. But watching *Roots* as a young boy started the process of re-evaluating his name.

'I wanted to walk my truth,' he explained when we talked over Zoom. 'My name, Kwame Kwei-Armah, roots me in the land my ancestors were taken from. Ian Roberts doesn't.'

For others, the question of whether to keep a name associated with brutal oppression or search for another name reflecting their true identity is complex. How do you say I have this name but am contesting it? For some, like Kwame Kwei-Armah, it is about finding an African name consistent with your heritage. For others, the answer lies in striking out a surname associated with a past slave owner. In a recent BBC World Service programme, the theologian, presenter and professor Dr Robert Beckford chose to strike out his surname. His last name is linked with the particularly brutal plantation owner, Alderman Beckford, in the Caribbean. When I contacted Robert Beckford, he explained that 'The strike-out signifies the contested history of my surname – a lived tension between a White slave name and an African-Caribbean history of overcoming. Writing my surname this way is liberating for me; it's the best of both worlds – resistance and celebration.'

Jamaica, June 2016

The plane lands at Montego Bay Airport and here I am thinking about Sanni.

I am reflecting on one of the letters I wrote to him, explaining my intention to visit Jamaica. It was a a brief letter, and I wasn't entirely transparent. I didn't disclose my true motivations for going to Jamaica. I didn't say I was curious about my maternal heritage. Or that I'd wanted to visit the island for years, but circumstance and affordability meant it was never a reality for me – only a distant dream. I failed to mention that going to

Jamaica would be only the second time I'd visited a predominantly Black country. The first time was in early 2000. I visited Tanzania with some girlfriends, and I was excited about the prospect of landing in a place where the people looked like me. I remember preparing for the hairs on my arms to stand up and my stomach to flutter with a sense of belonging. But it never happened. I felt no affinity with Tanzania. I gave Sanni scant details about Jamaica. I told him Mike and I would be staying on the island for two weeks, connecting the pieces of my ancestry together, but I didn't tell him part of my visit would be spent practising yoga in Negril. How could I tell him that? I wasn't entirely sure he was familiar with the concept of yoga. In one of our earlier letters, I tried to explain what I did for a living. I told him I'd practised yoga for over twenty years, and, in intricate detail, I explained the particular style of yoga that I practised. I said this ancient art, so precious to me, had never let me down. But what did yoga mean to him? Nothing. So, I told him I was 'in the health business' by way of an explanation, as I figured it covered all bases. Still, I was vague about my trip to Jamaica. Part of me knew our letters were fragile. His letters frustrated me. I questioned if I should continue writing to him. I was not sharing deep emotional truths with him, and he was not sharing deep emotional truths with me. Although we'd been writing back and forth over the last nine months or so, our letter-writing relationship felt like a plaster was holding it together.

As the plane comes to a complete stop, one of the passengers behind our seat says in a loud voice, 'Welcome to Jamaica. The island of smiles.'

And at that moment, Sanni is forgotten, momentarily. I am in Jamaica, my mother's birthplace.

Mike and I are greeted with a warm hug of air as we make our way down the steps of the plane.

I squint my eyes at the fierceness of the afternoon sun, rub the hairs on my bare arms and notice the sensation in my stomach. It flutters.

We are not staying in one of those all-inclusive hotels that are popular with tourists. The 30 or so yoga-course participants are staying in various types of accommodation in Negril, according to budget. Mike and I are staying in a small family-run guest house near the beach. We spend money in local restaurants, wander, and experience the *real* Jamaica, which suits me. I'm not a hang on the beach all day on a sun lounger kind of girl, and Mike is not a hang on the beach all day on a sun lounger kind of guy, so for the first few days we do yoga, and eat mangoes, so ripe, vibrant orange drips from the fruit and trickles down our cheeks.

Our yoga group is an eclectic bunch. Most are American, and they are not Jamaican first-timers like us. Some have visited the island many times. A handful, like me, are yoga teachers, while others are most definitely here for the holiday, not the yoga. And when some of the group discover my mother was born in Jamaica, they ask the same questions:

'Wow, and you've not been to Jamaica before. How come?'

'I could never afford it,' I reply truthfully.

'But you have family in Jamaica, right?'

'No,' I say, and I explain that, as far as I know, I don't have any family in Jamaica. They give me a 'that's too bad' smile and say, 'Oh, that's a shame.'

And it is a shame.

It wouldn't be an exaggeration to say I think about Sanni and my mother most days. I can't help myself. They are like permanent stains on my clothes; no matter how hard I try, I can't wash them off.

* * *

'Take what you need for savasana,' our white-haired American teacher says, five days into our trip, at the end of a particularly strenuous yoga class. (It always makes me smile when people presume yoga is easy. It is not; find the right teacher and the right style, and it is physically and mentally demanding.)

'I always struggle with this pose,' a tall woman in green leggings whispers to me. 'I just can't relax. I kinda struggle to let go.'

I raise my eyebrows because I do not struggle with this pose. I lie on my back and adjust my body to ensure maximum comfort.

The woman in green places her mat beside me and lies on it, and the teacher talks in soothing tones about surrendering our bodies to relaxation.

But I can't settle into the teacher's hypnotic delivery. While the woman in green snores, I think about my mother, and then my thoughts turn to my grandmother and grandfather. I think about the stories my mother told me about her childhood. Although some were stories of trauma, there was a lightness in the darkness. Once, I can't recall how old I was, but I remember asking her what she remembered about Jamaica, and she didn't mention being left there as a baby.

My mother talked of the aroma of pots cooking on an open fire, Jamaicans' sense of humour and the distinctive beauty of a hummingbird. She spoke of the lush mountainous countryside, where slave rebellions were born, and the nights she and her friends sat up till late, staring at the moon.

'When there was a full moon, we called it moonshine night,' she explained. 'The moon was so bright it illuminated everything. And that turquoise sea,' she said, her eyes staring into the distance. 'I'll never forget the colour of the sea.'

I remember this now as I lie on my mat, listening to the snoring woman next to me, and then, in a moment of sheer pleasure, at being here, on this island of my mother, this place that has seeped into my bones, I frantically calculate how Mike and I could move to Jamaica. Of course, I wasn't serious. It could never happen, but this was the fantasy. But at the same time, although I love this island, there is a sorrow about Jamaica I can't easily shake off. Over the increasingly loud snores of the woman beside me, I try to pinpoint the source of this sadness. Was it my mother's difficult upbringing in Jamaica or the brutal legacy of its past?

'Class has finished,' Mike says, gently tapping my shoulder and nudging me from my thoughts.

I rub my eyes.

'I wasn't snoring, was I?' I say, embarrassed.

'No,' he says, smiling. 'Just heavy breathing.'

'I was miles away,' I say, sitting up and surveying the rest of the group folding up their yoga mats.

Although, in reality, I am not miles away. I am still right here on this island that runs deep inside me, regardless of the past trauma of this place, I feel at home here.

One morning, over a delicately spiced breakfast of ackee and salt fish, eggs and fresh fruit, I make small talk with an American couple while Mike chats to our white-haired and laconic yoga teacher.

The couple are older than me, perhaps in their 60s. They have golden tans and toned bodies and, as we talk, I remind myself not to call them by their nicknames.

A few days ago, I discovered the hotel staff referred to this couple as Mrs and Mr Agassi, and in truth the woman's husband does bear an uncanny resemblance to the tennis player.

The three of us sit in comfortable silence.

We eat our breakfast and gaze out at the rocks dotting the ocean. The sky is pristine blue, but later it transforms into a deep blue-black. It surprises me how quickly the day turns to night here. One moment, the sun is beating down; the next, it is gone.

I pick up my glass of water and ask the 'Agassis' if they've seen any of the roadside adverts out and about.

They shake their heads, so I tell them about the billboard beside the delicious gelato place near the roundabout.

'Undertakers like overtakers,' I say, smiling at the memory. 'It made me giggle. That and Clarks shoes. I didn't realise they were so popular in Jamaica.'

Of course, as Americans, they had no idea that Clarks was an iconic shoe brand in the UK, so I explained.

Later, as I clear my plates, I overhear some of the hotel staff talking, and I know by the way they raise their eyes in my direction they are talking about me.

I walk over to say hello, and one of the girls, with braids and deep-set dimples in her cheeks, grins.

'We call you The English Girl,' she says.

Of course I had a nickname but why can't my nickname honour my Jamaican heritage? Can't I be 'The Jamaican/English Girl?' But how can I? I suppose, in their eyes, that's precisely what I am. I am The 'English Girl.' And you know what? I didn't mind. My trip to Jamaica and my strong sense of affinity with the country proved to me that it's possible to have more than one sense of home.

Norfolk, September 2016

It is early autumn in Swaffham, three months since my trip to Jamaica, and there is a palpable change. Visiting the island where my mother was born has changed our relationship. There is a new sense of kinship between us. I can see and smell the island when she talks about Jamaica now. It is no longer this abstract place I see on television adverts or in glossy holiday brochures, where racially ambiguous couples sip rum punches on sun loungers. The other change is my relationship with Sanni, if you could call our intermittent communication a relationship. He wrote to me a few days after I returned from my trip, but his letter felt forced, like he was going through the motions. I replied, and, when I read my letter back, it was similar to his letter. We were like two people trying to make a bad, incompatible date work. I posted my letter to him, but afterwards I thought, why did I bother? His letters frustrate the hell out of me. Why should I continue writing to someone who didn't raise me? I am my mother's daughter. My *Jamaican* mother's daughter.

One evening, after teaching my yoga class, I sit at the kitchen table and compose Sanni a letter.

I'd like to take a letter-writing break for a while, I write. ***I need some time to consider a few things. The last year or so has been a whirlwind of emotions, hasn't it? I need some time out to reflect. I hope you understand.*** And then I mention safer territory. I discuss the political situation in the UK and ask him general questions about Nigerian politics.

I don't post the letter straight away. It sits on my desk next to a plant. Some days, I think about throwing it in the bin; others, I think about rewriting it. Or I tell myself, perhaps the two of us could find a middle way, a once-a-year kind of letter-writing agreement.

The next day, I moot this idea to Jenny on our windless autumnal forest walk.

At a little after 6 o'clock in the evening, the woods are quiet, the trees watchful. As we tread between the weeds and overhanging bracken, I feel grounded by these woods: the fallen branches, the misshapen russet-coloured ferns and the silence.

'You're both finding your way,' Jenny says when I tell her about the letter to Sanni sitting on my desk. 'It's early days. Give it more time. Maybe talking on the phone is better than writing letters.'

'I don't have any more time to give,' I say. 'I'm not shutting the door completely. I'm just suggesting we have a break.'

She takes off her shades and places them on top of her head. Her skin is tanned from a recent trip to California to see her two children, and she radiates a West Coast glamour.

'What does Mike think?' she asks.

'That I should continue writing,' I reply, bending down to tie up my shoelace. 'You know Mike, ever the optimist. He thinks it's still early days too. But it doesn't feel like that to me. It feels like too much time has passed, and we're both scrambling around trying to find a connection.'

'He can't give you what you want,' she says quietly. 'I learned that with my dad.'

'He's never answered my question about why he contacted me now,' I say. 'There's . . .' I trail off, wondering if I should just say it. I start again. 'There's no bond, Jenny. He knows it, and I know it. It's too late. Too much time has passed.'

'At the end of the day, it's your decision. Do what feels right for you,' she says.

Later, in bed I think about what Jenny and Mike said.

I tell myself, maybe, just maybe, they are right. I should continue writing to Sanni. He'll answer my question in his own time, even though I knew, by then, my question had lost its potency and flavour. I wanted to make whatever we had between us work.

The next day, I throw my letter to Sanni into the recycling bin, and I start again.

Hello there, I write. ***Sorry for the delay in writing back. I've had a lot on my mind. How are you? How is Ifemi?***

I continue writing, asking the same old tired questions, and I think, you know what? I am sure my letters frustrate the hell out of him, too.

A few days go by, and then Teju calls.

I cradle my phone against my ear and ask if I could call him back.

'I'm heading out to see my mother,' I say.

'No problem,' he replies. 'It's just – well – Uncle Rimi asked for your phone number. He's—'

'Is he okay?' I ask, interrupting.

'He's fine,' he says. 'Of course, I didn't give it to him. I thought you were writing to one another?'

'We are,' I say, cradling the phone against one ear while hunting for my bag.

'I know he finds writing difficult,' he says.

'So you're suggesting I talk to him on the phone?'

'No,' he replies, chuckling in that lovely youthful laugh of his. 'Not at all. I understand that's a big step. I suppose Uncle Rimi mentions the telephone because it's his way of moving your relationship to the next stage.'

Part of me wants to say Sanni should have contacted me years ago if he wanted to build a proper relationship. Plus, if he was so interested why didn't he jump on a plane and come to see us? Teju tracked me down easily enough on his behalf, so why couldn't Sanni?

'I'm not ready to speak to him – yet,' I say, then I swallow and tell Teju the truth. 'I'm scared of getting hurt.'

'I understand,' he says in his quiet, reassuring voice, that over the last year or so I've appreciated and relied on. 'You'll call when you are ready.'

'I'm not sure I'll ever be ready to talk to Sanni.'

We are silent for a moment, so I take this as an opportunity to change the subject. I ask Teju about his upcoming trip to Senegal.

Thirteen

Say My Name

What's in a name? That which we call a rose by any other name would smell as sweet.

—*William Shakespeare*

Even now, decades later, I remember the exact location of the telephone at our house on Bradley Road. You opened the front door, and it was on your right. But instead of being relegated to a forgotten corner, dumped next to a wilting potted plant, the phone was perched like a peacock on a mahogany telephone table with a padded green seat and a side drawer for the phone directory and the Yellow Pages.

In those days, there was an unspoken telephone etiquette. When the phone rang, my mother did not say her name. She sat on the padded seat, crossed her legs, said 'Hello,' and reeled off the digits of her telephone number.

The person on the other end of the phone would then ask if they were speaking to Carmen.

'Speaking,' my mother replied.

Nowadays the penchant for repeating your telephone

number back to the person calling is a little outdated. They typically say their name, not their phone number.

If the landline rings in Swaffham, which is not often, and it's some kind of sales call, and they know my name, I'll brace myself, as the caller often presumes that making a 'funny' quip or two will build rapport. They will say:

'How is Charlie boy?'

'Bet you wish you had her money!'

'Are you fond of horses too?'

'Camilla, as in Parker Bowles?'

The person will giggle, oblivious to the fact that I have heard variations of the same jokes many times before. They do not realise the spectre of Her Majesty the Queen, née Camilla Parker Bowles, has followed me around since the 80s.

My mother was, and remains, a huge Princess Diana fan. She was #TeamDiana way before we used hashtags. And it wasn't only my mother who was fond of Diana. A few years ago, I discovered that other Black and Asian women saw in Diana someone who was forced into an arranged marriage and who struggled within a system of misogyny. Who cared if she was privileged and rich? These women related to her, as did my mother. She liked to think Diana and her were kindred spirits. Diana married a wrong 'un, and so did she. When Camilla Parker Bowles was outed as the other person in Charles and Di's faltering marriage, I had no chance. Camilla was the 'other woman'. How could my mother call me, her own daughter, Camilla, the given name of Diana's nemesis?

In the early 90s, when I was home from university at the height of the Camillagate scandal, my mother exhaled like a killer whale expelling air through its breathing hole when Camilla Parker Bowles graced the television screen.

'There's something about that Camilla Parker *Bowels* woman,' she said, shaking her head in disapproval.

I knew she was deliberately mispronouncing her surname, but I corrected her all the same.

'It's Bowles, Mum, not Bowels.'

'Who cares?' she replied. 'Turn that Camilla, Diana-hating woman off.'

In many ways I am fortunate. Sharing a name with Queen Camilla is a bit of a giggle, and there are unexpected privileges. During King Charles's coronation, for example, bars and restaurants in the UK offered free coffee and cocktails to anyone called Camilla or Charles or with the surname King. So, in the spirit of their royal nuptials, I whipped out proof of my name and gratefully accepted the offer of a double-shot Americano at my local cafe.

Thankfully, it is only Camilla that the Queen and I share. What must it be like to share both a given name and a surname with someone in the public eye?

In 2022, Shamina Begum returned to Manchester Airport from a holiday in Turkey. Like most people, she made her way to reclaim her baggage. However, unlike most people, a trip to baggage reclaim for Ms Begum resulted in her being detained by five officers and held under Schedule 7 of the Terrorism Act. And the reason? She shared a name similar to someone 'wanted', and was subjected to three hours of questioning about the origins of her name. The officers demanded to know why she was a Muslim. They asked questions about her family history and whether she thought bombing was okay. After hours of invasive questioning, Ms Begum was subsequently released once the officers were satisfied she was not *Shamima Begum,* the teenager who left the UK and travelled to Syria to join the Islamic State.

On a lighter note, what about Taylor Swift, not the pop star, but a male photographer from Seattle? Taylor has resorted to using his middle name, to differentiate himself from the singer. Or Donald Trump, a doctor and CEO of a cancer institute in Virginia. Or William Shakespeare. Unfortunately for Mr Shakespeare when the medical team who attended to him after a road accident asked for his name, and he replied, 'I'm William Shakespeare,' they presumed he was suffering the ill effects of severe confusion and concussion. He wasn't. That was his name. Or what about Kate Middleton, who lives in Cambridgeshire and not in the grounds of Windsor Castle? When I spoke to Cambridgeshire Kate, she explained that, whenever anyone comments on her name, she replies, 'Oh, but I was born first,' followed by an eye-roll or semi-wink to acknowledge her greying hair.

⋆

Reclaiming your name is a personal journey, and some people are reluctant to follow your lead. On the odd occasions my mother tries to call me Camilla it's like something lodged in her throat. She just can't quite get my name out. So how do I feel about that? For many years it annoyed the hell out of me. I grew tired of wearing those ill-fitting Mandy jeans. But now I'm a little more circumspect. *I've* reclaimed my name. If my mother can't accept that, then so be it. And in her defence, as the years have passed and I've explained my feelings around my name, she makes more of an effort. I liken her efforts to a baby learning to talk.

'Cam-ill-a,' my mother will say. 'How is the name book going?'

'It's okay,' I'll reply. 'I think I'm close to finishing. It's not just about names, Mum. It's about family and—'

She'll interrupt.

'That's good love. Keep going.'

'See, you can do it when you put your mind to it,' I'll tell her.

'Put my mind to what, love?'

'Camilla,' I'll say. 'You called me Camilla just then.'

'You'll always be Mandy to me. I can't help it.'

And I'll retaliate.

'Do you prefer Carmel or Carmen, Mum? Sometimes I don't know what to call you,' I'll reply semi-ironically.

But it's not just my mother.

Mike's father, Ken, couldn't call me Camilla either. He tried, but in his mind Camilla wasn't the person Michael brought to the family home in Lancashire for Sunday lunch in the early 90s. Where was Mandy? Mike and Mandy slipped effortlessly off the tongue. Who was this Camilla interloper? Ken tried, but it was like giving someone a standing ovation; it wasn't sustainable. So I gave up asking and he gave up trying. I was Mandy, not Camilla, to Mike's late mother, Shirley, too. How could I say, 'No, that's not me. That's not my name any more. I am Camilla,' given Shirley had dementia? In the very early stages of her diagnosis, when Shirley was beginning to show signs of confusion, Mike referred to me as Camilla, and I watched her forehead crinkle. Shirley stared at Mike and then at me. And I knew what she was thinking. She thought, who the bloody hell is Camilla? Where is Mandy? This Camilla person looks like Mandy. She looks like the person I taught how to make leek and potato soup. So, who is Camilla? Jesus Christ! Help! So, Mike and I came up with a naming plan. We agreed he should call me Mandy around his mum, and I would refer to myself as Mandy. We didn't want to confuse her any more than was necessary. My brother, Abdul, still calls me Mandy too; he doesn't even try to call me Camilla, and my interpretation of this is it is Abdul's problem, not mine, although his two children, my much-loved nephews, call me Aunty Camilla, as does Dunni's daughter, my much-loved niece.

For Dunni, it is Amanda, not Mandy, that is locked deep within her psyche. She's never referred to me as Camilla, which is why, on a recent 'siblings' family WhatsApp chat, I almost choked on my muesli when I read a message from her.

Good morning, C. Can you take Mum shopping this afternoon? If you can't, no problem.

An abbreviation of my name, yes, but a clear change. It's close. Give her a few more years, and I am hopeful she will write the remaining letters of my name.

A few years ago, I attended a funeral in Luton. Going back to Luton is a rarity, and, when I do visit, I don't usually hang around. But this trip was different. One of my mother's closest friends had passed away. She was known as 'Aunty Gloria,' and she was popular, kind and a little bit eccentric.

It was a warm day, and the church was packed. At the end of the service, I stood outside, put on my sunglasses and surveyed the group of well-dressed mourners in various shades of black. The service reflected Luton's multiculturalism and diversity. All races stood together, celebrating the life of a Jamaican-born woman who, ironically enough, was also known by two different names. I didn't realise this until I picked up the order of service, and there was Aunty Gloria, smiling from the brochure, except the name on the leaflet didn't say Gloria. It said Lynneth.

'I knew Gloria for over forty-five years,' my mother whispered over the sermon music. 'And I didn't know she was called Lynneth.'

Later, after the service, while my mother gossiped and caught up with her friends, I waved to a silver-haired woman in a pillbox hat who I recognised.

She waved back and shuffled towards me, unsteady, grasping a walking cane.

'Hello, Mandy,' she said, eyeing me up and down. 'What a way you've grown.'

'Hello, Aunty Maxine,' I replied, thinking, I hope I have grown, considering the last time you saw me I was doing wheelies on my Chopper bike.

'What a lovely send-off for our Gloria,' she said, dabbing her eyes with a tissue. 'All us Jamaican oldies are dropping like flies, Mandy. It will be my turn soon – but when the time is right, I'm ready to meet my maker.'

I told her that was a long way off because she was far too young, and she smiled at the compliment.

'Are you married?' she asked. 'Where is he? I want to say hello.'

I told her I was married, but Mike wasn't with me.

'We've been together since university,' I said, and, when I said this, I thought about how I'd managed to build and nurture a successful relationship against the odds? For a long time, because of my family history, I questioned whether that would ever be possible for me. But I did it. Mike and I did it.

'Good,' she said, smiling. 'I'm glad you found yourself a nice husband, Mandy. Men are like Monopoly. If you're lucky, you end up on Park Lane but, if you're unlucky, you end up in jail.'

I grinned.

'Oh Lord!' she said, covering her mouth with her hand. 'It's Camilla now, isn't it? Your mum told me you don't like being called Mandy. Why not?'

'It's okay,' I replied. 'It's a long story, Aunty Maxine.'

Her forehead wrinkled. She gave me an odd stare, and I was convinced she thought I was going through some kind of personal crisis, so I sought to reassure her.

'Camilla is my birth name; Mandy was a name given to me,' I explained. 'And after a long time, I reclaimed my birth name.'

'I told your mother I can't call you that name. You are Mandy. Mandy is such a pretty name. I don't know any Camillas. It's not a Luton kind of name, is it?'

We chatted some more and, when she left, I thought, you can't escape a past name easily. To her and much of the congregation, I was Mandy – Carmen's (Carmel to those in the know) youngest daughter. And I get it. Folks struggle with change. Maybe that's what happens when you reclaim or change your name late in life. But it doesn't matter. My name, my *real* name, is the final act of love and acceptance I give to myself, and no one can take that away.

Norfolk, November 2016

I told Teju I wasn't sure if I would ever be ready to talk to Sanni, and it took four months to be 'ready' to talk to him. When the time came, just before he left for Senegal, Teju was the intermediary.

We agreed I would call Sanni at a few minutes past seven on a Wednesday night which meant it was a few minutes past eight in the evening in Nigeria.

Mike is in the kitchen. I am in the living room, sitting bolt-upright on the edge of the sofa in a fleecy, black mohair polo-neck jumper.

The fire is blazing, and my heart is pumping at such a rate I worry I will collapse and not be able to speak to him. To say I am nervous is an understatement, so I am cradling a steaming mug of one of those insipid-flavoured, stress-busting promising herbal teas.

I take a sip and rehearse what I should call him in my head. I can't say 'Dad', that doesn't feel right. I can't refer to him by his given name. That's a no-no. Nigerian culture is all about respect, so the simplest option is neutrality. I will follow the same greeting I use in my letters to him. I will say, 'Hello there.'

'I'm going to call right now,' I shout to Mike.

But I don't call *right now.* I take a final gulp of tea and pull at the neck of my jumper. I am overheating in the mohair. And then, like a jack-in-the-box, I stand up, sit back down on the sofa, stand up, walk towards the window, sit back down on the sofa, and part of me wishes I could play this sit-and-stand game all night. I am afraid that I have made a rash move. I am afraid of what I will say. I am afraid of what I won't say. Biting my bottom lip, I decide not to sit on the sofa after all. I sit cross-legged on the floor, just like I did as a ten-year-old, except this time there is no MGM Judy Garland movie. This is real.

'I'm punching in the digits,' I yell to Mike, realising this sounds ridiculous. Why am I giving him a running commentary on my actions?

There is no ringtone at first, so I try again, waiting for a dialling tone, and the same thing happens. I try again, and this time I hear it ring.

'Hello,' a voice says.

It is his voice. My God, it is his voice.

'Hello,' the voice says again. 'Amanda?'

Hearing him say the name he used to call me as a child, in his elder-statesman-like voice, hits me in the gut. Perhaps that's why I tell myself not to correct him. I let Amanda slide; after all, this is our first phone call. I should cut the guy some slack.

'Yes, hi there,' I reply, swallowing.

Silence.

'How are you?' I say, fiddling with the sleeve of my jumper.

'What?'

'I said, how are you?'

'Speak up. My hearing is not so well.'

'HOW ARE YOU?'

'Oh – the usual aches and pains.'

Longer silence.

'Well – er – it's nice to hear your voice,' I say, glancing at the clock on the sideboard.

'How is your husband?'

'Mike is fine. He sends his regards.'

'When are you coming?'

'Coming where?'

'Nigeria. When are you coming to Nigeria?'

'I've no plans.'

'What?'

'I SAID I'VE NO PLANS.'

I brush my tongue along my front teeth. I am not fearful of silence. I am not intimidated by stillness, but these silences paralyse me.

'The family are looking forward to meeting you. Ifemi, all your cousins and your aunt send their best regards. When will you come?'

This wasn't in the script. Why is he talking about Nigeria again? In desperation, I change tack.

'I know you follow politics – and the political situation is pretty toxic in the UK right now,' I say.

'Please come to Nigeria. You can stay with your cousin Lolade.'

The name was familiar. When we first met in London, Teju mentioned Lolade, our high-flyer cousin, who attended a boarding school in England and then got an MBA at a prestigious American university.

'You'll come?' he asks.

I lick my lips and think, if I had children, this is the moment I would beckon them over to talk to their 'granddad'. I know how much children are esteemed and appreciated in Nigerian culture and I know, in situations like these, children are the secret 'Get out of awkward family phone calls' jail card. That's what a friend told me. She said if she ever has a tricky conversation with her mother over their Christmas plans, she calls out to the little people, and her kids dutifully trot out. She hands them the receiver and instructs the children to 'Speak nicely to your grandma' while she slopes away and pours herself a significant glass of gin.

But I don't have the buffer of babies. To Sanni now, I mention Dunni and Abdul, hoping to steer the conversation back to a safer topic.

'Abdul got promoted. He travels to the States and Europe quite often, and Dunni still works at a charity in London. I—'

'Very good. Will they come with you to Nigeria?'

'No – probably not, and I've no plans to come to Nigeria either. Going to Nigeria is a lot for me to consider. We're still getting to know one another,' I reply, failing to keep the exasperated tone out of my voice. 'So how are you doing?'

'What?'

'HOW ARE YOU DOING?'

'I told you I'm very well. How is your mother?'

I reply over a chorus of what sounds like pots and pans being banged over the telephone line.

'Hello. Hello,' I say. 'Are you still there?'

Silence.

I redial his number, but there is no ringtone.

I try again, and this time it rings. I hope this conversation will be the ONE – easy-going, less awkward, with no long silences.

'Can you hear me?'

Silence.

'Hello, are you still there? Hello?' I ask. 'Hello.'

Hours later, lying in bed, my mind in turmoil, Mike, ever the optimist, says my phone conversations with Sanni will improve.

'It's the first time you've spoken,' he says. 'Give it time.'

I grunt a response and pull the duvet cover around me tightly, and in the ink-black darkness I rehash our telephone conversation. But was it truly a conversation? Aren't you supposed to indulge in a two-way back-and-forth exchange of ideas and thoughts in a conversation? Aren't you supposed to say goodbye at the end of a phone call? Isn't goodbye a marker, a terminator to suggest an ending? And there's no getting away from it; tonight's call was awkward. What will I say if anyone asks how it went? Do I pretend it went well or do I tell the truth? Do I say talking to Sanni was similar to going to the dentist for a tooth extraction without any anaesthetic? And why the hell did I wear that fleecy mohair jumper? It will forever be a reminder of our damp squib of a phone call.

'I'm giving that mohair jumper to a charity shop,' I whisper to Mike in the darkness. 'I was never fond of it.'

A few weeks after I heard Sanni's voice for the first time in nearly four decades, Dunni 'pops' round to see me. And she can 'pop round to see me' now because, like my mother, she's made the big move to – drum roll, please – Norfolk. Not long after my mother and John moved to their bungalow 15 miles from Swaffham Dunni and her husband moved to a cottage in a slip of a village six miles from Swaffham. Only my brother is left. If he moves, that's it – Norfolk's diversity quota, courtesy of my family, is complete.

The two of us sit on high stools in the kitchen, slurping cups of tea and munching on homemade biscuits, and then I take a deep breath and tell her I spoke to Sanni.

'You what?' she replies. 'You spoke to him?'

I nod.

'This isn't about us leaping towards some sort of messy reconciliation,' I say. 'I told you we were writing letters; I suppose the natural progression was to talk to him.'

She chews her biscuit and swallows.

'Does Mum know?'

'No,' I reply. 'I will tell her, and can I do the telling, please?

I'll do it in my own time. It should come from me, not you or Abdul, okay?'

'There's no way on earth I'm telling Mum about you and Sanni,' she says, giving me a rather-you-than-me look. 'My lips are sealed.'

'When I tell her, I'll make sure I wear a bulletproof vest,' I say, smiling.

'So – er – what – er – how was he? Did you speak for long?'

'The line was terrible, and his hearing isn't great, so I spent half the call shouting at him, and to be honest, it was a bit . . .' I trail off.

'A bit what?'

'Dad was frustrating and a bit tricksy. It wasn't the easiest conversation, but I suppose it won't be easy.'

'He was always tricksy and frustrating.' She pauses. 'You called him Dad.'

'No, I didn't.'

'You did. You said *"Dad"* was frustrating.'

'Oh,' I say, hiding my embarrassment by getting up and refilling the kettle. 'He's always been Sanni in my head, but in the last few months – since we started writing – maybe he's become Dad – Bloody hell! I can't believe I said it. I feel a bit weird about saying that.'

'Why did you decide to call him?' she asks.

I don't answer straight away.

It's a question I've asked myself numerous times. How could I be in contact with someone who spent so much of my childhood letting me down?

'So,' I say, and then I hesitate because I want to find the right words. 'I didn't want to grow old consumed by anger towards him. Thinking, what if? I wanted to find out what happened between him and Mum and hear his side of the story.' I swallow. 'Whatever Sanni did, he is still my dad.' As I say this, I feel freer and lighter, like I've slipped off a backpack full of rocks. The world is full of people carrying some hurt or pain or sadness, and in this moment the burden I felt is lifted.

'Will you speak to him again?' Dunni asks.

'I will,' I say. 'I think we were both nervous. Maybe there will be fewer nerves next time.'

We sit in silence for a moment.

'Can you turn the heating up? It's freezing,' she says, buttoning up her cardigan. 'And can we change the subject? I don't want to spend the whole afternoon talking about Sanni.'

I don't either, so I mention Teju.

'It's unlike him,' I explain, getting up and switching on the dial for the heating. 'He's in Africa – Senegal, then Nigeria – but he hasn't replied to my emails or messages. I suppose he's pretty busy.'

Dunni shrugs her shoulders, and we listen to the hot-water pipe in the utility room howl like a ghoul.

'You'd like Teju,' I continue. 'He's serious, but when you get to know him he's got a crisp sense of humour – and he's incredibly knowledgeable about Nigeria, and Africa in general.'

'Oh yeah,' she says in a disinterested voice.

But I will not let Teju go.

'How about this?' I say. 'When Teju gets back from his travels, how about I invite him and his family over? I'll cook lunch, and then maybe we could go for a walk on the beach. What do you think?'

She chews her bottom lip and pushes the now-empty plate away.

'Maybe,' she says in a low tone. 'Don't get too excited. I'm not making any promises.' She pauses. 'So what's he doing in Senegal and Nigeria?'

'He's doing some sort of research,' I reply.

'I'm not making any promises,' she says again, but I detect a definite spark of curiosity.

'That's brilliant,' I tell her. 'He'll be glad to hear you want to meet him. I'll ask Abdul too, and Mum. I think she's curious about Teju. She won't admit it, but I know she is.'

'I'm not making any promises,' Dunni says again.

I nod, but in my head I imagine me, Mike, my mother, John, Abdul, Dunni, Teju, Hannah and their kids, my nephew and nieces, walking on Holkham Beach in north Norfolk – this glorious stretch of windswept coastline. I imagine us like any other extended family, our feet crunching on razor clams, shielding our eyes from the sun, dipping our toes in the sea, talking, laughing and getting to know one another.

But it never happened.

Teju didn't visit, and we didn't walk on the beach. By then, Teju was too ill.

Fourteen

Strange Phone Habits

As long as you speak my name, I shall live forever.
—African proverb

At the tail end of the 90s, I met a force of nature. Her parents were Nigerian, she was born in London and we met in South India on a yoga teacher training course.

She was called Bukky and one morning, as the sun beat down from a blue cloudless sky, we chatted over a cup of sweet-spiced chai, served in clay pots.

'I'm heading to Lagos in February to see my grandparents. Have you ever been to Nigeria?' she asked.

I shook my head. 'Because of my dad,' I said, wincing at the use of his name, but I couldn't very well refer to him as a nickname or surname, 'Nigeria isn't high up on my travel list. Or anywhere on my travel list.'

'You should go. Nigeria is fun,' she said. 'It's one crazy mass of infectious energy. But you know what?' she asked. 'Why does it get the "Oh, it's too dangerous" tag? I mean, look at New York. That's not exactly without its problems and people still visit. I wonder why Nigeria gets lumbered with the "it's too dangerous" tag?'

'And Jamaica,' I said, smiling. 'In fact, most of Africa and the Caribbean.'

'I wonder why?' she asked again.

We gave each other a silent, knowing nod. We knew exactly why.

When I think about that trip to India, I can see that Bukky planted a tiny seed about Nigeria. Although it was this alien place associated with estrangement part of me, a very small part, was keen to know more about this country. Needless to say, the other part wasn't interested. That part wanted to firmly close the door regardless of what Bukky called Nigeria's 'infectious energy'.

In the winter of January 2017, two months after our one and only stop-and-start telephone conversation, I made a mental note to relay Bukky's 90s Lagos and Jamaica 'it's too dangerous' anecdote to Sanni. I thought if I mentioned this, it might help build a rapport and create some kind of common ground. I also thought, maybe, just maybe, it might make him giggle; and, if that didn't work, my other option was to talk about the weather. I thought I'd tell him about the light dusting of snow on the front lawn and how, the previous night, I'd slipped on the ice. I was fine, no broken bones or anything like that, but it was a story. Our telephone conversations cried out for stories to tell or anecdotes to keep up the momentum. We required a new map, and a new sense of direction. Otherwise, like faulty satellite navigation, we were going nowhere.

Of course, Mike believed that 2017 would be the year of new, improved phone calls with Sanni.

I was desperate for them to improve, so this time I had a strategy – a plan. I would retell the Bukky anecdote. I would wear comfortable clothes: black trousers and a pullover. There was no fleecy mohair for me – not this time – and there was no mug of tasteless tea. Instead, I sipped a glass of warm water with a slice of lemon floating on top. And, unlike our last chat, this call was spontaneous, off-the-cuff and unplanned. Teju was in Africa. I had emailed him, but hadn't heard back, so there was no intermediary. I told myself that was fine. I figured spontaneity might create the right atmosphere for a less constrained chat.

I wasn't as nervous, but there was constant buzzing on the line again, so we both said, 'Hello, hello, can you hear me?' over and over.

'Amanda, when are you coming to Nigeria?'

'You called me Amanda. It's Camilla,' I said. 'You chose it, so why can't you call me Camilla?'

'What?'

'I'M CAMILLA.'

'When are you coming?'

'I told you. I'm not. I can't just drop everything and visit you.'

'Why not?'

'I have commitments – work, my mum, a husband – and I can't afford it.'

'How is Carmen's health?'

'Fine. Good.'

'Dunni and Abdul?'

'Brilliant.' I sighed.

Then, who knows what happened? I am reasonably robust but, boy, he pulled on those heartstrings. He told me he was getting old. He said there was so much to say, and meeting and getting to know one another would be easier if I came to Nigeria.

'My hearing isn't so good on the telephone. I want to see you in person. Come home.'

In the nicest way possible, I told him this was impossible.

'You'll enjoy Lagos very much,' he continued. 'The capital, Abuja, is quieter but very green and interesting. All the major embassies are there, and—'

'Hello,' I said. 'Are you still there?'

The line clattered, going dead. I was so fed up I am embarrassed to admit I considered not calling him back.

But I redialled the number.

'Hello, Amanda?'

I sighed like I was blowing out sixteen candles on a birthday cake.

'Will you come? I am an old man. Please come. You can stay with your cousins. They will help with your visa. Let's meet in person. I don't like the telephone. I can't hear well.'

I was so desperate to steer the conversation away from Nigeria that I considered telling a joke or asking if he was a cat or dog kind of person, or not a pet person. Where were the laughs, jokes, the serious questions?

'How's Ifemi, is she—?'

'Do you remember?' he interrupted. 'When you were a small child you used to sit on my lap and we watched *Doctor Who* together.'

I swallowed.

'You were afraid of the . . .' He paused. 'The machine men. I forget their names.'

'The Daleks,' I replied, blinking rapidly.

'I told you not to be afraid,' he said.

I had no memory of this, and then this hazy recollection rises. I remember watching television and falling against the weight of his body. My face pressed against his shoulder. In that single moment, I felt enchanted and comforted by him.

'Do you remember?' he asked again, his voice a whisper.

I sipped my now cold lemon water, and told myself to hold it together.

Don't cry. Don't you dare cry, I said to myself.

'When will you come?' he asked.

'All right,' I said, in a quiet voice.

'What?'

'Okay.'

'You'll come?'

This wasn't me hurtling towards some dewy-eyed resolution. This was a resigned acceptance that, if we wanted to move this relationship forward, this was the next logical step – a face-to-face meeting.

'Er – I – yes.'

'You'll come.'

'Mmm-hmm.'

'When?'

'April,' I spluttered without thinking. 'What do—'

'Good,' he said, and he slammed down the receiver without saying goodbye.

Half an hour later, Mike stepped through the door and shouted, 'Something smells nice.'

'I made a bean stew but was too liberal with the chillies. I think it's too hot,' I said absent-mindedly, stirring a pungent-smelling pot.

He grabbed a spoon from the cutlery drawer, spooned a mouthful of thick brown sauce, swallowed, gasped and coughed.

'Bloody hell!' he said. 'How many chillies did you use?'

'So, how was your evening?' I asked in breezy tone.

He gave me the long-term-couple glare – the one that said, 'What the hell is up with you?' The one that said, 'Come on, something is wrong, very wrong.'

'So,' I sighed, 'how do you fancy a trip to Nigeria in April?'

* * *

If you put something out in the universe, like *'I am going to Nigeria'*, you are swept up in the moment. At least I was, and, for the next few days, I was consumed by Nigeria. I reread the classics. Chinua Achebe's, *There Was A Country*, and *Things Fall Apart*. I read, *Looking For Transwonderland*, Noo Saro-Wiwa's, fiercely honest and funny account of her travels in modern-day Nigeria. I bought a book that promised I'd speak Yoruba like a local in a few weeks. And Google came into its own.

I punched in questions like:

How long does it take to get a visa?

What's the weather like in April?

Where are the best coffee shops in Abuja?

Where are the best book shops?

Are there any yoga studios in Abuja?

After an exhaustive hour of googling, I emailed Teju. By then, I'd lost count of how many emails I'd sent him, all unanswered.

In this message, I asked if he was okay and whether accessing the internet in Senegal was difficult, as I had not heard from him.

> *Teju, I have some news. I am going to Nigeria. It's tentative – nothing set in stone – but I am considering visiting in April if I get my visa. I've heard it can be an arduous process! Any advice is gratefully received. Let me know how you're doing. I'm not sure you're getting my emails.*
>
> *Best wishes,*
>
> *Camilla*

I paused before I pressed the send button. I noticed the flicker of doubt, the fluttering sensation in my stomach that maybe, just maybe, this impending caught-the-moment trip to Nigeria didn't feel right. But I ignored the doubts and hit send.

* * *

'What do we tell your mum?' Mike asked a few days after I sent the email to Teju about my trip to Nigeria.

I leaned against the kitchen door and scratched the top of my head. My mother now knew I was in telephone contact with Sanni and, surprisingly, had taken my revelation well, which was due in part to my exemplary timing.

Her favourite cooking show was on the television and she and John were swept up in the drama and the judges' comments to the competitors. Now, I wonder if she'd have reacted differently if there was no cooking show. How would she have reacted in a more focused one-on-one conversation?

Still, I took her distraction as my opportunity to tell her that Sanni and I talked on the phone 'from time to time'. She tore her eyes from the screen and, through gritted teeth, said, 'Okay, love. Well – you know what you're doing. It's your choice. You've made your bed. You have to lie in it.'

We didn't discuss him again and this suited her and me, but my going to Nigeria to visit him was a step up.

'Are you going to tell your mum you're seeing Sanni?' Mike asked once more.

'I'm going to tell her I'm going on a yoga retreat in Spain, and I'll pick up a fancy bottle of olive oil from Waitrose as a gift,' I replied.

'Is that a joke?'

'I don't like lying,' I continued, 'but I can't very well tell her I'm swanning off to Nigeria to visit Sanni. I'll explain everything when the dust settles, and she's drizzling hearty amounts of delicious Spanish olive oil over her salad. That's the plan.'

By his silence and shake of the head, I inferred he disapproved of the plan.

I didn't care. I was on a mission.

When I spoke to Sanni again on a Sunday, two weeks after

our last call, there was an energy, a vibrancy, a renewed zip to our conversation despite the torrential downpour outside. And I knew why. Going to Nigeria focused our previously lacklustre conversations.

He called me Amanda, and I laughed good-naturedly.

Over a faint and fuzzy connection, he asked about Dunni's, Mike's, Abdul's and Carmen's health, and I laughed in a cheery tone and thought, you know what, asking about people's health is just one of his interesting quirks!

But then, given that I was the one travelling to see him, I asked the question that had been floating around my head since we first contacted one another – the question I'd asked in my letters, and he'd never responded.

'Why did you never think of coming to see us?' I asked. 'You could have easily tracked us down and jumped on a plane.'

'I couldn't come.'

'Why?'

'I'm scared of flying,' he said.

'You're scared of flying,' I repeated.

'Yes,' he said. 'That's why I couldn't come. I don't like aeroplanes.'

'Fine,' I said, not laughing good-naturedly now, at his pathetic excuse.

'What's your telephone number?' he asked.

'Why do you want it?' I said, which was a stupid question. Why does anyone ask for a number? They want to call it.

He said he had a pen, so I shouted out the digits in a ridiculously loud voice because he said he couldn't hear.

'Very good,' he said after he'd finished jotting my number down.

I started to say something, and he slammed the phone down without saying goodbye, or 'it's been nice talking to you.'

I was left standing there, holding the receiver in my hand, feeling like a failure.

In February, a few days after my birthday, I finally heard back from Teju.

I read his email quickly, re-reading the first line, apologising for his long radio silence.

I am currently on sick leave. I picked up some sort of stomach bug in Senegal, and its ferocity has virtually grounded me ever since. The good news is I'm back in Oxford, and tests are being conducted at the local hospital. I hope things will begin to change soon.

I am thrilled you are going to Nigeria, Camilla. Will Mike come too? Your cousins and aunt will look after you.

Pack lightly and bring chocolates to Nigeria! Aunt Ayo is a big fan of Ferrero Rocher; they don't melt in the heat. Have you organised your visa? You haven't got much time. The visa process is notoriously taxing. When you visit the Nigerian High Commission, I recommend you take a book. A long one!

As soon as I feel stronger, I'll be in contact again.

Warm Regards to Mike

Teju.

I emailed straight back.

Hello Teju,

It's good to hear from you! I've been worried. I'm so sorry you've been unwell. Let me know if I can help in any way.

I've not got very far with Nigeria, I'm afraid. To be honest, Teju, I'm a little nervous. Sometimes, I wonder if I've been a bit hasty.

Let me know how you are doing. If you feel up to it, I can come and visit you in Oxford.

All best wishes,

PS: I have a quick question! Sanni has a habit of not saying goodbye at the end of our calls. Is this a Nigerian thing? I just wondered.

Camilla

Days passed, and Teju didn't reply to my email.

A week later, after I taught a frankly unfocused yoga class, I sloped downstairs and joined Mike on the sofa.

'What's wrong?' he asked, shifting to one side to accommodate me.

That was a tricky question to answer. I was worried about Teju, but there was something else – a feeling, a realisation. My Nigeria visit was stuck in quicksand because, the truth was, I was conflicted. Going to Nigeria would be like a declaration of peace, and I wasn't sure I wanted to sign the declaration.

'When you speak to your dad, do you sometimes feel a bit deflated?' I asked Mike.

'What do you mean?'

'Do you come off the phone feeling a bit frustrated with him?'

'God, yes,' he said. 'Sometimes my dad annoys the hell out of me. But that's families for you. They're not perfect. No one is perfect,' he said, pausing. 'Present company excluded, of course.'

'But you don't come off the phone feeling empty,' I said.

'No.'

'Well, I do,' I replied. 'And that doesn't feel right.'

The next day, after a night spent tossing this way and that, I called Sanni's number a little after seven in the evening. But I couldn't get through, so I tried 30 minutes or so later, and he picked up.

'Amanda?'

'Yes, it's me,' I said, not bothering to correct him.

He asked after everyone's health.

I told him everyone was well and fine, but I didn't mention Teju's stomach bug; something told me not to.

'Hâve you obtained your visa?' he asked.

'Well – no – not yet.'

'Why not?'

I paused, and then, in a flurry of sentences, I explained the time wasn't right. I couldn't go in April after all.

'I'm sorry. I hope to come soon,' I said.

'Oh,' he replied, in a barely audible voice.

'I will come at some point,' I said 'I may—'

Sanni slammed down the phone, and I held the receiver in my hand, thinking about what I'd said. A tremendous wave of guilt washed over me, and I didn't feel clean and fresh. I was covered in disappointment. I thought about what Mike said: no family was perfect, so guess what? I redialled Sanni's number.

'Perhaps I can come at the end of the year,' I said quickly, in case I changed my mind.

'You'll come.'

'Yes,' I said, finally. 'I'll come in November.'

'You'll come in November?' he repeated. 'But that's too far away.'

'I'll come in *November*,' I said again.

He made a grunting sound and the receiver clattered down. I stood there like a fragile glass ornament on a shelf. If dropped, I would fall into pieces.

A couple of days later, the landline rang. It was a Sunday, a few minutes after three, and we were heading out to friends for a late lunch I was upstairs, rooting through my cupboard for a scarf. Spring was establishing itself, but despite the shoots of new-season beauty there was a chill in the air.

Mike was in the living room, and he shouted, 'I'll get it.'

Once I retrieved my scarf, I ran downstairs. I heard Mike in the living room and detected a hint of a 'polite telephone voice'.

'Yes,' he said. 'It's – er, been nice talking to you, too.'

'Who is it?' I mouthed, standing at the door.

'Here's Camilla,' he said, quickly handing me the receiver.

'Who is it?'

'Sanni,' he mouthed back.

I took the receiver from his hand, and we spoke for a few stilted minutes about how my trip to Nigeria was progressing.

Once we finished, I placed the receiver back in its cradle, and sat on the sofa, scarf in one hand, staring into the distance.

Mike sat next to me.

'Well – you spoke to Sanni,' I said. 'What did you chat about?'

'Football,' he replied.

'Football?' I said. 'But you're not massively into football.'

'I know.' He sighed. 'To tell you the truth, it was a bit awkward at first – and then he randomly mentioned sport. He started talking about the Nigerian football team.'

'Really?'

'Yeah, I think he said they were called the Super Eagles – and the conversation flowed for a bit – then you came down.'

I swallowed and wondered, if I were a man, would it be easier to talk to Sanni? Nigeria is an extremely patriarchal society. Perhaps if Abdul were calling him, and not me, they'd chat away for hours. Maybe they'd discuss next year's World Cup, or they'd talk about my brother's children, and there'd be no awkward pauses. At the end of their phone conversation, Sanni would say goodbye and Abdul would say goodbye and my brother would put down the phone feeling elated, not flat.

'At least I've spoken to him,' Mike said.

'Yeah,' I said quietly. 'At least you've spoken,' and I gave him a sad stare.

Over the next few weeks, I did not contact Sanni, and he did not call me. Perhaps we both required a period of silence – time out. I wanted more. But more of what? And each time I spoke to Sanni, Teju wasn't far from my thoughts. I was concerned about him.

Needless to say, when Teju did finally call, I was so excited to hear his voice that I said, 'I've missed you,' which wasn't our usual greeting. We were not demonstrative like that, but it was the jolt of affection I felt hearing his voice after so long.

'Are you still calling Uncle Rimi?' he asked.

I told him I was, and the last time we spoke, I'd agreed to go to Nigeria at the end of the year, not April as I'd initially planned.

'I'll call him again in a couple of weeks – we're still finding our way.' I paused. 'Are you all right? Are you over your stomach bug? Are you feeling any better? I've been worried about you.'

There was a sharp intake of breath, then he replied but his words didn't immediately register. Teju didn't use battle metaphors. He didn't talk of defeating the late-stage tumour in his stomach. He said he was hopeful, and asked if, once he felt stronger, I would visit him in Oxford.

'I'll make sure there's bags of coffee for you,' he joked, trying to remain upbeat.

I tried to sound optimistic too but, when I placed the receiver on my lap at the end of the call, the tears fell.

Fifteen

Named

Nomen est omen – name is destiny.

—Unknown

'Did you bring the banana skins?' my mother asked. 'The roses love them. It's the potassium.'

It was a Saturday, a few weeks after I'd spoken to Teju, two days since I last spoke to Sanni, and I was at my mother's bungalow, standing at the conservatory window, gazing into her back garden. It was early March, and her garden was on the cusp of breaking free of the shackles of a particularly harsh winter.

'The bananas are in my bag. I'll get them later,' I said, thinking about Teju, and the last brief conversation I'd had with Sanni. There was a constant rattle on the line. He couldn't hear me, and I struggled to hear him. Despite this, we soldiered on. We talked about my trip in November. He said my cousins hoped to take me to Wuse market. I had read about this market, located in the heart of Abuja. It sounded fun. I told him I looked forward to going. He couldn't hear, so in a louder voice, I said, 'I would love to visit!' He replied 'very good,' and the phone crashed down.

'I'm going to grow red peas over there,' my mother said now, pointing to a corner plot next to a fig tree.

'Mmm-hmm,' I replied, not fully listening.

'How is Teju?' she asked.

I realised she was making an effort. She was trying.

'He's okay . . .' I trailed off, still unable to explain Teju's terminal diagnosis without completely losing it.

'When you speak to him, give him our regards,' she said.

I told her I would pass on her good wishes. I uttered the same words to Dunni too. She called and said, 'Pass on our regards to Teju.' When Abdul called, he said the same thing, but he went further than Dunni. He asked for Teju's address.

'I'm going to visit him in Oxford,' he said. 'I'll take the boys.'

'Teju would like that,' I replied and, although I didn't say it, I liked it too. It was Teju's illness that promoted change, but I was glad my brother was finally meeting his cousin.

'John!' my mother yelled. 'It's back,' she said, turning to him, sitting in his chair. 'The pigeon I told you about. It's not normal. We didn't have pigeons that big in Luton. Why are they so big in Norfolk?'

I smiled and watched the engorged bird shuffle over the shingled path until it flew off, settled onto their shed roof and stared defiantly towards us.

My mother banged the conservatory window.

'Shoo, go away, you big brute,' she yelled.

'Mum,' I said, walking towards one of her wicker chairs. 'How did you feel when you met your mum in Panama?'

She paused for a moment, searching her head for the memory.

'I'd just turned 50. My goodness, where does the time go?' she said, fluffing a scatter cushion and sitting next to me, while simultaneously craning her neck to check the pigeon had flown off. It hadn't. It was still there, its head bobbing around her pear tree.

I remembered when she returned from her reunion, having travelled to Panama to meet the woman who left her in Jamaica as a baby, my mother was energised. She had pressed a photograph into my hand of a smiling, seventy-something, sparkly-eyed woman and said, 'This is your grandmother.' I spoke to my grandmother on the telephone myself a handful of times. She apologised for her English and said warmly, 'You must learn Spanish, Camilla.' We chatted about this and that and, at the back of my mind, I wondered what life would have been like if I'd *really* known my grandmother and I'd visited her in Panama. What kind of relationship would we have had? And what kind of relationship would my mother have had with her? But it didn't last. The calls between my mother and her mother gradually petered out, their relationship reverting to how it had always been – an unfinished sentence.

'How did I feel?' My mother repeated my question. 'There was no bond, love,' she replied. 'Too much had happened between us, but I was glad I had met her.'

'Why?'

'If I hadn't met my mother again, I would still be bitter towards her,' she said. 'And for a long time I carried a lot of anger towards her. I was an angry woman.'

'You certainly were, Carmen,' John quipped.

'But I had to let it go,' she continued.

Looking back, this was an opportune moment to tell her I intended to visit Sanni in Nigeria at the end of the year. But I didn't. It didn't feel right. I hadn't worked out what I would say to her. One day, I would, but I sensed my mother was lost in her own thoughts about her mother. And there was that gigantic pigeon in the back garden. There would be other moments. I would tell her all about Sanni and my tentative plans to visit Nigeria in November, but not now, not yet.

Two months later, at the beginning of May, on a rainy Monday evening, I was at home, teaching a yoga class to an enthusiastic, keen-to-learn, smiley bunch of students – who laughed at my cheesy jokes and asked for extra yoga 'homework' at the end of the session.

After the class, I went downstairs, messaged Mike at his acupuncture clinic and flicked through my notebook.

I was working on an untitled short story, set in Tokyo, and I'd scribbled a few ideas here and there. I thought it had 'something', but I wasn't entirely sure what. That's the thing with any creative endeavour. You have to accept that there are mazes of nuances to be uncovered. So, when my phone rang, I almost didn't pick it up. I was preoccupied with my story, figuring out if magic might emerge from the words.

I glanced at my phone, and Teju's name flashed up on my screen.

I picked up.

Teju said my name, but his voice was weak, ravaged by months of gruelling chemotherapy and radiotherapy, and then he paused.

'Camilla, I'm so sorry, but your father's had a stroke,' he said. 'He's in hospital but don't worry.'

'Is he okay?' I asked, my mind racing. 'I spoke to him last week, the line wasn't great so we didn't talk for long, but he didn't sound unwell. He was – Oh God – Teju. Will he be okay?'

'Don't worry,' he said again. 'He's in very good hands at the hospital. I'll call again once I know more.'

We said goodbye, but I couldn't settle. I called Abdul and Dunni, but their phones went to voicemail, so I left the same breathless message on each of their phones.

'Sanni's had a stroke,' I said. 'We're waiting for more news. I'll call once I know more.'

An hour later, my phone rang.

It was Teju.

As soon as he uttered my name, there was no need to say anything more. I knew my father was dead.

*

Growing up, I used to worry about my mother dying. I suppose all children do but, when I was very young, I went through a stage of hoping I would die before her. Or that she would live to be a hundred or two hundred. Or that we would die at precisely the same time. That way, no one would be sad. Back then, I rarely considered Sanni dying. He was so far away I had no concept of whether this person, who was barely more than a series of nicknames, pronouns or a surname, was dead or alive.

In the haze after my father's death, I spoke to Teju, and he explained what happens when someone of the Muslim faith passes away. I googled the nearest mosque to Swaffham. It was in Norwich, some thirty-five minutes' drive away, but it wasn't far enough away. I wanted a longer distance - time to process my thoughts. There was another mosque in Cambridge. The city was an hour's drive from Swaffham or longer, given it was a Friday. Mike asked to come with me, but I said no. It was a challenging journey I needed to make alone.

On that Friday, five days after my father's passing, I drove to Cambridge. For distraction, I switched on the car radio and the presenter and her guests laughed at some throwaway comment. I thought how can you laugh? I turned it off, thinking of my father. Our stop-start conversations, our stop-start letters, the wasted years and the wasted opportunities.

I stopped the car multiple times.

I cried on the hard shoulder of the A11. I cried in the petrol-station toilets until someone knocked on the door, asked if I was all right and then apologised.

'I'm sorry to ask,' the person outside the door said, 'but will you be long? I'm desperate for the loo.'

I cried in the car park on the corner of Mill Road, a few metres from the mosque.

I cried so hard I thought I would never stop.

The entrance door to the mosque, on the corner of Mill Road, was open, but the building was eerily quiet, except for a young man, who asked if I was okay.

'Can I help? Prayers have ended,' he said.

I explained that this was my first time in a mosque and I wasn't sure of the etiquette.

'I'm – here—' I stuttered and started again. 'My father passed away on Monday – and I wondered if you'd mention his name at your next prayers. My cousin said this was something you might do—'

He said he was sorry for my loss.

I thanked him and told him we had been estranged for a long time.

'He lived in Nigeria,' I said. 'I was supposed to go out and see him, but I changed my mind and now it's too late—'

Talking about my father was like an out-of-body experience. I can't recall what else I said to this kind, unfalteringly calm and considerate young man.

'What was your father's name?' he asked in a gentle voice.

I handed him a carefully folded piece of paper.

He opened it and silently read my father's name.

Abdul Raheem Sanni.

Nigeria, July 2017

Grief travels by air, sea, foot, bike or plane, and names travel too.

Here I am, bleary-eyed, weathered by a long flight navigating this new kind of grief. I am grieving for a father I came to know but who remained strangely unknowable. Our relationship was chaotic and complex, and the grief I feel is chaotic and complex.

Mike is with me and, as we wheel our lightly packed suitcases towards the arrivals gate, although I am tired, it feels like the whole world is opening up. I can't help myself. I stare at the people shuffling past, wheeling much larger suitcases, talking, laughing, living in the hustle and bustle. And there is bustle. The airport feels like someone has turned up the brightness on the television. Everything is enhanced to its maximum potential. I steer my suitcase behind me, trying not to bump into anyone. Trying to find the space in my head for all these people in the airport who look like me. I watch a young family ahead of us. We were on the same flight and the two boys grip their parents' hands, complaining of the noise and the heat. I wonder if, like me, this is their first trip to Nigeria. Are their stomachs churning like mine? Are they in Nigeria for a life and a death? For an instant, the circumstances of my own trip hit me again. I imagine what it would be like if my father were at the gate waiting for me. But he's not. I will not meet my father. It's too late. Perhaps it was always going to be too late.

'Are you all right?' Mike asks, wiping a bead of sweat from his face.

'I'm thinking about my father,' I say, which sounds morbid, but I don't feel sad or melancholy. In this moment, I am energised by the possibilities of life here in Nigeria for a week, to meet a family I don't know, where I will talk about a father I didn't know. And I *will* talk about my father. Teju said there will be a memorial service for a hundred or so guests. In two days' time, on a sticky and humid Wednesday morning, I will stand up and survey the assembled faces who are waiting to listen to me speak about the man known affectionately as 'Uncle Rimi'. I will look out at those faces and adjust the fabric of my blue and white head wrap. It will be the first time I have worn a traditional Nigerian gele. I do not know how to tie a head wrap. I am all fingers and thumbs, until my cousin comes to the rescue and helps me. Then, in a quivering voice, as the early morning sun beats down, I will say I made peace with my father, and then I will stop, overcome by a crashing wave of emotion. Voices in the audience begin to mumble. One of my cousins will stand up and prepare to step in. But I will not crumble. I shall continue. Louder now, I will say I made the decision to come to Nigeria now because I couldn't wait. The need was too strong. I will say my father was a complicated man. A flawed man. A man I have few memories of, but the scant memories I have of him, both good and bad, I will hold on to. As I say this, the decades-long knot I have carried deep within my pelvis will loosen its grip. Later, one of my father's friends, a regal-looking man in a trilby hat and glasses, will introduce himself. In a kind voice, he tells me how much I look like my father.

'You are your father's daughter,' he says, smiling. 'You have his ears and eyes.'

'Madam,' a man on the arrival concourse shouts now. 'You want some help, Miss?'

I shake my head, and reply, 'no,' and then I think perhaps I resemble some sort of furrowed-browed tourist, who is out of her depth. Lost in the confident swashbuckling swagger of this place called Nigeria.

And yet, I don't feel out of my depth. In a strange way I feel like I belong.

'Didn't Teju say someone would be here to meet us?' Mike

asks, his eyes, like mine, scanning the sea of expectant faces on the concourse.

'One of my cousins' drivers,' I reply, my eyes squinting into the distance.

'Sir, sir, taxi,' a man in the crowd yells to Mike. 'Come. I have a very nice taxi. Miss. Miss.'

I smile politely, my eyes darting this way and that, but all I can see are hordes of people, some clutching name placards, others simply watching and waiting.

Then I see him – an older man in a khaki shirt, well-ironed trousers and polished black shoes, holding a handwritten sign with my name spelt out in black capitals.

He waves the placard in the air, his head bobbing, his eyes searching for me.

CAMILLA ADEBISI

The man holding the placard catches my gaze. His eyes narrow as if to ask. Is it you? Are you this person? Are you this woman? Are you this story of a name?

I am.

Afterword

When I came back from Nigeria, I spent a lot of time on my own. I wasn't avoiding other people as such, I needed time to process the enormity of my trip. Frankly, my head was in a mess. Although I was flooded with kindness and an incredible amount of love in Nigeria, I returned to Norfolk with more questions than answers. Everyone spoke fondly of 'good old Uncle Rimi', but I came back with no clear sense of who this man really was. As my grief ebbed away, it was replaced by a quiet acceptance. I knew him briefly, and I must accept that. Now I was home, I faced new challenges. I was worried about the ramifications of going to Nigeria in the first place. I was unsure how I should discuss this extraordinary country or, indeed, how I should talk about my father, with my mother. I agonised about her feelings. Did my mother think she was now surplus to requirements? I wasn't sure if I should share the photos I'd taken. Like an over-enthusiastic tour guide, I had taken snap after snap of my grinning cousins at Aunt Ayo's sprawling house in Abuja. If I shared these photographs with my mother what would she think? Some part of me felt uncomfortable sharing my experiences. If she asked about Nigeria, what would I say? Should I be honest and admit that

I missed Nigeria's energy and confidence. I missed the feeling of walking into a packed cinema with my cousins and experiencing my first, and certainly not my last, Nollywood movie. Or that I missed talking and learning about aspects of my heritage and culture. Should I be honest and tell my mother that my cousins were already planning my next trip to Nigeria. No, I couldn't. Those first few days I wasn't ready to be honest.

So I retreated.

I didn't immediately call my mother. Instead, I messaged her, explaining my fatigue and jet-lag. Minutes later, a message pinged through from her telling me to 'rest up, love', accompanied by a heart emoji.

I took my mother's advice. I did rest up. I read, or I walked in the woods with Mike. And we walked and walked. It was good to walk. I did very little walking in Abuja. Mostly, I sat in the back seat of an air-conditioned car, staring out the window at the city's have and have-nots, the wide tree-lined avenues, pristine highways and hawkers weaving through the traffic.

But now, as Mike and I walked along a path of overgrown ferns, I talked about the whirlwind that was Nigeria. I talked about my father. I talked and talked. Mike didn't respond; he just listened. And then we walked in silence. I relished not speaking. Lost in my own thoughts. I thought about Teju. The person who was so instrumental to me, who in a few months will be taken from us, leaving a gaping hole in my life and this story.

I've carried this book within me for a long time. It hasn't been easy. There have been many sleepless nights wondering whether or not I was doing the right thing. But the conversations running around my head about our names, family, where we are from, and the stories we must tell were too loud to ignore. There comes a moment in life when you have to tell your story.

And I was ready to tell mine.

Three days after I returned from Nigeria, one fine summer afternoon, I finally called my mother on her landline.

She was slightly out of breath when she picked up.

'I was watering the garden, love,' she said. 'How was your trip?'

I leaned against the kitchen counter, wondering how best to answer this question.

'Well,' I replied, choosing my words carefully. 'I came across lots of names,' I said. I explained to her that I wrote down all of the names I came across in Nigeria in my notebook. She probably thought I was a bit daft, but then, like now, I continued to be obsessed with names. I am still the kind of person you meet at a party who introduces themselves and morphs into an archaeologist. I dig around. I want to know if the person I am talking to likes their name. I want to know who chose their name. I want to know if they secretly wished they had another name. By the time I'm finished with my name interrogation, the person I am talking to scarpers. Named out, exhausted by my machine gun questioning.

'Two of my cousins organised a spa day,' I said to my mother now, remembering how my cousins told me I needed a day for myself after the emotion of my dad's memorial.

My mother said that was kind of them.

'What was the food like, love?' she asked.

I detected the hesitation in her voice, the sense she was trying, really trying to be generous and curious.

'It's spicy,' I said. 'But delicious just like Caribbean food.'

She laughed, and I was struck by how hopeful she sounded. I was hopeful, too, but I was also a realist. This wasn't some sugar-coated rom-com. There was a long road ahead. I needed to figure out where I would go from here, and, strangely, she did, too.

'I've got a present for you,' I said.

'A present?'

'Well, it was a surprise, but I know you don't like surprises.'

'What is it, love?'

I told her about the morning I had spent in the teeming Wuse market. I watched as two of my cousins haggled good-naturedly with market stall holders, my stomach rumbling from the aroma of delicious-smelling food wafting through the air.

'I've brought you a kaftan and some bits and bobs for the house,' I said.

'Is it a cotton kaftan?' she asked. 'A Nigerian lady at church told me Nigerian cotton was the best. Is that true?'

'Yes,' I replied, smiling. 'It's the best.'

She thanked me again.

'See you later, with my not a surprise,' she said. 'I'll put the kettle on.'

'Lovely,' I replied.

The word goodbye lingered on my lips, and then I remembered something Teju, this remarkable man I was proud to call my cousin, had told me before my father died. I had asked him why my father never said goodbye at the end of our phone calls, and Teju said, 'Maybe your dad had said everything he needed to say.'

Thinking about this now, I knew my father hadn't said everything he wanted to say, and neither had I.

'Well, see you later, Camilla,' my mother said again.

'See you later, Carmel,' I said with a wry smile, and then I paused, thinking of my father now. 'Goodbye,' I whispered.

And we hung up.

References

Chapter One: Mandy, Mandi, Mandeee

A large and remarkably fine: [accessed 13 March 2023] https://www.the-saleroom.com/en-gb/auction-catalogues/bloomsbury/catalogue-id-blooms1-10012/lot-f02e4f01-05c4-40cd-89ed-abca00f75eb6

29,086 measures barley 37 months Kushim: [accessed 13 March 2023] https://www.nationalgeographic.com/science/article/whos-the-first-person-in-history-whose-name-we-know

A total of 29,086 measures of barley: Yuval Noah Harari, *Sapiens: A Brief History of Humankind* (London: Vintage Books, 2011) p. 139.

Chapter Two: All Change, Please

I often ask my clients about their names: Jeremy Schultz interviewed by telephone 8 March 2024.

Craig Moore to Bowser I-Just-Wanna-Drift Moore: [accessed 3 April 2023], https://www.bbc.co.uk/sounds/play/p04vc5bx

In 2024 Dustin Ebey became Literally Anybody Else: *Guardian*, 25 March 2024.

According to Deed Poll UK, most people change their names: [accessed 4 April 2023] https://www.deedpoll.org.uk/why-do-people-change-their-name

I never liked the name, and I couldn't think of anyone I liked or who was successful who was called Gideon: Andy Beckett, The real George Osborne, *Guardian*, 28 November 2011.

Before she became widely known as Chimamanda Ngozi Adichie: [accessed 4 December 2024] https://bagusng.com/2021/01/02/i-invented-it-chimamanda-ngozi-adichie-and-the-story-behind-her-name

I knew that my ex-husband would try any means, legitimate or otherwise, to find me, so I changed my name: Mary interviewed by email 20 October 2023.

My husband and I felt strongly about this: Tracy interviewed by email 3 October 2023.

But there are many, many more changes of male names than of women in the Scriptures: The Reverend Alice Goodman interviewed by email 9 February 2024.

Choosing a name is often one of the first ways trans people: Online Symposium, Finding Joy in a Name, Trans Youth Experiences of Names and Naming Practices, Julia Sinclair-Palm, 29 September 2022.

My name is just a few letters different from my birth name: Jai interviewed by telephone 27 September 2023.

When you are trans, you can write your own story: Sophie interviewed by email, 23 October 2023.

Emma was perceived as warm and competent [accessed 16 May 2022] https://www.newscientist.com/article/2169622-how-your-name-shapes-what-other-people-think-of-your-personality

2016, when the dating app Tinder released its list of the most popular: [accessed 23 August 2024] https://www.elle.com/uk/life-and-culture/culture/news/a33092/tinder-most-popular-names-tinder

From around the age of 11, or thereabouts, I really started to dislike my name: Queenie-May interviewed by email 7 October 2024.

In my father's paradigm, changing my name was against everything he stood for: Kebbah interviewed by telephone and email, 4 December 2023.

Dion discovered people who liked their first names also liked themselves more generally: Kenneth L. Dion, Names, Identity, and Self, *A Journal of Onomastics*, Vol 31, No 4 (1983).

Sixty-three per cent of the respondents explicitly referenced their names when indicating who they were: Kenneth L. Dion, Names, Identity, and Self, *A Journal of Onomastics*, Vol 31, No 4 (1983).

The most momentous thing to have happened in Swaffham: Harry Cole, James Heale, *Out of the Blue: The Inside Story of the Unexpected Rise and Rapid Fall of Liz Truss.* (London: Harper Collins, 2022) p. 65.

Chapter Three: Miss Abara

The most important anchorage to our self-identity throughout life remains our own name: [accessed 3 January 2022] https://www.bbc.com/future/article/20210525-how-your-name-affects-your-personality

Students were asked to address their parents in an unconventional (for them) manner: Paul L. Leslie and James K. Skipper, Jr, Towards a Theory of Nicknames: A Case for Socio-Onomastics, *The Journal of American Onomastics*, Vol 38, No 4 (December 1990) p. 274.

By then, most names were from Normandy. Names like Hugh, Robert, and for women Matilda and Rosamund: [accessed 3 February 2022] https://www.historyextra.com/period/norman/baby-names-popular-royal-history

By the 1530s, after Henry VIII broke away from the Roman Catholic Church: [accessed 3 February 2022] https://www.historyextra.com/period/norman/baby-names-popular-royal-history

In 2014, Mohammed was the most common name for men in Norway's capital city, Oslo [accessed 3 June 2022] https://www.bbc.co.uk/news/blogs-news-from-elsewhere-28982803

In the UK, from 2016 to 2021, Muhammad was the number-one name for baby boys [accessed 20 February 2023] https://www.newarab.com/news/muhammad-uks-favourite-boy-name-second-year-row#:~:text=From 2016 to 2021 Muhammad,the title again in 2023.

On a recent overseas trip, the Labour MP, Mohammad Yasin, was stopped from boarding a flight to Canada: MP stopped boarding a flight, his name was Mohammad *Guardian*, 23 October 2023.

I didn't know in Nigerian culture your name was unique to you: Dr Ayokunmi Ojebode interviewed by email 30 July 2024.

In a 2022 YouGov poll, 30 per cent of American parents admitted they chose a given name because they like the sound: [accessed 8 May 2023] https://today.yougov.com/society/articles/44077-where-american-first-middle-names-come-from-yougov

Chapter Four: Made in Luton

Choosing a name is an early, crucial parenting behaviour: Jean M. Twenge, Lauren Dawson, W. Keith Campbell, Still standing out: children's names in the United States during the Great Depression and correlations with economic indicators, *Journal of Applied Social Psychology* (2016).

It's a shared practice … A baby's birth is a recognition of someone coming into the community: Dr Ebunlomo Walker interviewed on Zoom 3 May 2024.

Language and speech therapists think most babies begin to recognise the pattern of sounds: [accessed 3 May 2023] https://www.bbc.co.uk/tiny-happy-people/articles/zb4t7yc

A name is in accordance with the belief that a baby who is not named within seven to nine days: [accessed 8 September 2022] https://locallearningnetwork.org/wp-content/uploads/2021/08/yoruba.pdf

In his statement the judge said the name made a fool of the child: [accessed 1 May 2022] https://www.theguardian.com/lifeandstyle/2008/jul/24/familyandrelationships.newzealand

The 'unusual name' had 'unfortunately slipped through': Jordyn Beazley, Australian journalist calls her baby 'Methamphetamine Rules' as a test of naming regulations, *Guardian*, 19 September 2023.

Parents who give their kids weird names are weird themselves: Justin Kaplan, Anne Bernays, *The Language of Names* (USA: Simon & Schuster, 1997) p. 125.

In a recent survey of 2,000 grandparents in Australia: [accessed 2 November 2023] https://www.goodhousekeeping.com/life/parenting/a31213216/grandparents-hate-millennial-baby-names

In the sixteenth century, virtue names like Grace, Faith, Hope and Charity: [accessed 3 June 2022] https://www.historyextra.com/period/norman/baby-names-popular-royal-history

Daisy, Hazel, Holly and Ivy were popular girls' names in the nineteenth century: Leslie Alan Dunkling, *First Names First,* (London: J. M. Dent & Sons Ltd, 1977) p. 116.

Irrespective of gender, the older twin is always called Taiwo: [accessed 17 June 2022] https://www.reuters.com/article/idUSKCN1RL1A8

Renault Clio was called Nicole, and this sparked a baby name boom: *The Sunday Times*, Style Magazine, 10 July 2022, p. 39.

Father from Uttar Pradesh named his newborn son Sanitiser: [accessed 2 March 2022] https://indianexpress.com/article/india/lockdown-corona-covid-sanitiser-baby-name-6428445

I picked Richard supposedly after St Richard of Chichester: Patricia interviewed by email 16 February 2023.

So, Philip became Philippa, Nicolas, Nicola, and Alexander became Alexandra: [accessed 3 June 2022] https://www.historyextra.com/period/norman/baby-names-popular-royal-history

The biggest change we've seen in the past decade is the rise of gender-neutral names: Pamela Redmond interviewed by email 18 July 2022

Names that reflect this gender neutrality will become more and more appealing: Pamela Redmond interviewed by email 18 July 2022.

Chapter Five: Carlton Long

The word 'nickname' originates from the Old English *ekename*, meaning an additional (or supplementary) name: Justin Kaplan, Anne Bernays, *The Language of Names*, (USA: Simon & Schuster, 1997) p.114.

Many Filipinos go by nicknames like 'Baby,' commonly given to the youngest child in a family: [accessed 5 May 2023] https://www.cbc.ca/news/canada/british-columbia/filipino-names-and-nicknames-1.6074647

In Nigerian Yoruba culture it is taboo for a new bride: Dr Ayokunmi Ojebode, Professor Idowu Ojebode, *Titbits on Onomastics Among The Yoruba Africans* (2019).

'*I like Ike*,' based on the nickname of Dwight Eisenhower, was one of the most memorable: [accessed 5 May 2023] https://americanhistory.si.edu/collections/nmah_529457

Chapter Six: Sorry, Can You Spell That for Me?

We've found a lot of people feeling embarrassed – ashamed of their name: [accessed 14 June 2023] https://www.kuow.org/stories/a-rose-by-any-other-name-would-not-be-me

From 1982 to 1986, St George's Medical School in London was so inundated for applications: BBC Radio 4, *The Artificial Human*, Can AI get me a new job? 3 July 2024.

Potential employers were attracted to names that rolled off the tongue. They used the term 'name fluency': [accessed 3 May 2023] https://people.hamilton.edu/documents/Name Pronunciation 2 February 2022.pdf

Yoruba is a tonal language: Dr Ayokunmi Ojebode interviewed face-to-face 5 July 2023.

The survey found 71 per cent of Chinese-speaking students who used English names: Simon Cotterill, Call me Fei: Chinese-speaking students' decision whether or not to use English names in classroom interaction, *Language, Culture and Curriculum* (Routledge Taylor & Francis Group, 2019) p. 6.

On the campaign trail for the 2024 presidency against Harris, Trump said he 'couldn't care less' if he mispronounces her name: https://www.independent.co.uk/news/world/americas/us-politics/donald-trump-kamala-harris-name-b2587260.html

In a 2022 Diwali celebration at the White House: [accessed 21 October 2022] https://www.independent.co.uk/news/uk/politics/uk-prime-minister-rishi-sunak-biden-truss-b2210241.html

Chapter Seven: Not a Camilla

They wanted to find out whether a name matched someone's face: Yonat Zwebner, Nir Rosenfeld, Anne Laure-Sellier, Jacob Goldenberg, We Look Like Our Names: The Manifestation of Name Stereotypes in Facial Appearance, *Journal of Personality and Psychology*, 2017.

Blacks in the US were allowed the dignity of a surname, and many chose the surname of the first US president: The surname Washington [accessed 12 December 2022] https://www.nbcnews.com/id/wbna41704238

However, that pattern changed dramatically as most Blacks.... adopted increasingly distinctive names: Hewan Girma, Black Names, Immigrant Names: Navigating Race and Ethnicity Through Personal Names, *Journal of Black Studies*, 2020, Vol 5, p. 19.

Some given names (such as Shanice and Precious) were found to be relatively popular among Blacks for girls: Jane Pilcher, Names and "Doing Gender": How Forenames and Surnames Contribute to Gender Identities, Difference, and Inequalities, *Feminist Forum Review Article*, 2017.

In the landmark 2004 study, 'Are Emily and Greg More Employable than Lakisha and Jamal?': https://www.nber.org/digest/sep03/employers-replies-racial-names

Whereas names that sounded Asian, Middle Eastern or African had the fewest: https://d.newswise.com/articles/study-examines-job-recruitment-racial-discrimination-in-europe

In 2017, social scientists at Bristol University sent out two identical CVs: [accessed 2 February 2023] https://www.bbc.co.uk/news/uk-england-london-38751307

Let's take the surname Iqbal: BBC Radio 4, What's In A Name?, 24 June 2017.

The British-Asian comedian Romesh Ranganathan's: *The Sunday Times* magazine, interview with Romesh Ranganathan, 24 December 2022.

Résumé whitening is the practice of removing or downplaying cues that may reveal a candidate's: Dr Sonia Kang interviewed by email 11 September 2023.

Kang interviewed 59 Asian and African-American candidates between the ages of 18 and 25: Sonia K. Kang, Katherine A. DeCelles, Andras Tilcsik and Sora Jun, Whitened Resumes: Race and Self-Presentation in the Labor Market, Cornell University, *Science Quarterly*, 2016, Vol 61.

Imagine my kid in kindergarten having to explain his name and other kids making fun of him: Hewan Girma, Black Names, Immigrant Names: Navigating Race and Ethnicity Through Personal Names, *Journal of Black Studies*, 2020, Vol 5, p. 19.

The results found recruiters were more likely to hire Simon over Susan: [accessed 3 June 2023] https://fortune.com/2016/06/08/name-bias-in-hiring

Room seekers with the Muslim name Mohammed were less likely to receive a positive: [accessed 27 June 2023] https://www.theguardian.com/uk-news/2018/dec/03/flatshare-bias-room-seekers-with-muslim-name-get-fewer-replies

I'm not White. I'm Black, and so I would like a name that is given to Black people: Mary Lassiter, *Our Names Ourselves* (London: Heinemann Ltd, 1983) p. 62.

Chapter Eight: Big in Japan

18-year-old high school student from Yamanashi prefecture: [accessed 2 December 2024] https://mainichi.jp/english/articles/20190411/p2a/00m/0na/012000c

On my birth certificate I'm Justin, a name my mother favoured and my father barely tolerated: Justin Kaplan, Anne Bernays, *The Language of Names* (USA: Simon & Schuster, 1997) p. 11.

Trevors Together: [accessed 1 March] https://www.theguardian.com/lifeandstyle/2024/feb/23/experience-i-run-an-online-support-group-for-people-called-trevor

I feel like I'm home at last: Trevor Cunningham interviewed by telephone 2 March 2024.

A person's name is fundamental to who they are: [accessed 5 April 5 2022] https//www.canada.ca/en/immigration-refugees-citizenship/news/2021/06/minister-mendicino-minister-bennett-and-minister-miller-announce-that-indigenous-peoples-can-now-reclaim-their-traditional-names-on-immigration-ide.html

That's my name. It's always been my name. I'm taking back what's mine: Thandiwe Newton [accessed 5 April 2022] https://www.vanityfair.com/hollywood/2021/04/thandiwe-newton-reveals-correct-spelling-and-pronunciation-of-her-name

The whole time I was on *Blue Peter*, I was known by my Catholic middle name, Andy or Andrew: Ayo Akinwolere interviewed on Zoom October 2023.

Chapter Nine: The Tricky Middle

In 2014, a study set out to discover whether initialised middle names increased other people's perceptions of someone's intelligence: Wijnand A. P. Van Tilburg, Eric R. Igou, The impact of middle names: Middle name initials enhance evaluations of intellectual performance, European Journal of Social Psychology, published online April 2014.

In other areas like sports, physical labour or down the pub, using middle initials: Dr Eric I Igou interviewed by email 11 September 2023.

The writer Nicholas D Kristof believed the middle initial added a bit of authority and gravitas: [accessed 13 March 2022] https://archive.nytimes.com/kristof.blogs.nytimes.com/2014/01/01/whats-missing-in-my-byline

I don't see a comeback as any more likely than that of the clip-on tie: Pamela Redmond interviewed by email 23 September 2023.

By the 1900s they were so commonplace that the American enlistment form used in World War 1: Stephen

Wilson, *The Means of Naming* (London: UCL Press Limited, 1998) p. 300.

Five of the dozen American presidents who have held office in the yard since 1945: Stephen Wilson, *The Means of Naming* (London: UCL Press Limited, 1998) p. 300.

He is more commonly known as Salman, but Ahmed is his given name: *Knife: Meditations After an Attempted Murder* (London: Vintage. Penguin Random House, 2024) p. 25.

Count me down as somebody who underestimates Barack *Hussein* Obama: [accessed 6 June 2023] https://slate.com/news-and-politics/2006/12/barack-hussein-obama-and-the-history-of-bad-middle-names-in-politics.html

It's not about the disagreements Governor Romney and I may have: YouTube, President Barack Obama addressing the Alfred E. Smith Memorial Dinner, 16 October 2008.

When I spoke to Matthew Barratt, the CEO of the UK Deed Poll Service, he explained that Danger was among the UK's most popular middle names: Matthew Barratt interviewed by email 11 October 2024.

In 2021, the then Labour leader, Sir Keir Starmer, revealed to a live audience that his middle name was Rodney: Helen Pidd, 'Almost everyone hates theirs': Keir Starmer reveals middle name is Rodney,*Guardian*, 2 June 2021.

In 2024, at the Conservative party conference, gasps were heard around the auditorium: [accessed 2 Oct 2024] https://www.theguardian.com/politics/2024/oct/01/tory-gasps-as-robert-jenrick-reveals-daughters-middle-name-is-thatcher

The singer Michael Kiwanuka, British born, with Ugandan heritage, was initially encouraged to release music under a pseudonym: [accessed 13 September 2024] https://www.theguardian.com/music/2024/sep/13/singing-about-faith-was-scary-i-wanted-to-be-cool-michael-kiwanuka-on-god-fatherhood-and-his-secret-to-great-art

Chapter Ten: Chardonnay

In 2013, the controversial media personality and former reality-television contestant Katie Hopkins: [accessed 3 July 2022] https://metro.co.uk/2013/07/04/katie-hopkins-incurs-wrath-of-holly-willoughby-with-this-morning-name-debate-3869897

A chav is an insulting word for someone, usually a young person, whose way of dressing: [accessed February 2022] https://dictionary.cambridge.org/dictionary/english/chav#

A 2014 study found almost half of UK teachers said they conjured up a mental picture of the student: [accessed 3 July 2022] http://news.bbc.co.uk/1/hi/education/8243684.stm

Gregory Clark and his colleagues compared the names of students at Oxford University: [accessed 2 July 2022] https://www.bbc.co.uk/news/magazine-26634477

Recently I read about the case of Emmanuel Taché de la Pagerie: [accessed 23 June 2022] https://www.theguardian.com/world/2022/jun/23/french-mp-sued-emmanuel-tache-de-la-pagerie-aristocratic-name

Surprisingly, in the early 1990s, the first name Kevin: Angelique Chrisafis, We need to talk about Kévin: French namesakes fight national mockery, *Guardian*, 5 August 2022.

Working-class families began choosing their own names, often English-sounding: [accessed 31 October 2022] https://france-amerique.com/in-france-a-first-name-is-more-than-just-a-name

Perhaps this explains why some 2,700 Kevins in France apply for a name change: [accessed 31 October 2022] https://france-amerique.com/in-france-a-first-name-is-more-than-just-a-name

In 2023, a discussion about workplace culture in relation to an incident on ITV: [accessed 29 June 2023] https://

www.independent.co.uk/arts-entertainment/tv/news/this-morning-itv-tower-block-tracys-b2357326.html

Jane Garvey, BBC Radio 4, *Woman's Hour,* What's in a name? 17 April 2017.

***Tatler*, the magazine of choice for a certain kind of reader:** [accessed October 2023] https://www.tatler.com/article/poshest-baby-names-of-all-time

It revealed more than a quarter of young people in Britain thought it was easier to obtain a work placement with a double-barrelled surname: [accessed 3 October 2023] https://www.theguardian.com/lifeandstyle/2017/nov/02/keeping-up-with-smith-joneses-no-longer-posh-double-barrelled-surname

Chapter Eleven: Last Orders

A recent survey by the Pew Research Center:[accessed 3 June 2023] https://www.pewresearch.org/short-reads/2023/09/07/about-eight-in-ten-women-in-opposite-sex-marriages-say-they-took-their-husbands-last-name

In the UK, around 94 per cent of women married to a man change their surnames after marriage: Jane Pilcher, Names and "Doing Gender": How Forenames and Surnames Contribute to Gender Identities, Difference, and Inequalities, *Feminist Forum Review Article*, 2017.

In about 95 per cent of cases, wives in Japan: [accessed 30 April 2024] https://www.theguardian.com/world/2024/apr/02/japan-sato-only-name-by-2531-marriage-law

Hannah Willow, recently crowned Glasgow's first champion tree hugger: [accessed October 2024] https://www.theguardian.com/uk-news/2024/oct/09/glasgow-tree-hugging-champion-early-years-teacher-hannah-willow

Brett Pelham, a professor of psychology at Montgomery College in the US, who has studied the strange

phenomenon of apt surnames: Dr Scott Pelham interviewed by email 10 October 2024.

In the US, as recently as the 1970s, married women could not use their birth surname to vote: Lucy Stone [accessed 3 June 2023] https://time.com/5537834/lucy-stone-maiden-names-womens-history

Perhaps Mrs Hauptly's need was not for a change of name but for a competent psychiatrist: Deborah Antony, Eradicating Women's Surnames: Law, Tradition, And the Politics of Memory, *Columbia Journal of Gender and Law*, 2018, p. 15.

In a recent article in the *Independent*, a wedding planner from Sydney: [accessed 4 May 2023] https://www.independent.co.uk/life-style/love-sex/marriage-surname-women-feminist-change-b2314536.html

The sociologist Norbert Elias says that our given names: Jane Pilcher, Names and "Doing Gender": How Forenames and Surnames Contribute to Gender Identities, Difference, and Inequalities, *Feminist Forum Review Article*, 2017.

Chapter Twelve: Wood and Water

Slaves recognised the humiliation implicit in the names that they were given: Trevor G. Burnard, Slave Naming Patterns: Onomastics and the Taxonomy of Race in Eighteenth-Century Jamaica, *Journal of Interdisciplinary History*, Vol 31, No 3, Winter 2001, pp. 325–46.

When Negroes are sick, their relations and friends usually give them some very ugly New Name: Trevor G. Burnard, Slave Naming Patterns: Onomastics and the Taxonomy of Race in Eighteenth- Century Jamaica, *Journal of Interdisciplinary History*, Vol 31, No 3, Winter 2001, pp. 325–46.

The US is tied to more recent vestiges of slavery and the civil rights generally: Diane Allen West, Holness Fellow for Atlantic World History at the University of the West Indies, Jamaica, interviewed by email 3 October 2023.

There were 185 names for male children and 91 names for female children: [accessed 3 October 2023] https://www.cbc.ca/radio/ideas/how-nazis-used-personal-names-to-spawn-the-holocaust-1.5818120

In prisons and concentration camps, names were replaced with numbers: Jane Pilcher, Names, Bodies and Identities, *Sociology*, Vol 50(4), 2016.

You're one of those Black people who changed their names: Justin Kaplan, Anne Bernays, *The Language of Name* (USA: Simon & Schuster, 1997) p. 88.

My name, Kwame Kwei-Armah, roots me in the land my ancestors were taken from: Kwame Kwei-Armah interviewed on Zoom 16 February 2024.

In a recent BBC World Service programme: BBC News, World Service, *Heart and Soul*, Should I change my name? 21 April 2024.

The strike-out signifies the contested history of my surname - a lived tension between a White slave name and an African-Caribbean history of overcoming: Dr Robert Beckford interviewed by email 3 October 2024.

Chapter Thirteen: Say My Name

Bars and restaurants in the UK offered free coffee and cocktails to anyone called Camilla: [accessed 30 April 2023] https://www.manchestereveningnews.co.uk/whats-on/food-drink-news/manchester-bar-offer-free-drinks-26801385

They asked questions about her family history and whether she thought bombing was okay: [accessed 8 April 2023] https://www.independent.co.uk/news/uk/home-news/shamima-begum-shamina-airport-name-b2313806.html

They presumed he was suffering the ill effects of severe confusion and concussion: BBC Radio 4, *Saturday Live*, 6 April 2024.

Further Reading

Authors and their publications that have influenced and inspired this book, and I now pass on to you.

Chinua Achebe, *Things Fall Apart* (1958)

Chinua Achebe, *There Was a Country: A Personal History of Biafra* (2012)

Trevor Burnard, *Mastery, Tyranny & Desire: Thomas Thistlewood and His Slaves in the Anglo-Jamaican World* (2004)

Teju Cole, *Everyday is For the Thief* (2007)

Leslie Alan Dunkling, *First Names First* (1977)

Buchi Emecheta, *Second Class Citizen* (1974)

Roy Feinson, *The Secret Universe of Names* (2004)

Hewan Girma, *Respecting Names: Ethiopian Transnational Adoptee Name Changes, Retention and Reclamation (*2023)

Alex Haley, *Roots* (1976)

David Hey, *Surnames, DNA, & Family History* (2011)

Mavis Himes, *The Power of Names* (2016)

Carole Hough (ed.), *The Oxford Handbook of Names and Naming* (2016)

Justin Kaplan, Anne Bernays, *The Language of Names* (1997)

Mary Lassiter, *Our Names, Ourselves* (1983)

William Lewis, *What's in Your First Name?* (2014)

Toni Morrison, *Song of Solomon* (1977)

Ayokunmi Ojebode, Idowu Ojebode, *Titbits on Onomastics Among The Yoruba Africans* (2019)

Ayokunmi Ojebode, Idowu Ojebode, *African Onomastics and Gender in Chimamanda Adichie's Purple Hibiscus* (2018)

Stephen Wilson, *The Means of Naming* (1998)

Noo Wira-Saro, *Looking for Transwonderland* (2012)

Acknowledgements

Writing this book has been an incredible journey. So many people, so many names, have been instrumental in believing in me and this story. Thank you to Katie Bond, who read my article in the *Observer* and set the idea for this book in motion. You ignited the flame, Katie, and your early vision pushed this book forward. A massive thank you to Kate Ballard, editor extraordinaire, for your wisdom, perception, intelligence, sensitive editing and support. I can't thank you enough, Kate. An enormous hug of gratitude goes out to my brilliant agent, Emma Shercliff, who works so hard for all her authors and has always been there for me.

To all the experts and academics who helped sharpen my understanding of the vast and daunting ocean of personal names. I was frequently lost down the rabbit hole of research, and Dr Rebecca Gregory and Dr Ayokunmi Ojebode kept me on track.

Thanks to my MA Creative Writing tutors at Goldsmiths. Morrison, Diana Evans, and particular thanks to Francis Spufford, who read an early chapter of this book and encouraged me to keep writing my story. Thank you, Bel Greenwood. Thanks, too, to the late novelist and screenwriter Stephen Thompson, who identified the kind of writer I could be – huge thanks also to Dr Midge Gillies and everyone at Madingley College.

I am eternally grateful to the early readers of this book. Your insight and sensitive critique were invaluable. Thank you, Tan Frank, Kemi Lawson, Christine Marshall, Patricia Schaefer, Katri Scala and the Black Writers Guild for providing mentoring support. Thank you to everyone who's contributed to this book and shared their name stories.

To the people who are an integral part of this book and are no longer with us, your spirit remains.

Love and gratitude to my family. Mum, thank you for all your encouragement. Thanks for all your messages telling me to 'keep going' on those challenging days. Shout out to Mr Baxter, our rescue dog, for providing restorative strokes.

Huge thanks to all my friends for your patience, for keeping me going with coffee and walks and for how keen you were to talk about the book but also distract me from it.

And finally, thank you, Mike. I could not have written this without you. Your love, patience and kindness humbles me. This book is for you.

About the Author

Photo credit © Michael Balshaw

Camilla Balshaw grew up in Luton. Her work has been published in the *Observer* and the *Guardian*. She has an MA in Creative & Life Writing from Goldsmiths and is an Honorary Research Fellow in the Institute of Name Studies at the University of Nottingham. She lives in rural Norfolk. This is her first book.

@camillabalshaw
camillabalshaw.uk

Bedford Square Publishers

Bedford Square Publishers is an independent publisher of fiction and non-fiction, founded in 2022 in the historic streets of Bedford Square London and the sea mist shrouded green of Bedford Square Brighton.

Our goal is to discover irresistible stories and voices that illuminate our world.

We are passionate about connecting our authors to readers across the globe and our independence allows us to do this in original and nimble ways.

The team at Bedford Square Publishers has years of experience and we aim to use that knowledge and creative insight, alongside evolving technology, to reach the right readers for our books. From the ones who read a lot, to the ones who don't consider themselves readers, we aim to find those who will love our books and talk about them as much as we do.

We are hunting for vital new voices from all backgrounds – with books that take the reader to new places and transform perceptions of the world we live in.

Follow us on social media for the latest Bedford Square Publishers news.

@bedsqpublishers
facebook.com/bedfordsq.publishers/
@bedfordsq.publishers

https://bedfordsquarepublishers.co.uk/